Building Everyday

LEADERSHIP

in All Teens

Revised & Updated

Building Everyday LEADERSHIP in All Teens

Revised & Updated

PROMOTING ATTITUDES AND ACTIONS FOR RESPECT AND SUCCESS

MARIAM G. MACGREGOR, M.S.

free spirit
PUBLISHING®

Library of Congress Cataloging-in-Publication Data
MacGregor, Mariam G.
   Building everyday leadership in all teens : promoting attitudes and actions for respect and success / by Mariam G. MacGregor. — Revised and updated edition.
        pages cm
   Earlier edition: 2006.
      ISBN 978-1-63198-042-8 (paperback)
 1. Leadership—Study and teaching (Secondary) 2. Leadership in adolescents. I. Title.
   HM1261.M32 2015
   303.3'42—dc23

                                                                                          2015006974

ISBN: 978-1-63198-042-8

Cover and interior design by Percolator
Edited by Ruth Taswell, Eric Braun, and Darsi Dreyer

10 9 8 7 6 5 4 3 2
Printed in the United States of America

Free Spirit Publishing Inc.
6325 Sandburg Road, Suite 100
Minneapolis, MN 55427-3674
(612) 338-2068
help4kids@freespirit.com
www.freespirit.com

FSC
www.fsc.org
MIX
Paper from
responsible sources
FSC® C005010

Free Spirit offers competitive pricing.
Contact edsales@freespirit.com for pricing information on multiple quantity purchases.

DEDICATION

To my mom (1935–2004) and dad,
who have always believed in me, and more
importantly, taught me to believe in myself,
especially when I was a teenager.

ACKNOWLEDGMENTS

I am grateful that *Building Everyday Leadership* is being used to inspire 21st Century youth leaders worldwide. This book—both the original and this updated edition—would never exist without the insights, engagement and support of the following:

Jeanne Rosenberger, vice provost for student life and dean of students at Santa Clara University, who served as an incredible mentor in my early career, became one of my dearest friends and who continues to inspire me today.

Tom Mordue, retired principal of Vantage Point Alternative High School in Thornton, CO. Years ago Tom took a chance by hiring me and allowing me to teach leadership to youth-at-risk in a way that was very different than the norm. This launched the prototype curriculum, which is now the *Building Everyday Leadership* curriculum.

Kristin Aarestad, *still* one of the best language arts and diversity teachers out there, who eagerly and consistently engages her students as leaders no matter the subject being addressed.

Every student with whom I've had the honor of working, especially those who doubted they had the "right stuff" to be leaders, and who often proved everyone including themselves wrong.

Ruth Taswell, Eric Braun, and Darsi Dreyer, my talented editors at Free Spirit over the years, who each provided support in my quest to create a "better mousetrap" in terms of how leadership talents are nurtured in kids and teens.

Alyssa Riggs, who kept my kids happy, healthy, and safe, and serves as a sounding board for talking through activities and ways to keep students engaged when learning to lead.

Hayes, Colt, and Lily, each of whom reinforces everyday how young leadership can be taught and how it is learned. Together, they face and deal with daily situations that require "attitudes of leaders" to succeed.

My sweet husband Michael, who unfailingly supports me in my pursuit to write and teach about leaders in ways that make a difference in the lives of teens, the adults working with them, and generations of everyday leaders to come.

CONTENTS

BONUS MATERIALS IN THE DIGITAL CONTENT

(These materials can be accessed at **www.freespirit.com/belt-forms**, use password **potential4**.)

Additional Teen Leadership Activities

In My Lifetime Action Plan

Leadership Word Play

Choose a Button

Pick-Up Sticks

Pass It On

Can't Judge a Book

Guest of Honor

Leadership Quotes for Discussion and Writing

Using Movies for Leadership Discussions

Summaries and Discussion Questions for Movies

Additional Movies for Leadership Discussions

Standards for Earning a Varsity Letter in Leadership

Leadership Project Group- and Self-Evaluation

LIST OF REPRODUCIBLES

These reproducible forms can also be downloaded or printed out at **www.freespirit.com/belt-forms**, use password **potential4**.

FOREWORD

by Barry Z. Posner, Ph.D.

Every day there are opportunities for teens to take the lead among their peers, and all teens have the potential to learn the attitudes and skills that enable them to do this. It's a myth that leadership can't be taught. Viewing leadership as non-learnable character traits or believing that only certain kids can lead dooms society to limited leadership. It's far healthier and more productive to recognize it's possible for everyone to lead. With *Building Everyday Leadership in All Teens* and its companion guidebook for teens, *Everyday Leadership*, you can make a tremendous difference in helping young people learn how to become everyday leaders.

Leadership development is fundamentally self-development. The primary instrument of a leader, teen or adult, is one's self. To teach leadership, then, requires helping teens explore "inner territory"—who they are and what they care about. If, for example, in teaching leadership skills, we say, "Leaders stand up," we also must help teens figure out what they're going to stand up on (their foundations). For teens to grapple with this idea amidst their struggles for independence can be intense. But if you help teens realize they are indeed leaders, then you can assist them in using their unique talents to serve the common good while pursuing individual interests.

Using the tools and techniques within this book and the teen guidebook, you can counsel and provide an important perspective for teens to help them practice leadership skills. Author Mariam MacGregor provides ample opportunities for teens to discover, strengthen, hone, and enhance their leadership skills. A talented educator, she acts every day on her passion for youth leadership and for liberating the leader within every teen, including those outside the traditional leadership venues of student government and athletics. In both her books, she's captured teens' interests, language, struggles, and dilemmas as they seek to find out more about who they are and what they care about.

In my own work with teens, as well as adults, I'm constantly reminded of the power within every person. Each of us has a capacity to do more than what we're usually asked. Again and again, when given the assignment "to go out and lead" (for example, make a difference in some organization), teens magically do just that. It's awe-inspiring to see what young people are capable of bringing forth within themselves when motivated to do so. Educating young people is truly the lever to change the world. I join Mariam MacGregor in saying, "With your guidance, teens can gain a greater understanding of who they are and how that translates into *how* to lead."

Barry Z. Posner, Ph.D.
Dean and Professor of Leadership
Santa Clara University, Silicon Valley, California
Coauthor, *The Leadership Challenge* and *A Leader's Legacy*

Inspiring Teens to Take the Lead

You probably know many young people who have a positive outlook about themselves and their future. Just as teens can choose to have a positive attitude, they can acquire a "leadership attitude." With a leadership attitude, people take action when they see the need and encourage others to do the same.

Yet many people in the world, young and old, are not *prepared* to take the lead. Some may not know how; others may not realize their own potential to do so. This curriculum guide is written specifically to support your efforts as an educator or youth worker to instill in *any* adolescent a leadership attitude. It helps you teach young people how to take responsibility and action—how to take the lead.

With the accompanying guide for teens, *Everyday Leadership,* you can help teens develop confidence in their own leadership attitude and potential. You can encourage them to discover the rewarding challenges and successes of being a leader, regardless of whether they're building leadership skills from the ground up or improving skills they already have. You can help them discover that leadership opportunities, both great and small, arise in seemingly unremarkable everyday situations.

Connecting Teens to Leadership

Typically, leadership experiences have been reserved for those students who are the "best" or the "brightest." Often these are teens who are already inclined to run for student council or plan the prom, or who demonstrate certain leadership attitudes and actions before beginning a leadership class or program. If we focus only on these teens as candidates for leadership roles, however, we limit the potential so many other students have to offer. We draw a line rather than open up possibility. With boundaries created before some young people even have a chance to try taking the lead, it is no surprise they often hesitate to do so when an opportunity arises.

Some teens also may doubt themselves or think being a leader means knowing the right thing to do all the time. They see only so-called good kids or successful students having what it takes to be a leader.

As educators and youth leaders, however, it is our job to teach teens that leading is as much about promoting positive attitudes and respect as it is about achieving success. *Building Everyday Leadership* is an engaging, age-appropriate approach to teaching and preparing teen leaders. Rather than modify adult texts or copy handouts and articles that usually relate leadership to business or politics, this curriculum guide relates leadership to situations specific to teens. You can create a safe setting where participants actively practice and test leadership skills and learn what it means to be an effective leader. Teens will get up and move, think and write, consider their individual ideas, work together, and act as leaders.

Making a Difference

Given the chance, teens who learn leadership skills will benefit in many ways. During the five years I taught leadership classes as a counselor at an alternative high school, students who successfully completed the leadership curriculum generally had:

- better attendance rates
- higher retention rates and fewer failed classes
- positive participation and contribution to class discussions
- greater confidence in speaking at meetings or assemblies and taking on peer leadership roles

- greater confidence in resolving conflict without the assistance of adult staff
- increased participation in optional extracurricular activities (those not required by probation or diversions programs)
- increased empathy during community service projects
- higher average quarterly GPAs than nonleadership participants
- increased involvement in school decision-making processes
- increased interest in attending postsecondary school or a vocational training program (for example, voluntarily taking the ACT, attending college information sessions, completing entrance exams, and applying for financial aid prior to graduating)

Most importantly, the opportunities in this curriculum guide are intended for *all* youth, not just a select few. Every teen has the potential to lead. Challenge the teens you work with to try new skills, and they will succeed. This success will come from the self-satisfaction that occurs when they realize they are capable and respected for taking a stand, taking the lead, and making a positive difference.

Teaching teens about leadership also will allow you to solidify your own leadership values and expectations, and your role as a leader.

Please join me on Twitter (@mariammacgregor) for conversations, questions, or to share your experiences on youth leadership and engaging kids and teens as leaders. Or you can reach me at:

Free Spirit Publishing Inc.
6325 Sandburg Road, Suite 100
Minneapolis, MN 55427-3674
help4kids@freespirit.com

Mariam G. MacGregor, M.S.

INTRODUCTION

Leading the Way

Teens often are as self-assured as they are uncertain: one moment they're ready to take on risks without thinking, the next they're critical and cautious. Learning about leadership can help support the important process of figuring out "Who am I?" "What do I care about?" and "How can I contribute?"

This guide and the accompanying teen guide, *Everyday Leadership*, are divided into 21 sessions covering different topics of leadership. Prior to starting the sessions, you may want to have teens complete the Everyday Leadership Skills and Attitudes (ELSA) Inventory, found on pages 161–163 of this guide. This tool is designed for teens to gain self-awareness of their leadership skills. You can conduct it one time to launch your leadership program, or use it as a pre- and post-session tool for students to identify their leadership gains from participating in *Building Everyday Leadership* sessions.

Coordinating the Sessions with Your Setting

Both this guide and the book for teens are easy to follow and applicable in a range of settings: classrooms, after-school groups, advisory or family groups, service learning and leadership programs, and community- or faith-based programs. Whether you're exploring leadership throughout a school year or unrelated to an academic timeline, such as during a weekend youth group, you have a complete curriculum with *Building Everyday Leadership*.

Each session is designed to take 45 minutes. You can modify the session sequence to fit your needs depending on how often your group meets and participants' maturity and leadership experience. It is worthwhile to conduct the sessions in the order they appear, but should your schedule not allow you to conduct all the sessions,

identify those topics most important to your group. When time allows, build upon what you've already covered by doing additional sessions.

At a minimum, begin with session 1 to set the fundamentals for your leadership teaching effort. And conclude with session 21, however many sessions you conduct, to emphasize the value of a leader's role in acknowledging the contributions of others and to celebrate everyone's participation in this leadership development experience.

You'll find a sample sequence of sessions and a class syllabus at the end of this book (see pages 178–183). If you decide to follow (or modify) these, set up your own specific timeline of dates before beginning the sessions.

Ideally, each participant in your group will have his or her own copy of *Everyday Leadership,* which is meant to be written in and filled out by the participant. Teens might also want to use a folder to store handouts and to add pictures or other mementos from experiences they have throughout the sessions.

Have a couple extra copies of the teen guide on hand in case some teens forget to bring their copies to a session. Alternatively, ask teens to leave their copies where the group meets so they're sure to have them at each session.

The ideal group size for teaching teens leadership can vary depending on participants' ages, maturity, and previous leadership experiences. For high school teens, a group of 16–25 seems to work well. If the group is too small, the variety of perspectives that makes learning about leadership more dynamic may not be as possible. If the group is too large, everyone may not get an opportunity to share their opinions or try out new skills. For middle school students, a group of 12–18 is more optimum, since younger teens generally need more time and attention to express their thoughts and practice skills. If conducting the sessions in a classroom, your class size may be larger. To engage as many students as possible, you may need to divide the class into smaller groups that will simultaneously participate in an activity or rotate more teens as observers. If your group size is much smaller, decrease the number of teens per group when working in small groups or eliminate observers during role playing.

Using the Sessions

Many teens have had few opportunities or lack confidence or self-awareness to take on specific leadership roles. This curriculum helps these participants, as well as the more experienced individuals in your group. Teens who have self-confidence and insight into themselves and others will be equally challenged to fine-tune their leadership abilities. Each session in this guide is organized as follows:

- **Goals**—the purpose of the session and what teens are to learn or accomplish

- **Materials Needed**—what you'll need to conduct the session; teens can bring their copies of *Everyday Leadership* to each session or leave them where the group meets so they're sure to have them

- **Getting Ready**—steps to prepare for conducting the session

- **Getting Started**—topic introduction; some sessions include "Find Out More About It" handouts with background information

- **Teach This**—step-by-step guidance through the planned activity, which correlates with "Try This" sections in the teen guide; may include "Instructions for Try This"

- **Talk About It**—discussion questions to use with the group following the activity

- **Think and Write About It**—questions in the teen guide, *Everyday Leadership,* for each participant to think about and respond to following group discussion or the session

- **Do Something About It**—list of ideas at the end of each session in the teen guide to help each participant put their leadership learning into action

Each session in the teen guide includes the following parts:

- **Quotes**—at the beginning of each session, quotes to help teens think further about the leadership

skills they're learning—you may want to solicit teens' reactions to these quotes or encourage them to share their thoughts about them with their peers; a brief introduction to the session topic also is included following the quotes

- **Think and Write About It**—questions for each participant to think about and respond to following group discussion in the session

- **Do Something About It**—the list of ideas at the end of each session to help each participant put her or his leadership learning into action

Some sessions in the teen guide also include:

- **Try This**—material for teens to complete either during or after the session that coordinates with a session activity

- **Find Out More About It**—background information about the session topic to read before or after a session activity

Read through each session completely before conducting it to familiarize yourself with the goals and focus, plan for conducting the activity, and review the background information. This preparation will assist you in anticipating any concerns from participants and in determining a possible emphasis for discussion, according to the needs of your group. Be sure also to consider any specific directions for the reflection writing in "Think and Write About It" and goal setting in "Do Something About It" (see the next section "Choosing a Strategy").

At the beginning of each session are the corresponding pages for the session in the teen guide. The "Try This," "Think and Write About It," and "Do Something About It" pages from the teen book appear in this guide as smaller, readable images with corresponding page numbers as well. "Find Out More About It" background information is in both this guide and the teen book, also with corresponding page references. The information provided in the teen book is often abbreviated in relation to the corresponding information in this guide. It's important to be familiar with both versions so you know what information you may want to fill in during discussions. The "Find Out More About It" sections in this guide are presented as reproducible handouts, which can be photocopied or downloaded (see page viii for how to access digital content) to provide teens more in-depth information. In some sessions, the extended "Find Out

More About It" material in this guide is essential and *must* be made available to teens. In these cases, the handouts are listed under "Materials Needed" to highlight them. At times, you'll want to direct teens to read "Find Out More About It" background before an activity. In other instances, you'll find it valuable to hold off on providing more information in order not to influence behavior in the activity.

Choosing a Strategy

Before beginning any of the sessions, choose a general strategy for when you'd prefer participants to answer the questions in "Think and Write About It" and to select goals in "Do Something About It," and when you will review their written reflections and goals achieved. Here are a few different possibilities to consider for "Think and Write About It":

- Allow 10 minutes at the end of each session for teens to do their reflective writing. Before the session ends, scan what they've written and initial and date the page to indicate that they've completed the assignment and you've reviewed it.

- Ask teens to complete their reflective writing outside of the session. At the beginning of the next session, check in to see if participants have any questions or comments to share. Depending on participants' maturity and rapport with one another, suggest teens take 5 minutes to partner with another person and share their responses. As teens practice leadership skills throughout the sessions, their comfort with sharing their reflective writing with a partner will increase.

- Periodically collect the teen books to review their writing. If possible, schedule brief (10 minutes) individual meetings at least once at some point during a later session in the schedule to talk about what teens have learned through the "Think and Write About It" process. Offer feedback and recognition specific to the teen and his or her achievements in the program. If brief meetings aren't possible, provide written feedback.

- If time is more limited, assign only one or two of the questions, or have teens select a few themselves. Either way, encourage teens to write on any of the other questions to further explore their leadership thoughts.

In choosing a general strategy, keep in mind that because some "Talk About It" discussions during a session can get quite involved, your group may occasionally want more time to think about the particular material. When that becomes apparent during a session, consider a change in your strategy and wait until participants meet next to assign "Think and Write About It" and "Do Something About It" and wrap up the topic. If your group meets for longer than 45 minutes, however, feel free to expand group discussion.

For "Do Something About It," consider a similar strategy for reviewing teens' progress. They can use the checklists on these pages to identify one or two personal goals or as inspiration to make a commitment to do something. The lists offer three to four suggestions and include additional blank lines for teens to add their own ideas. The goal statements are written to echo what teens experienced in the session. Some of the goals can be completed in a day; other actions will take longer. Teens are to indicate a date by which they plan to put their goals into action, the date they completed them, and a description of what they did.

"Do Something About It" sets the stage for teens to incorporate leadership behaviors into both everyday activities and more formal leadership roles they may already be involved in or that they want to take on. Encourage teens to take risks and try new things when engaging in the actions they select. Talk about how people often learn the best lessons doing something unlike anything they've done before.

Setting the Tone

Because you are asking teens to write about (as well as discuss in sessions) topics that inspire self-reflection, it is essential to promote a safe environment that encourages supportive attitudes for and from everyone.

Confidentiality

Remind teens to talk and write honestly and sincerely in discussions and in their books while still only describing what they are comfortable sharing with others. Maintain an atmosphere within your group that's respectful of diverse opinions. Instruct group members to honor everyone's confidentiality. Caution them not to mention other people's personal information or to use real names when recounting interactions or conflicts, both within and outside of the group.

When conducting the sessions, you may discover that some topics evoke personal admissions and highly charged situations. It's hard to predict exactly when someone may become affected by emotion or when conflict may arise within the group. But if you establish trust early on with the group and monitor any particular dynamics between members, you likely will be able to anticipate potentially difficult circumstances. If intense moments occur, remind teens about maintaining confidentiality and help those disagreeing talk it through.

Maintaining confidentiality is increasingly challenging for digital natives, where thoughts and comments can be distributed with the touch of a text. Remind students that sending information virtually—even if only to one person—violates confidentiality and can lead to larger problems because of the speed with which information moves online and in the cloud.

The same is true with seeing comments made by peers in social media. If teens are ever concerned by what they read in posts made by friends or peers, encourage them to reach out for help on behalf of someone who may be struggling.

Skills Practice

Some of the session activities depend upon one or more of the teens taking a leadership role or guiding a group discussion. Ask different volunteers to assume these roles throughout the sessions so everyone gets a chance to practice skills. At times, you may want to randomly pick participants' names out of a box or hat. Encourage reluctant teens to give it a try and promote the activity as an opportunity rather than a requirement. However, if you're evaluating teens' learning (see "Evaluating Learning" on page 5), remind them that their participation counts toward part of their assessment or grade. (See also "Goal Setting," which follows.)

As the facilitator, you can help teens practice skills comfortably by providing participants plenty of opportunities to try new skills, looking for what's "right" in what teens are doing, and giving helpful, positive feedback. Take some time to think about your own definitions, expectations, biases, and personal behaviors related to leadership before you begin any of the sessions. Whatever your facilitation style, when you make the sessions come alive for the teens in your group, they more likely will feel your energy and why you want them to take the lead. And demonstrating leadership will better enable you to *let* teens take the lead.

Goal Setting

Some teens initially may be uncomfortable taking the risks necessary to lead or participate fully in session activities. This can be stressful for those who haven't had much experience taking the lead or participating in group activities (such as team-building exercises). Your sensitivity to their perspective is essential.

One helpful approach to facilitating learning is "Challenge by Choice" (CbC), endorsed by Project Adventure, a nonprofit education and training organization known for its innovative experiential education approach and ropes challenge courses (see "Resources and Additional Reading" on page 212). CbC promotes individuals taking responsibility to participate in an activity. Specifically, a person learns to set a goal that offers enough of a challenge to improve skills and contribute to the group rather than one that is too easy or too difficult or contributes nothing. For example, a shy or reserved group member is willing to take on a speaking role in an activity but is not quite ready to lead the activity.

Role Playing

Another helpful approach is role playing, which some of the session activities use. Role playing provides participants a fun opportunity to experience different perspectives in small or large groups. They assume the roles of certain characters to act out in various scenarios. Review the roles with participants before starting an activity and remind them to stay in character throughout the role play.

When teens practice different leadership and group roles, the learning takes on a real-life aspect making it easier to apply particular strategies when actual situations arise. Much of the role playing in the sessions is scripted to support an expected outcome. Even so, the role playing allows participants to connect personally to the topic. Role playing is most meaningful when participants and observers also discuss their reactions to the role play afterwards and its application to real life.

Be sure to address with teens some basic ground rules for role playing. As with "Talk About It" and "Think and Write About It," remind participants that they do not have to reveal personal information in role playing. If teens start to act overly silly or lose focus, stop the role playing and remind them of its purpose.

As participants develop self-confidence and comfort in practicing and developing leadership skills, increasingly promote their involvement within the group.

Because the activities in this book are designed to be engaging and appealing, they tend to draw teens in from the beginning. But even if at first some choose to participate minimally, it isn't long before they feel they are missing out by not joining in.

Evaluating Learning

Whatever setting in which you teach teens leadership, you may be asked or choose to measure teens' growth.

Core Leadership Competencies

Although there are no recognized or agreed-upon national content standards for teaching leadership in the United States and Canada, standards are being developed and established at the state and provincial levels. Teens participating in all 21 sessions in the *Building Everyday Leadership* curriculum guide can expect to acquire and enhance 12 core leadership competencies (listing follows). These leadership competencies align closely with developing and established content standards for leadership, service learning, or workplace preparation in the states of Arizona, Hawaii, Maine, Michigan, Montana, New Jersey, Pennsylvania, and Virginia (see "Resources and Additional Reading" on pages 207–208).

- Develop a personal definition of what it means to be a leader and identify opportunities to demonstrate leadership in everyday situations.

- Discern the variety of ways people lead and how to promote others' leadership potential.

- Understand the role and use of a leader's power, influence, and authority.

- Make well-considered ethical decisions confidently, even when facing negative peer pressure.

- Demonstrate sensitivity to attitudes, issues, and responsibilities of leaders related to a diverse society, including confronting prejudice and stereotypes and creating an inclusive team atmosphere.

- Accept responsibility willingly, follow through on projects, balance commitments, and support others in doing the right thing and standing up for their beliefs.

- Work with others on a team and recognize the differences individuals bring when becoming part of a team.

- Identify productive approaches to conflict resolution and problem solving.

- Identify personal motivators and ways to motivate others, as well as recognize the importance of establishing a team vision and goals.

- Identify appropriate role models and demonstrate effective leadership for others.

- Accept and learn from mistakes respectfully and celebrate team successes appropriately.

- Act confidently as a leader and be recognized for leadership actions that demonstrate a capability to make an ongoing difference, whether big or small, as an everyday leader.

If there are no established content standards for leadership classes in your area, first identify the learning outcomes within other subjects or classes, such as social studies, language arts, family and consumer science, service learning, or other relevant content areas. Then you can connect the leadership core competencies for this curriculum to these other areas.

Even with increased requirements to meet standardized testing goals in other academic subjects (such as those listed previously), you can easily incorporate leadership development into these classes and in doing so support and enhance core subject matter. For example, writing prompts in language arts courses can involve leadership topics and a typical civics lesson in social studies can include a discussion on how decisions are made in various community settings.

The Everyday Leadership Skills & Attitudes (ELSA) Inventory

The Everyday Leadership Skills & Attitude Inventory (see page 159) was developed specifically with young people in mind. Rather than adapt an inventory designed for adults or college-age students to measure leadership awareness and growth, this inventory evaluates leadership concepts from younger perspectives. As anyone working with kids recognizes, tweens and teens have distinct expectations and constructs in which they measure leaders and leadership.

It doesn't matter if they are applying these frameworks to themselves or others. In general, when given opportunities to test and try out leadership behaviors, most teens will use similar language and examples to describe what they've learned and how their leadership skills can (or will) be applied. And granted, some kids are better than others at identifying leadership talents, let alone doing something with this awareness.

Prior to having the teens with whom you're working complete the ELSA Inventory, identify your goals for utilizing the inventory. This can help you select additional activities, enrichments, connections, or projects to infuse leadership development. As with any leadership inventory, you may find various ways for using this tool. Suggestions for use include:

- As a pre- or post-assessment tool with a leadership experience to measure changes in attitudes and skill development

- As a goal-setting tool within a youth leadership experience to identify strengths and challenge areas and establish leadership goals with those areas in mind

- As a personal-awareness tool to help teens gain a greater understanding of their leadership abilities, whether or not they do more with that information

- As a team-awareness tool to help teens assess the skills and talents—as well as shortcomings—of their team or group and set goals to enrich how the team works together

- As part of a leadership curriculum where you can collect data to determine the effectiveness of your leadership education and development efforts

No two leadership programs are alike. Yet, as with adults, leadership skills and attitudes in young people run along similar paths, regardless of the experiences in which teens are involved. While the inventory aligns directly with the *Building Everyday Leadership* curriculum, field tests with a wide-range of leadership programs and courses involving teens and tweens indicate its validity with youth leaders regardless of the program.

The ELSA Inventory, step-by-step instructions for administering it, and supporting materials related to using the Inventory begin on page 159. The ELSA supporting materials are designed to enrich how you and the teens completing the inventory can use the results. The data sheet (page 166) can be used by you or your organization to keep track of the demographics of teens completing the ELSA.

Measuring Leadership Learning

The ELSA Inventory can be used to measure leadership learning by asking teens to complete it before participating in leadership training and again at the end of the training experience. To measure learning, keep students' first completed ELSA Inventories and compare them to the results of the inventory after students have completed your program, allowing students to review and reflect on personal changes.

Determining Reasonable Outcomes

It's valuable to establish expectations of teens and tweens to demonstrate leadership competence at the outset of any leadership training. The following list identifies examples of leadership behaviors that are reasonable to expect of teens and tweens. The level of competence will depend upon age, preparation, and opportunities provided in leadership engagement.

Teens and tweens can:

- Design and manage their own projects from start to finish. They may benefit from having support from adults in the form of setting format, clarifying timelines, and identifying specific boundaries.

- Set master outlines and conduct project follow-through.

- Delegate group responsibilities for various activities.

- Be expected to appropriately confront others about inappropriate behaviors; having these behaviors modeled consistently by adult mentors is important, as are opportunities to learn and practice this skill in a safe setting.

- Demonstrate right from wrong behavior as a student leader.

- Stand up for themselves against peer pressure.

- Stand up for individual beliefs among peers and adult mentors.

- Organize meetings, planning events, committees, etc.

- Demonstrate appropriate behavior at mixed (adult and youth) events.

- Develop public speaking skills.

- Develop anger management and conflict resolution skills.

- Mediate conflicts among peers.

- Demonstrate sensitivity and tolerance with diverse populations.

- Differentiate between fact and opinion.

- Establish and model reasonable standards of responsibility among peers.

- Fairly select members or leaders for projects, committees, organizations.

- Set and manage budgets for youth activities and projects.

- Design public relations campaigns and other appropriate promotion activities.

- Solicit donations and coordinate fundraising efforts.

- Conduct group problem solving.

- Prepare and present to key stakeholders.

- Interview and assist with staff (program, teaching, board, etc.) selection.

- Develop, review, evaluate, modify, and monitor policies that directly affect youth.

- Facilitate group activities, lead discussion, guide debriefing, and apply what is learned through leadership activities.

To determine if your expectations are reasonable, build time into the project, activity, or program process to ask teens:

- What do you want to learn to become a better leader?

- In what situations is it difficult to be a leader?

- How can you get others to see you as a leader, especially if you have never been looked at like that before?

- What can I do to help you become a better leader?

- What can other teachers, staff, or mentors do to help you?

- How can we work together as a school or an organization to show everyone that leading and leadership are "cool"?

- How do you think adults in our school or organization could be more sensitive to your leadership talents and contributions?

- What is your perspective on this issue, topic, or policy? How does this affect your motivation for this project?

After completing a project or presentation, consider these reflection questions:

- Did you feel prepared to conduct that project?

- In what ways could you have been better prepared?

- Do you feel that this project allowed all teens in our program the chance to become leaders and showcase their abilities?

- If people didn't follow through with their responsibilities, what do you suggest we do?

"The Leadership Project Group- and Self-Evaluation" handout (part of the bonus materials in the bonus digital content—see page viii for how to access) is a useful way for teens to give and receive leadership feedback. After completing a group project or program, give teens the opportunity to complete a handout for themselves as well as one for each member of their team. Use this information as you wish such as establishing grades or for one-on-one feedback to improve teen leadership skills.

Similar to "360 Degree" feedback used in the workforce, this form is most effective when members of the group are asked to fill out individual evaluation forms for each group member as well as one for themselves. Remind teens that their forms will be kept confidential, even though they are asked to sign their name to the form, to get greater honesty. Allowing teens to submit the forms anonymously is an option; however, it can result in flippant complaints about peers rather than valuable critiques about individual contributions.

Measuring School-Based Teen Leadership Learning Outcomes

Additional ways to measure outcomes for the *Building Everyday Leadership* curriculum is to consider having teens research a leader, observe an organization and present a report to the group, or complete a midterm or final exam. (You will find guidelines for a research report and the observing-an-organization project as well as a midterm exam and a final exam covering the content in the 21 sessions for *Building Everyday Leadership* in the back of this book. See "Supplemental Materials" beginning on page 177.) If grading is necessary, here is a suggested breakdown for distributing points toward grading that you can modify for your own needs:

- Participating in sessions
  10 points each session

- Reflective writing
  15–25 points each

- Achieving personal goals
  15–25 points each completed goal

- Researching-a-leader project
  125 points

- Observing-an-organization project
  50 points

- Completing exams (midterm and final)
  100 points each

The total possible points participants can earn will depend upon how many sessions you conduct and the number of other requirements you establish for your group.

Alternative Methods for Measuring Teen Leadership Learning Outcomes

The process of "learning leadership" may pose challenges for individuals who seek only statistical measurements of how a teen's leadership abilities have improved. Teaching teens the value of creative thinking enables educators and instructors to model how creative thinking can provide methods for measuring learning. Here is a list of field-collected ideas that go beyond paper-and-pencil testing to understand the leadership gains made by teens:

Artwork/Drawing

Leadership topics can be understood in the form of a drawing or photograph. Give teens opportunities to express themselves through art. Provide them with a large piece of paper, propose a leadership topic or issue, and have them express what it means to them. Create a gallery for the projects to be shown. Build in time for discussion and interpretation.

Community Projects

Teens can demonstrate the results of work they have done in the community by collecting feedback from the program served, writing an essay about their personal experience, or getting a letter of recommendation from a program staff member. Or they can create a leadership project that will have a direct, positive, and measurable impact on their community and interview individuals affected by their efforts. Consider projects that are social, ecological, or done with a business.

Create a Story Board

Many teens, especially boys, like graphic novels. Start with a sequence of roughly drawn pictures that capture key moments in their leadership journey. Put them up on a wall to create and trace the history of the project or the issue. This can be powerful with leadership issues such as ethical dilemmas, leadership project design, social issues facing teens, and communication topics.

Create a Wall-Size Mural

Have teens paint a mural, which can be a vivid representation of leadership. Endless topics can be expressed and promoted in a mural. Discuss the "leadership" differences between creating a mural and graffiti or tagging, such as knowing the property owner, having permission to create the mural, coordinating location with law enforcement so the end result contributes positively to the community, including signage on the mural indicating who did it and who sponsored it, and so on.

Debates

A significant value of debates is in preparing for the actual debate! Create a specific rubric or other criteria for assessment so teens know what you'll be watching for. Watching a professional debate between leaders (such as a political debate) is a powerful discussion and learning tool as well.

Game Design

Ask teens to take any game, such as Simon Says, Monopoly, Scrabble, Jeopardy, Trivial Pursuit, Wheel of Fortune, Concentration, card games, or ball games, and redesign it so it relates to leadership. For example, Scrabble can be played as instructed with the parameters that every word used must relate to leadership (see Leadership Word Play in the digital content for a "human-sized" version). Certain versions of Trivial Pursuit are excellent for discussing and learning about leadership-related topics (or people). Some games played as instructed allow leadership behaviors to emerge naturally (such as Risk). Even video games played in a group setting lend themselves to leadership discussions.

Interviews

Leadership learning can be assessed if teens are given time to talk freely about it. Casual, stress-free discussion or interview time is rarely used, and yet can be of great benefit. If teens can't interview real people, have them formulate questions and extrapolate hypothetical answers. Even more powerful is when teens can interview existing leaders and interpret and present the results of that interview.

Leadership Inventories

Facilitate the ELSA Inventory with teens as an additional way to measure leadership learning. Have them set goals based on the inventory and strive to strengthen skills based on the self-assessment that comes from the inventory results.

Leadership Letter

Just as teen athletes earn varsity letters for athletic participation and accomplishments, create standards and guidelines for teens to earn similar letters for their leadership participation and accomplishments. Invite teens to create the guidelines or consider the guidelines found in the digital content.

Leadership Portfolio

Have teens produce a portfolio (notebook, video, other medium) that demonstrates any leadership building activities or programs in which they've been involved. A useful approach can be found by looking at the Wisconsin Youth Leadership Skills Standards Certificate program, most notably, the "transcript" found at cte.dpi.wi.gov/cte_ylssindex (see page 208).

Journals and Learning Logs

For teens who are private and introspective, use personal written reflection to learn about what they know. Through journaling, the content becomes specific and teens can create or answer questions about what and how they learned. They can also add their own feelings and possible leadership applications of their experiences.

Montage or Collage

This format is a way to collect and put together thoughts and ideas. Have teens explore traditional collages (using magazine clippings, photographs, scrapbooking supplies, etc.) or create PowerPoint presentations or design a Web page. The more choice and freedom you give teens, the more likely you'll get something really innovative.

Multimedia

Teens can make a video, audio recording, podcast, or website related to leadership. Insist that it be quality and provide access to the necessary resources. Have teens organize into small teams, pick topics from a hat (or have the large group work together to self-select topics), and let teens create and post a video to YouTube. Encourage teens to create leadership public service announcements (PSA) for a local TV station. Create a little friendly competition based on votes for best leadership video (increase exposure even further by having teens create Facebook fan sites to draw more votes).

Music

Most leadership materials and issues can be written about, set to music, or performed as music. Lyrics of existing songs can also be used to help teens understand how they learn leadership, including evaluating songs for negative or positive leadership influences. Or have teens rewrite an existing song to emphasize leadership issues.

Newspaper Articles

Let teens create a mock-up front page on a leadership topic. They can take different points of view. Have each teen relate their "column" to their own life. That way the front page will cover leadership from personal, financial, sociological, historical, literary, mathematical, physical, or scientific perspectives.

Performance

Have teens create a movie or theatrical script with a leadership theme. Point out existing plays (such as *West Side Story*, *Wicked*, or *Rent*) that have leadership themes intertwined with the main plot. Some leadership topics lend themselves to being performed (such as social issues, controversial topics, and role modeling). Allow time for teens to do a quality job preparing or writing their script. Then create a fun stage for them to perform upon.

Plan and Produce a Mini-Conference

Teens plan a mini-conference on leadership. They gather speakers, plan the talks and workshops, organize the logistics, put it on, and evaluate it. This assessment requires tremendous teamwork and time, but it is well worth the effort.

Sculpture

Let students represent their learning through artistic models. In addition, existing sculptures or objects can be used to prompt teens to discuss the issues surrounding the piece or what leadership issues arise by looking at the design.

Student Teaching

Provide teens time to create a lesson on leadership. Encourage them to use the leadership skills they've learned. Educate teens on the basics of different learning styles prior to teaching a lesson so they know how to make the lesson interactive and engaging. Keep the experience fun by letting students choose their leadership topic and promoting peer support. Give each teen (or team of teens) time to teach their topic to the class.

Surveys

Have teens design and administer surveys to peers, adults, and any other stakeholders. Encourage teens to use any formats such as box-checking and short essay or answer. Ask questions such as "how did you feel about leadership when we first started?" Move through progressive questions to find out if the learners have changed their feelings about leadership as well as asking questions specific to leadership skills and abilities they have learned and developed.

Teen Written Tests

Let teens figure out what's important and what's not. Ask them to create their own test—you can set some basic criteria and still leave plenty of room for creativity.

Webs or Mind-Mapping

Let teens create huge, poster-sized maps of what they know about leadership or leadership topics. Thematic webs and graphic organizers offer tangential and interconnected thoughts about a main idea. Mapping is a great way for teens to show they understand relationships, themes, and associations of leadership ideas.

Before beginning the sessions, determine what methods, if any, you will use to measure participant learning (for example, will you require a project to observe an organization, exams?) and set grading standards. If using the ELSA (page 159), build time into your session schedule to allow for conducting and interpreting the inventory. Suggestions for when to plan exams, project presentations, and research papers are included in the sample sequence of sessions (see pages 178–182). If you are using an evaluation or pre- and post-assessment, review the one you have selected to determine when teens might complete it.

Additional Information on Youth Leadership

Youth leadership is a growing interest area in the field of leadership development, with programs being developed in schools and communities worldwide. This is exciting because for many years, leadership training has been associated with business or management. Much of the existing research and anecdotal observations apply to the business world or other corporate environments.

But while adult leadership programs can provide a starting point for developing effective teen leadership programs, teen leaders prefer age-relevant instruction rather than that geared toward adults.

A wide range of leadership opportunities exist for kids and teens. Even so, young leaders often are not provided enough training to succeed in their leadership roles. Student leaders, particularly in middle school and high school, are put into positions of leadership through popular vote, teacher and staff selection, or parental urging. Frequently, students in leadership roles have little in-depth understanding of the significance of their role or the personal development that can come with the experience.

Many of my interviews with teen leaders indicate that their experiences would be more meaningful if someone took the time to explore what being a leader meant to them and how they could get the most from

a particular leadership position. In addition, teen leaders express that not everyone is interested in being in student council, yet often, those students are the only ones given opportunities to take leadership classes or participate in leadership workshops or trainings.

Too frequently, youth leadership education lacks consistent and deliberate connection between the leadership experience and the application of these skills to the real world. Because of this, some teen leadership experiences remain stagnant or superficial rather than truly promoting youth empowerment and leadership ability. Many teens begin to perceive their leadership experiences—athletics, student government, youth group, clubs, school participation, class involvement, or volunteering—as "fun and games" without meaningful connection to daily life and lifelong goals. In cases where leadership is part of a "turn around" program (diversions, intervention, etc.), teens may even participate because they feel they *have* to, rather than doing so to enhance personal development.

At the college level, the sophisticated integration of leadership development has increased tremendously since the late 20th century. The advent of organized leadership programs means there's no excuse for college-bound students not to be sufficiently prepared to take on the responsibilities of leadership. For secondary students who don't intend to attend college, the need for sufficient preparation at the middle and high school level is even greater. As teens enter adulthood, they will find themselves working with an increasingly diverse and complex workforce. When competing with college-educated peers who have participated in leadership experiences, a lack of these skills will be obvious. Employers will be looking at how capable each person is at being a leader within their own field and with colleagues.

It's disappointing that comprehensive teen leadership education is rarely included in most curricula. And although many activities of adolescence contribute to positive leadership development, these activities repeatedly occur without concentrating efforts on discussion, reflection, application, and mastery. For example, teens elected to lead their student council may recognize the power of their new position without recognizing how capable or prepared they are to carry out the responsibilities of that position. The same is true of teens who are involved in volunteer efforts yet are unprepared to interact with community citizens or the populations they're excited to serve. Unfortunately, advisors lack the time necessary to conduct appropriate leadership training so teen leaders are prepared. Yet, teen leaders are still expected to demonstrate consistent and balanced leadership abilities.

Recognizing that teens benefit from assistance identifying, developing, and fine-tuning leadership skills is a key step. Recognizing that youth leadership is different from adult theories of development is also an important step (see the Josephine A. van Linden and Carl I. Fertman book *Youth Leadership* for research support). The challenge is how to dedicate time and energy to developing leadership skills and sensitivities in teens.

It's important to recognize the pivotal role all adults (educators, youth workers, camp directors, youth ministers, mentors, etc.) play in helping every teen develop leadership abilities to this potential.

Rather than viewing leadership ability as something one either has or doesn't have, and employing this attitude with all teens, it is more effective to embrace the idea that every teen has the potential to be a leader. This perspective is effective because it:

- is action oriented
- is present tense ("here and now")
- is personal and individualistic
- is reinforced when teens work with others
- promotes locus of control skills
- promotes self-esteem and confidence
- combines thought, action, feelings, and physiological responses
- recognizes that there are various definitions of leadership yet common terms that apply to leaders and leadership
- recognizes that leadership is a collection of skills and behaviors that can be taught, practiced, and improved upon
- prepares teens for their future

Read on to understand teen perspectives on leadership, what's missing for teen leaders, and ways to serve as an exceptional leadership educator and role model for all teens you encounter.

Understanding the Teen Leadership Frame of Reference

- Teens tend to embrace a "philosophical" (what does leadership mean in my life; how do I feel about being a leader) approach to leadership. They develop individual and personal beliefs about leaders and leadership instead of trying to fit into predefined leadership categories.

- Teens have similar experiences as their peers and can apply these experiences to their daily life. What they do in school and in the community are closely linked and may involve interacting with the same people in all settings. Organized leadership development efforts are particularly effective because of this interconnectedness.

- Many teens realize, but may not accept, their strengths and challenges as leaders. They may bend to social pressure to act "cool" even if their internal compasses struggle to guide them differently.

- Teens are savvy in identifying acceptable and appropriate standards for socially recognized leaders. They have difficulty identifying heroes as compared to earlier generations because of the rise in "famous" yet unnoteworthy individuals in society.

- Teens expect a lot from peers who are elected or selected into leadership roles. In situations where selection standards are ill-defined or minimal, poorly prepared teen leaders may find themselves in positions that result in peer and/or adult dissatisfaction.

- Teens have greater opportunities than in the past to take on increasingly responsible leadership roles in school or the community. Even though teen opinions are sought by adult leadership (for example, by community agency boards, mayors, senators, city councils, school boards, etc.), opportunities for teens to impact decisions directly affecting youth "quality of life" in the community are still limited.

- Teens have grown up being taught to accept diversity and tolerance and to have a multicultural attitude when serving as leaders.

- Teens tend to embrace leaders who are team-oriented, a style that works well for teens who have grown up believing in teamwork and inclusivity. This is not all positive, however, because some teens have difficulty taking the lead when others won't.

- Teens are provided opportunities to take on leadership roles to assist peers in developing personal power and control in daily conflicts. More mediation and intervention programs rely on the power of teen involvement—from telling their story to serving as formal role models.

- Teens are increasingly encouraged to seek out (or are set up with) mentors within their school or community. Research continues to indicate the beneficial role mentors play in the lives of kids and teens.

- Teens value the importance of building relationships and showing care for others.

- Like adults, teens struggle with the stereotype that leaders are popular and attractive, and that only good kids are good leaders. At-risk teens more often than not believe that to be a leader there must be something special about you.

- Teen leaders grapple with how to deal with peers who want them to confront authority, change the system, or otherwise counteract status-quo and may accuse them of "selling out" when they agree with adult-driven leadership decisions.

Making Teen Leadership Preparation More Meaningful

Preparing teens to lead takes dedication and deliberate attention. Consider using the following guidelines as a foundation for making teen leadership opportunities meaningful, and in turn, more sustainable:

- Provide opportunities for teens to make mistakes without having these mistakes held against them.

- Help teens identify appropriate contemporary social role models, even if these role models seem few and far between.

- Value teens for who they are now rather than wanting them to "grow up."

- Establish consistent, reasonable leadership standards that parents, teachers, and other close adults can expect from teens.

- Provide real leadership experiences that apply to daily life and the future.

- Recognize that real life experiences (positive and negative) often shape the leadership attitudes of tweens and teens, and adapt leadership training to transform these attitudes if necessary.

- Look for ways to provide at-risk teens with leadership roles, so negative social influences won't take precedence (for example, gangs, negative peer-pressure, adult acquaintances, drug culture, etc.).

- Acknowledge and embrace the diversity and cultural differences of modern teens.

- Connect teens with adult mentors who are comfortable allowing them to take on significant responsibilities and leadership roles.

- Encourage teens to envision the difference and power one person can make.

- Provide consistent, frequent opportunities to take on leadership roles within the communities or organizations most influential to teens (schools, youth groups, community centers, etc.).

- Be willing to learn from spontaneous classroom or group discussions rather than restraining teen energy through over-programmed, sterile, or climate-controlled situations.

Tips for Developing Your Skills as a Leadership Educator

Kids and teens want to see that you're as serious as they are about being a leader. Here are ideas for infusing a leadership attitude into your classroom or program:

- Use leadership language in everyday conversation with teens (remark when you notice how they take charge, make a difference, believe in themselves, make good decisions, serve as role models, etc.).

- Acknowledge and recognize teens who make good leadership decisions in their mental health, peer activities, and other involvements.

- Use leadership development activities as sessions for groups.

- Use debriefing and reflection that relate the experience to the issues of the group as well as to what they can do in their daily lives.

- Dedicate specific sessions to developing leadership.

- Depending upon the subject matter of individual sessions, incorporate leadership skills development as part of group action plans or homework.

- Develop a leadership library from which teens can check out books or videos. A brief selection of books and movies are included on pages 215–218 of this book. Also, visit mariammacgregor.com for additional resources.

- Show movies with leadership themes, discuss them, and apply them to the issues at hand.

- Offer an organized, ongoing leadership development class. Have this class provide consistent experiences for every student who completes it. As time goes on, the culture of your program will begin to reflect the ideals you develop in the class, regardless of when teens participate in the class.

- Communicate the importance for leaders to recognize and value diversity. Create activities that assist in developing these skills and sensitivities.
- Create or enhance peer mediation training.
- Create teen review boards or decision-making committees to help with organizational decisions and meet regularly.
- Develop a schedule for teens to introduce current events for leadership discussion.

Here are ideas for personal and professional development to enhance one's skill as a leadership educator:

- Read about leadership theories, attitudes, and trends.
- Talk with teen leaders around your school and community.
- Observe teen leaders in action.
- Teach a leadership class: like teens, adults learn best through hands-on experience.
- Participate in a ropes course.
- Take a training class to learn how to facilitate a ropes course.
- Attend a lecture or presentation given by a business leader or other individual who is recognized for leadership skills and use what you learn when working with teens.
- Volunteer in the community—service experiences are excellent ways to develop leadership skills.
- Develop an evaluation form of your skills that teens can complete and give back to you. (Allow for anonymity—you get better feedback.)
- Participate in the school improvement process; volunteer to chair a committee or lead some other group process.
- When reading (books, newspapers, blogs, Web content, etc.), read with an eye for the leadership issues being addressed (such as ethics, creative thinking, problem solving, communication, appropriate conflict resolution, etc.).
- Co-plan and/or co-teach with a teen leader a class session on a leadership topic. Take time after the experience to discuss successes and challenges.
- Attend professional development trainings on leadership topics.

- Co-teach with teachers in various academic disciplines a class session on leadership or a lengthier leadership class.
- Coach a teen athletic team.
- Sponsor a school club or other youth activity.
- Serve as detention monitor one day, but instead of the usual detention schedule, design and conduct relevant leadership lessons (for example, on how to stay out of detention)—leadership lessons *do* apply to truancy and misbehavior.
- Find a mentor who can help you strengthen your skills as a leadership educator.
- Enroll in a course on organizational behavior, leadership styles, communication, or something similar (check local colleges and universities—this coursework often counts toward continuing education for professional licenses/credentials).
- Watch and discuss movies that relate to leadership (many movies do!).
- Practice, practice, practice.

Here are tips for building a culture of leadership into classrooms or program space:

- Partner with teens to establish a definition of "leadership" and "leader" and post them in a prominent place for all to see.
- Identify the leadership characteristics you desire teens in your program to possess, and create opportunities to learn them. Examples include:

  —volunteering at a shelter (empathy and tolerance)

  —participating in a community forum (community leadership)

  —registering to vote and understanding the voting process (political leadership)

  —attending a cultural event of a culture different from your own (tolerance and diversity)

  —practicing ethical decisions (ethics, values, and decision making)

- Seek teen perspectives when shaping policies and programs.
- When teens in your program or school make a mistake, allow time to discuss what they learned from the experience and how they can use what they learned. In other words, allow for mistakes, process through them, and apply the learning.

- Explore ways that teens can learn new things and apply what they have learned. As with most things, learning leadership takes practice. Talk about experiences along the way.

- Make "leadership" and "becoming a leader" part of daily conversation, program activities, school, and family activities.

- Include youth leadership tips and youth leadership recognitions in your newsletter or at your website.

- Relate leadership to all activities.

- Identify what is important to the young people in your program and find ways to create leadership opportunities around those topics and issues.

- Learn and practice appropriate conflict resolution with youth.

- Consistently recognize leadership accomplishments for all teens, all situations.

- Be attentive to "teachable leadership moments."

- Listen and be patient . . . developing leaders is an ongoing process.

- Be supportive and encouraging.

- Model what you expect, and let teens lead.

Leadership Education for Digital Natives

Today's teens are the first of many generations who will grow up in a technologically driven world. A few years ago, cell phones were designed for basic text and talk interactions, and other mobile devices were limited in the classroom. Now, students learn in wired environments, complete assignments individually or in groups using various Internet platforms, and are expected to BYOD (bring your own device) to some classes.

It's an exciting and challenging endeavor to prepare kids and teens that are highly connected to one another (and their learning) via the cloud to be leaders in real life. While technology can enrich most academic learning environments, when it comes to this type of experiential learning, technology can distract or distance kids from hands-on, interactive leadership lessons.

Participating in sessions from *Building Everyday Leadership* is a bit like attending summer camp where, unless you're at technology camp, campers are asked to leave their devices behind in order to fully participate in group activities. By facilitating lessons where students take on various leadership roles or actively participate from beginning to end, teens learn critical relationship skills needed by good leaders. Curtailing technology use during interactive leadership lessons minimizes the busy "split-brain" approach to life that is becoming normalized for kids and teens. In many ways, good leadership education relies on old-school techniques—building face-to-face relationships, teaching and practicing conflict resolution in real life, laughing together, problem solving through tough situations, and strengthening critical thinking skills instead of allowing wishy-washy multiple-choice decision making.

Adult facilitators also excel when modeling high-touch teaching by putting away their own devices during discussions and processing. Teens learn how to give their full attention when they receive our full attention.

But . . . when it comes to enriching and extending the learning, technology is an excellent and relevant tool! Recording videos, snapping and artistically editing photos, creating funny viral memes, using modern resources to measure authentic learning, interacting in real time on multiple social platforms (which change rapidly), and creating connected youth communities on these same platforms is worthwhile and relevant.

It bears repeating: everyone can learn to lead. But truly learning to be a leader requires more than a Google search to identify the best ingredients. It requires practice and "being present in the present." Young people who look others in the eye, offer a hand for a hand shake, and speak clearly and confidently stand out in a crowd full of teens with eyes glued to a device, thumbs tapping away, and responding with mumbled, distracted, fragmented comments in conversation.

Inspiring the Way

Teen leaders are not just the leaders of the future; they are our leaders of today. As an educator or youth worker using this curriculum guide, aim to actively seek out teens' insights and contributions in school, in businesses, in the community, and in families. If you can motivate teens with high expectations and an attitude that lets them know you believe in them, they rarely will set their personal standards any lower.

Leading with your own heart is what teaching teens about leadership and being a leader is all about. With this guide, you'll discover many ways to personally inspire teens to embrace leadership and take the lead. But no matter how well you know the subject matter, the true inspiration comes from within you. Your passion for working with teens and nurturing their potential for leading will only increase as you embrace and experience their passions. And imagine what that can mean for all the leaders to come!

INTRODUCING LEADERSHIP

(PAGES 5–8 IN *EVERYDAY LEADERSHIP*)

GOALS

Participants will:

- consider their own potential for leadership
- gain insight into the value of leadership in everyday activities
- introduce themselves to the group
- review program or class expectations and goals

MATERIALS NEEDED

- *Everyday Leadership,* one book for each participant
- Class sequence and syllabus (optional)
- Everyday Leadership Skills & Attitude (ELSA) Inventory, one for each participant (optional)
- 8½" x 11" colored paper
- Markers, colored pencils, or crayons

GETTING READY

Make copies of the "Class Sequence" and "Class Syllabus" on pages 181–182 and 183 and if necessary, modify for your specific use.

Getting Started

Gaining an understanding of why leadership is important in everyday ways, big and small, is key to teens developing their own leadership ability. This session provides an entertaining way for teens to consider their potential as leaders. It also enables teens to introduce themselves to one another if they don't already know each other.

Welcome everyone to the group. During the first 10 minutes, acknowledge the specific reasons teens are learning about leadership. Briefly express your reasons for teaching leadership. Then explain why leadership is important. You might say:

How often do you find yourself complaining or disappointed about things you wish you could change? Do you ever feel frustrated about not knowing how to make a change happen? Or wish you felt more

confident to speak up and say something? By learning and building the skills to step forward and stand up for your beliefs, or to follow through on your dreams, you can put yourself in a better position to make your voice heard. In other words, learning how to take the lead can help you achieve what you want.

Leading doesn't mean you have to do something big, such as be president of a group or a famous individual who campaigns for political causes. And it isn't something just a few people in recognized positions of authority do either. There are lots of smaller, more modest ways to take the lead every day, such as routinely doing volunteer work or welcoming a new kid at school into your group of friends.

Learning to lead enables you to learn about yourself and try new skills. It's about putting into action who you are and what you care about to make a positive difference for yourself and the world around you.

Pass out copies of *Everyday Leadership*. Highlight the ways this book will be a "work in progress" for teens. You might say:

After the group sessions and our discussions, you will be thinking and writing in your book on the topics we learned about. By doing so, you will be creating a collection of your thoughts and ideas on leadership. Hopefully, this book will become your personal guide and resource to refer to throughout any leadership experiences.

Ask teens to read the "Introduction" on pages 1–4 of their books, and allow them a few minutes to flip through the pages. Then, for the next 10 minutes or so, cover the following steps, excluding any that are not relevant to your setting:

1 Hand out the syllabus and the sequence of sessions. Ask teens to look over them, and briefly point out any required projects, papers, and exams. Tell teens you will address details about these requirements during future sessions.

2 Distribute copies of the Everyday Leadership Skills & Attitude (ELSA) Inventory (page 159), and instruct teens on completing it. If there's time, ask them to do it during the session or instruct them to complete it later and return it by the next session.

3 Explain that in addition to doing one or more activities and having a group discussion during a session, they'll be using their books both in and outside of the sessions. Go through the general format of *Everyday Leadership* and point out each of the sections and how they relate to what takes place in each session. You might say:

- "Quotes" pages help trigger your thinking about the leadership topic for each session. You may want to share the quotes and your reactions to them with friends and family and ask what they think. Keep the quotes in mind throughout the activities we'll be doing.

- "Try This" pages you may do individually or in a small group during the session.

- "Find Out More About It" pages provide background reading. Sometimes you'll read this information before an activity. Other times, you'll read the information afterward so it doesn't influence how you act or what happens during the activity.

- "Think and Write About It" pages include questions to think about and respond to individually after our group discussion.

- "Do Something About It" pages give you ideas or actions to "do something" with what you are learning about being a leader. Each time, you'll select one or two of these ideas to set as personal goals to achieve. If you have an idea or two of your own that you prefer, there's also space to add these to the list.

4 Explain how you will review their writing to provide feedback (or if grading is necessary) based on the strategies you've selected. For example, you might say:

Time allowing, you'll get 5 to 10 minutes to write at the end of each session. If we do not have enough time, you'll need to complete your responses to the required reflective writing questions in the "Think and Write About It" section by the next session. Feel free to answer any additional questions on your own to further explore leadership.

Sometimes, we'll share responses with the group or a partner to learn from each other. Please respond honestly to the questions in your books, keeping in mind that what you write may be read by or discussed with another person. If you have written something you'd prefer just me to read, let me know and we can meet individually.

5 Encourage teens to be creative with their books. They can use the book or a separate folder to store handouts, notes, pictures, or other mementos from leadership experiences they have throughout the sessions or later.

Allow a few minutes for questions. To summarize, you might say:

> **Make the book your own. Having fun with it and being creative is part of this leadership learning experience. Think about what leadership means for you, why you are here, and what kind of a leader you want to be.**

TEACH THIS

At the Newsstand

In this warm-up activity, teens will draw fictitious magazine covers featuring themselves. This activity helps teens consider their potential for being leaders. Some of the covers might be funny, others more serious.

Distribute the colored paper and markers (or colored pencils, crayons) to each person. Ask everyone to focus on her or his piece of paper while you describe a scenario. As they are looking at the sheet of paper, say:

> **It's years from now and you're looking at a magazine on the newsstand. The cover shows a successful leader in the world. The person on the cover is you.**

Explain that each person is to design his or her magazine cover during the next 5 to 10 minutes. Give fictitious examples such as "Javier Discovers New Comet!" on *Star Gazer,* "Meet the Parrot Lady—Jennie Smith Starts a Sanctuary" on *Animals Today,* or "Book Lover Donates Collection" on *Library Archives.* Tell teens to include their names in the cover headline and emphasize they do not have to be splendid artists to make their point. To get them started, ask:

> **Imagine why you are on the cover. What magazine is it? What's the headline? What have you done to deserve recognition? What makes you the leader everyone is admiring? What do people see in you? Think of what matters to you: big or small. Imagine what you really care about or would like to positively affect.**

When everyone is finished, ask for volunteers to stand up, introduce themselves, and show their covers. Invite teens to explain their covers and the leadership characteristics highlighted. At a minimum, provide an opportunity for everyone to introduce themselves even if they don't share a lot about their cover.

Talk About It

Lead a 10-minute group discussion about the various ways different people view what makes a leader. Ask:

> • **How did it feel to think about yourself in the future and on a magazine?**
>
> • **What makes it difficult or easy to think of yourself as a leader?**
>
> • **When you see a magazine cover with a well-known person, what distinguishes the person as a respected leader versus a celebrity?**
>
> • **Do you think being on a magazine cover means the person is a leader? Why or why not?**
>
> • **Why do you think many people believe a person has to do something monumental to be considered a leader?**

Wrapping Up

For "Think and Write About It" (pages 6–7 in *Everyday Leadership*), let participants know whether they are to answer specific questions or all of them, or if they're to choose a few themselves. Suggest as they write their responses they consider what their magazine cover means to them and keep in mind what others in the group shared.

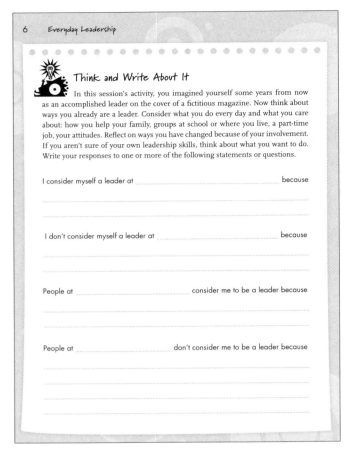

Think and Write About It

In this session's activity, you imagined yourself some years from now as an accomplished leader on the cover of a fictitious magazine. Now think about ways you already are a leader. Consider what you do every day and what you care about: how you help your family, groups at school or where you live, a part-time job, your attitudes. Reflect on ways you have changed because of your involvement. If you aren't sure of your own leadership skills, think about what you want to do. Write your responses to one or more of the following statements or questions.

I consider myself a leader at _____ because

_____

_____

I don't consider myself a leader at _____ because

_____

_____

People at _____ consider me to be a leader because

_____

_____

People at _____ don't consider me to be a leader because

_____

_____

---

to select what resonates for them individually but also involves challenging themselves to improve their skills. To close, you might say:

Remember, what may be simple for an outgoing person may be more difficult for someone who is shy or reserved. Also, even if you've practiced some leadership skills previously, you may feel a bit uncomfortable at first about doing something new. Believe in yourself and keep practicing.

Do Something About It

To commit to learning about leadership, it's important to put your thoughts into action. Choosing to act can help you take being a leader to the next level, assist you in finding out more about yourself, or inspire you to do something that before now you couldn't imagine doing.

Check the goal(s) you will set to demonstrate your leadership abilities. If you have ideas of your own that you prefer, add them on the lines provided. Then write a date by which you plan to put your goal(s) into action on the "To Do By" lines and the date you completed them on the "Did By" lines. Be sure to fill in "What I Did to Achieve My Goal(s)."

	To Do By	Did By
○ I will do what I can to help a new teen in my neighborhood, school, or youth group feel welcome.	_____	_____
○ I will sit next to someone other than one of my friends in one of my classes or other activities and offer my help.	_____	_____

When you think of yourself as a leader, what expectations do you have of yourself?

_____

_____

_____

What expectations do you feel others have of you as a leader?

_____

_____

For future reference, you may want to put a check next to the questions you are assigning.

Before ending the session, remind teens to choose a couple goals from "Do Something About It" (pages 7–8 in *Everyday Leadership*) and create an appropriate time-frame to achieve them—a week, two weeks, a month, and so forth—and write it down. Instruct participants also to write down the actual date they achieved the goals and to describe what they did to achieve those goals. Make clear that there are no right or wrong choices; encourage all

---

	To Do By	Did By
○ I will find out what teen leadership positions are available at school or with a community group or program.	_____	_____
○ I will talk with my friends or family about the ways they think I am already a leader.	_____	_____

Other "Do Something About It" Ideas

○ _____

_____

○ _____

_____

What I Did to Achieve My Goal(s)

_____

_____

_____

_____

WHAT LEADERSHIP MEANS TO ME

(PAGES 9–13 IN *EVERYDAY LEADERSHIP*)

GOALS

Participants will:

- learn basic leadership concepts
- identify various leadership characteristics
- define leadership
- reflect broadly on the significance of leadership in everyday circumstances

MATERIALS NEEDED

- Markers or chalk
- Chart paper (recommended since you can keep it) or whiteboard
- Masking tape

GETTING READY

If using chart paper, tape three or four sheets on the wall, bulletin board, or whiteboard.

Getting Started

In this session, teens explore their own definitions of leadership and gain an awareness of how differently people define leadership. Understanding group members' various views of leadership can help teens lead more effectively.

To introduce the session, tell participants that people have studied and talked about leadership for many years and defined it in many different ways; even the experts don't agree on a single definition. You might highlight and briefly discuss these two definitions:

- From *Merriam-Webster's Collegiate Dictionary*[1]: "the office or position of a leader; the capacity to lead; or the act of an instance of leading." This definition is typical of those that refer to the position of leadership that someone holds—often with a title of control over a group.

- From *On Becoming a Leader*[2]: "knowing yourself, having a vision that is well communicated, building trust among colleagues, and taking effective action

---

1. *Merriam-Webster's Collegiate Dictionary, Eleventh Edition* (Springfield, MA: Merriam-Webster, Inc., 2003).

2. Bennis, Warren G., *On Becoming a Leader* (New York: Perseus Publishing, 2003).

to realize your own leadership potential." This definition comes from Warren Bennis, who many people call the "leadership guru" because of his contributions worldwide to the field of leadership.

Make sure teens understand Bennis' definition. To continue, you might say:

> While Bennis' definition of leadership comes from the world of business and management, it also captures the way you will be exploring leadership to develop your individual talents. Because there are so many different perspectives on what leadership is, Bennis, along with his coauthor, Burt Nanus, say in their book *Leaders: Strategies for Taking Charge*[3] that: "Like love, leadership continue[s] to be something everyone [knows exists] but nobody [can] define." Today, you are going to work on your own definitions of leadership.

TEACH THIS

Defining Leadership

(page 10 in *Everyday Leadership*)

Ask teens to count off by threes to form small groups. Then direct everyone to turn to "Defining Leadership" in his or her books. Tell them:

> In your groups, take 5 to 10 minutes to brainstorm words or terms, positive and negative, that come to mind when you think about leaders or leadership. Think about words that describe characteristics of leaders and write them in your books. Do not simply list names of leaders.

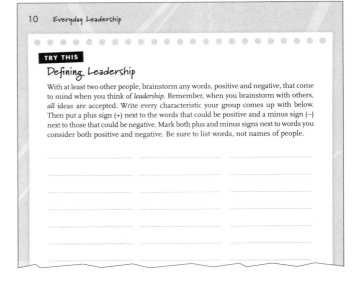

10   Everyday Leadership

TRY THIS

Defining Leadership

With at least two other people, brainstorm any words, positive and negative, that come to mind when you think of *leadership*. Remember, when you brainstorm with others, *all* ideas are accepted. Write every characteristic your group comes up with below. Then put a plus sign (+) next to the words that could be positive and a minus sign (–) next to those that could be negative. Mark both plus and minus signs next to words you consider both positive and negative. Be sure to list words, not names of people.

Ask teens to tell you their understanding of brainstorming; if necessary, remind them that brainstorming means all ideas are accepted and written down and no one comments either positively or negatively on any of the ideas. As the groups are brainstorming, circulate around the room to comment on their lists and make sure they stay on task.

Take the next 10 to 15 minutes to have each group vocally share its list of leadership characteristics on the chart paper or whiteboard. Ask for one or two volunteers to write all of the words on the chart paper or whiteboard as each group shares its list. The recorder can use hatch marks to identify duplicates. You may want to leave the chart paper hanging to keep these leadership characteristics in mind during additional sessions. (If possible, following the session, create a community list by typing all of the words onto a master list. Distribute copies of the list at the next session for teens to keep with their leadership materials.)

Talk About It

Lead a 10-minute discussion about the groups' experiences defining leadership. Ask:

- **How easy or difficult was it to come up with descriptive words?**

- **How many words or phrases on your lists do you consider negative descriptions of leadership or leaders? What are a few examples? Why do you think these words show up on the lists?**

---

3. Bennis, Warren G., and Nanus, Burt, *Leaders: Strategies for Taking Charge* (New York: Collins, 2003).

- **What characteristics did every group list? Why do you think these terms are so common?**

- **When you think of the people who are leaders in your life, which of these characteristics do you associate with their leadership?**

- **If you want people to think of you as a leader, what characteristics do you hope they would use to describe you?**

- **What characteristics are unrealistic to expect in a leader?** (for example, *perfect, flawless, immortal,* or others that the groups shared)

- **In general, what overall expectations do you have of leaders? Do you think your expectations are realistic? Why or why not? What do you think, feel, or do when leaders don't live up to your expectations?**

Wrapping Up

"Think and Write About It" (pages 10–12 in *Everyday Leadership*) encourages teens to keep in mind the community list as they answer the selected questions in their books and reflect further on their personal definition of leadership.

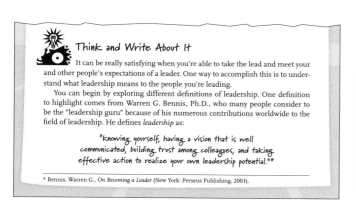

Think and Write About It

It can be really satisfying when you're able to take the lead and meet your and other people's expectations of a leader. One way to accomplish this is to understand what leadership means to the people you're leading.

You can begin by exploring different definitions of leadership. One definition to highlight comes from Warren G. Bennis, Ph.D., who many people consider to be the "leadership guru" because of his numerous contributions worldwide to the field of leadership. He defines *leadership* as:

"knowing yourself, having a vision that is well communicated, building trust among colleagues, and taking effective action to realize your own leadership potential."*

* Bennis, Warren G., *On Becoming a Leader* (New York: Perseus Publishing, 2003).

Session 2: What Leadership Means to Me   11

More simply, leadership is being clear about who you are and what you care about, and doing what needs to be done. Consider this definition, and any others you know, as you write your responses to the questions and statements that follow.

Review the characteristics of leadership from your list on page 10 (or the larger group's list). Select the ones that mean the most to you and explain why each one is important to you.

_____

_____

_____

When people refer to you as a leader, what do you hope they are saying or thinking about you?

_____

_____

_____

I want others to consider me a leader because:

_____

_____

_____

People who are considered leaders should be expected to:

_____

_____

---

12   Everyday Leadership

_____

_____

I define *leadership* as:

_____

_____

_____

For future reference, you may want to put a check next to the questions you are assigning.

"Do Something About It" (pages 12–13 in *Everyday Leadership*) offers goal choices that reinforce the development of leadership characteristics identified in the brainstormed lists.

Do Something About It

Think about your own definition of leadership and the characteristics you associate with it. What steps will you take to demonstrate or build these traits in yourself?

Check the goal(s) you will set to demonstrate your leadership abilities. If you have ideas of your own that you prefer, add them on the lines provided. Then write a date by which you plan to put your goal(s) into action on the "To Do By" lines and the date you completed them on the "Did By" lines. Be sure to fill in "What I Did to Achieve My Goal(s)."

	To Do By	Did By
○ I will ask someone I respect to tell me about a more experienced and admired person he or she got advice from and how that person affected him or her.		
○ I will pick a subject I'm good at and ask a teacher if I can tutor younger students or peers for 8 to 10 sessions.		

	To Do By	Did By
○ I will interview a community leader and ask for his or her definition of leadership. I will share what I learn with this group.		
○ I will cowrite with a friend an article for the school or local newspaper, or a community program newsletter about the leadership abilities of teens.		

Other "Do Something About It" Ideas

○ _____

○ _____

What I Did to Achieve My Goal(s)

_____
_____
_____
_____

SESSION·SESSION·SESSION·SESSION·

3

THE LEADERS IN MY LIFE

(PAGES 14–19 IN *EVERYDAY LEADERSHIP*)

GOALS

Participants will:

- learn about basic qualities that make a person a leader

- correlate individuals who are leaders with the characteristics that make them leaders

- identify people they consider leaders

Getting Started

In this session, teens identify well-known individuals who exhibit overall qualities people generally look for in leaders. It's helpful to have teens note well-known individuals so everyone can relate to how others interpret each quality. By also considering people important in their own lives (which teens do in "Think and Write About It"), teens link the very personal nature of leadership and how every person has the potential to be a leader.

To introduce the topic of leadership qualities, you might say:

A single characteristic alone—like self-confidence or enthusiasm—does not make a person a leader. Today we're going to think about qualities we seek in effective leaders or that you may want to strive for to be seen as an effective leader. We're going to

look at these qualities by identifying famous individuals who demonstrate them as well as by selecting people you know personally.

TEACH THIS

Qualities of Leadership

(pages 15–16 in *Everyday Leadership*)

Ask teens to turn to "Qualities of Leadership" in their books on page 15. Allow them 20 minutes to read about the qualities and to write the name of a well-known leader who demonstrates each one. You might say:

As you read the list of qualities, write on the blank line the name of a well-known person who demonstrates each quality. It's not unusual for well-known leaders to have more than one quality, but try to

think of a different person for each quality. Choose someone for the quality he or she most obviously exhibits. If you're stuck, think about people locally or nationally you've read about in newspapers or magazines, or heard about on radio or TV recently.

TRY THIS

Qualities of Leadership

Identifying well-known people who demonstrate effective leadership qualities helps you relate to how others interpret those qualities. Read each of the following qualities and fill in the blanks with the name of a well-known person who shows that quality. It's not unusual for well-known leaders to have more than one quality, but try to name a different person for each quality. If you get stuck, think about people locally or nationally you've read about in newspapers or magazines, or heard about on radio or TV recently.

A Well-Known Leader Who
DOES THE RIGHT THING: _____

Leaders who do the right thing know how they feel about issues and take the high road, even in difficult situations and when others aren't watching. They are ethical, act with integrity, have good morals, and know how to stand up for their beliefs.

A Well-Known Leader Who
HAS A SENSE OF DIRECTION: _____

Leaders with a sense of direction have a "built-in GPS system." They know how to move from Point A to Point B, even when things get in the way. Their vision extends beyond the present day and beyond themselves; they recognize that setting goals and being purposeful keeps them and others motivated on the journey.

A Well-Known Leader Who
RESPECTS POWER: _____

Leaders who respect power recognize their responsibility in using their power. They do not use their power carelessly or irresponsibly or to take advantage of situations.

A Well-Known Leader Who
THINKS CREATIVELY: _____

Leaders who think creatively know how to look at opportunities and problems in new ways or differently from others around them. They see the possibility that exists and ask, "Why not?"

A Well-Known Leader Who
EMBRACES DIFFERENCES: _____

Leaders who embrace differences recognize how diverse our world is. They recognize that people with different beliefs, backgrounds, and expectations often need to work together. They strive to promote understanding from all sides and bring dissimilar groups together to explore new directions.

A Well-Known Leader Who
ACTS WITH PASSION: _____

Leaders who act with passion inspire others. They communicate their excitement about a task in both subtle and obvious ways.

A Well-Known Leader Who
MANAGES UNEXPECTED SITUATIONS: _____

Leaders who manage unexpected situations know that success requires more than good planning. They think before acting and try to consider the outcome of options, even when time is limited.

A Well-Known Leader Who
MODELS HUMILITY: _____

Leaders who model humility (or modesty) act to make a difference. They don't call attention to their accomplishments and talent. They don't brag, seek praise for achievements, or have any hidden motives.

Talk About It

Allowing at least 10 to 15 minutes for group discussion, start by asking different participants to explain a quality in their own words. Invite each person to share who he or she named for a few qualities and one or two reasons why. Then ask:

- (If applicable): **Several of you named the same person for the same quality. What do you think that tells us about that leader?**

- **Will this activity influence you to think more broadly about the ways people around you and in the world behave as leaders? Why or why not?**

- **How does this activity influence thinking about yourself as a leader?**

- **What other qualities can you think of that are not on this list that other well-known leaders demonstrate? Name the leader and describe the quality she or he exhibits.**

Wrapping Up

"Think and Write About It" (pages 16–18 in *Everyday Leadership*) provides an opportunity for teens to focus on qualities of leaders they know well (for example, parents or other family members, coaches, teachers, supervisors, mentors). To encourage teens with their reflective writing, you might say:

> **Selecting people who are important in your life helps you see that leadership happens all the time and that every person has the potential to be a leader.**

Think and Write About It

Leadership happens all the time; every person has the potential to be a leader. For each of the following leadership qualities, write the name of someone you know *personally* who demonstrates it. Choose a different individual for each quality, even though one person in your life may possess more than one of these qualities. Describe in what ways each person demonstrates the quality.

The actions in "Do Something About It" (pages 18–19 in *Everyday Leadership*) get teens thinking about *how* they achieve a goal. Challenge them to concentrate on what qualities they demonstrate to others in accomplishing a specific act, such as coordinating a food drive or planning an event.

A Person I Know Well Who
DOES THE RIGHT THING:
_____
_____

A Person I Know Well Who
HAS A SENSE OF DIRECTION:
_____
_____

A Person I Know Well Who
RESPECTS POWER:
_____
_____

A Person I Know Well Who
THINKS CREATIVELY:
_____
_____

A Person I Know Well Who
EMBRACES DIFFERENCES:
_____
_____

A Person I Know Well Who
ACTS WITH PASSION:
_____
_____

A Person I Know Well Who
MANAGES UNEXPECTED SITUATIONS:
_____
_____

A Person I Know Well Who
MODELS HUMILITY:
_____
_____

For future reference, you may want to put a check next to the questions you are assigning.

▶ Do Something About It

Think of people who are leaders in your life and the qualities they demonstrate. Now consider the qualities you show others in accomplishing what you set out to do.

Check the goal(s) you will set to demonstrate your leadership abilities. If you have ideas of your own that you prefer, add them on the lines provided. Then write a date by which you plan to put your goal(s) into action on the "To Do By" lines and the date you completed them on the "Did By" lines. Be sure to fill in "What I Did to Achieve My Goal(s)."

	To Do By	Did By
○ I will write a thank-you letter to someone who has been a leader to me.		
○ I will nominate a friend, mentor, or family member for a community award (sponsored by a local TV station, newspaper, organization, government office, or other agency) that recognizes valuable contributions to our community.		

	To Do By	Did By
○ I will interview an elder to get a different generation's perspective on leadership qualities as well as to get advice for young leaders. I will share what I learn with this group.		
○ I will write about three other leadership qualities (not included on the "Qualities of Leadership" list on pages 15–16) that are important to me and explain why I value these traits.		

Other "Do Something About It" Ideas

○ _____
_____

○ _____
_____

What I Did to Achieve My Goal(s)
_____
_____
_____

SESSION · SESSION · SESSION · SESSION · SESSION · SESSION

WHAT I LOOK FOR IN A LEADER

(PAGES 20–24 IN *EVERYDAY LEADERSHIP*)

GOALS

Participants will:

- explore their expectations of leaders

- discuss other group members' expectations of leaders

- balance personal and group expectations of leaders

Getting Started

It's important for teens developing leadership skills to recognize that what one person looks for in a leader may vary from what another person seeks. Understanding different expectations of leaders helps teens more effectively meet individual and group needs when they take the lead. In this session, teens examine what they may need to do to balance their expectations of leaders with those of others.

To introduce the session focus, you might say:

Today, you are going to explore what you personally need and expect of a leader, as well as what a group may need and expect of a leader. In the process, you'll also discover what it takes to balance individual and group priorities.

TEACH THIS

An Effective Leader

(pages 21–22 in *Everyday Leadership*)

Ask teens to sit in a circle with their books and a pen or pencil and to turn to "An Effective Leader" on page 21. Then instruct them to:

Read the directions at the top of this page. You have 5 minutes to individually rank the top five actions you believe a leader can take to effectively direct a group project that you're working on. Read through the entire list first and then go back to do the ranking. If you feel any important or necessary behaviors are missing, write them on the blank lines at the end of the list before doing the ranking. Please don't share your choices or consult with others while you are doing this.

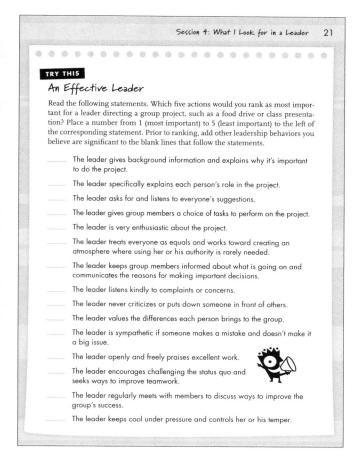

TRY THIS

An Effective Leader

Read the following statements. Which five actions would you rank as most important for a leader directing a group project, such as a food drive or class presentation? Place a number from 1 (most important) to 5 (least important) to the left of the corresponding statement. Prior to ranking, add other leadership behaviors you believe are significant to the blank lines that follow the statements.

_____ The leader gives background information and explains why it's important to do the project.

_____ The leader specifically explains each person's role in the project.

_____ The leader asks for and listens to everyone's suggestions.

_____ The leader gives group members a choice of tasks to perform on the project.

_____ The leader is very enthusiastic about the project.

_____ The leader treats everyone as equals and works toward creating an atmosphere where using her or his authority is rarely needed.

_____ The leader keeps group members informed about what is going on and communicates the reasons for making important decisions.

_____ The leader listens kindly to complaints or concerns.

_____ The leader never criticizes or puts down someone in front of others.

_____ The leader values the differences each person brings to the group.

_____ The leader is sympathetic if someone makes a mistake and doesn't make it a big issue.

_____ The leader openly and freely praises excellent work.

_____ The leader encourages challenging the status quo and seeks ways to improve teamwork.

_____ The leader regularly meets with members to discuss ways to improve the group's success.

_____ The leader keeps cool under pressure and controls her or his temper.

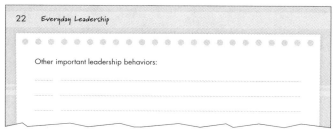

Other important leadership behaviors:

_____

_____

_____

Talk About It

Invite one teen to be a tally keeper to track everyone's top five rankings. Instruct the tally keeper to place a small mark in front of each statement in her or his book each time someone *includes* it in the ranking. (The tally keeper is not to track who ranks the statement or whether the ranking is number 1, 2, and so on.) Take 5 to 10 minutes to track the rankings and then discuss the results. Ask:

- **Which five statements got ranked the most?**

- **What do the five most frequent rankings tell you about individual expectations for a leader?**

- **What themes do you notice based on how everyone ranked the statements?**

- **What might the outcome be for completing a project if everyone in a group ranked "The leader is sympathetic if someone makes a mistake and doesn't make it a big issue" as a top expectation for a leader? Would the type of mistake matter?**

- **What might the outcome be for completing a project if no one in a group ranked "the leader explains each person's role in the project" as a priority?**

TEACH THIS

An Effective Leader: The Group's View

(page 22 in *Everyday Leadership*)

Keeping teens in a circle, ask them to reread the effective leader actions on pages 21–22. Then instruct them as follows:

> **You're now going to do a similar ranking; however, this time you will complete the ranking as a group. Discuss as a group if you feel any important or necessary behaviors are missing. Add them to the list before doing the ranking. Select one person in the group to keep track of time. You have 15 minutes to complete this activity.**

Depending upon group dynamics, this activity can take a while. As facilitator, observe how participants interact. Usually, one person inevitably emerges from the group as a leader to facilitate discussion about the ranking. Take note of this process. Subtly acknowledge it by relinquishing your facilitator role and guiding the teen leader to encourage the "talkers" to listen and the "listeners" to talk or other leadership behaviors necessary for the group to complete the activity.

An Effective Leader: The Group's View

Read the Effective Leader statements again. Work with the rest of your class or group to rank *together* the top five actions needed for a leader directing a group project, such as a food drive or class presentation. Place a number from 1 (most important) to 5 (least important) to the left of your original rankings. Prior to ranking, add other expectations the group believes are significant to the blank lines that follow the statements. Your group must agree on the final ranking, even if individually you prefer to rank them differently. If you have time, consider identifying (not necessarily ranking) the next top five actions and the five actions the group feels are least important.

Talk About It

Allocate at least 10 to 15 minutes for discussion exploring differences in what teens learned from ranking expectations of leaders individually and as a group. Ask:

- **How did ranking the most important actions as a group compare to doing this on your own? Are there other situations in which you think you might rank these actions differently, on your own or as a group? Explain.**

- **Did someone in your group take the leadership role? What roles did different people take?**

- **Did some of you have to change your rankings to accommodate others' preferences? If you had to change your rankings, were you willing to do so? Why?**

- **How many of you gave up a high-ranking priority to keep another statement high on the list? How do you feel about this? How could you relate this experience to everyday situations, such as making decisions with your friends about what to do, completing homework, or taking care of responsibilities at home or at a part-time job.**

Wrapping Up

Working with others to make a group decision can evoke a range of reactions and emotions. Encourage teens to keep their reactions to the group activity in mind while completing "Think and Write About It" (pages 22–23 in *Everyday Leadership*).

Think and Write About It

Prioritizing what *you* want from a leader versus what the *group* wants requires different mindsets. When you're working with a group to agree on some goals (as in the session activity), each person in the group may experience interesting reactions or emotions. Keep your own reactions in mind as you answer the following questions and statements. Use the lines provided to write your responses.

What is it like to have to compromise or negotiate on your priorities for the benefit of your group?

What do you think it takes for a group to make a decision together?

What role do you think the leader should play when a group needs to make a decision?

I often find myself thinking/doing _____ when I'm part of a group making a decision. During the next group activity I participate in, either with this group or in a different setting, I will try to:

For future reference, you may want to put a check next to the questions you are assigning.

"Do Something About It" (pages 23–24 in *Everyday Leadership*) goals this session offer participants opportunities to act in ways that require them to balance their own needs with the needs of one or more other people. You might also point out:

The goals may inspire you to act differently than you usually do. For example, if you're a quieter person, you may feel challenged to practice speaking up in a group. Or the goals you select may enable you to explore further some skills or reactions you experienced in the activities you just did.

Do Something About It

Try selecting actions from the following goals that inspire you to act in different ways than you're used to in groups. The skills you'll build in various situations will help as you participate in other groups. And whether or not you're the leader, you can help balance everyone's priorities, including your own.

Check the goal(s) you will set to demonstrate your leadership abilities. If you have ideas of your own that you prefer, add them on the lines provided. Then write a date by which you plan to put your goal(s) into action on the "To Do By" lines and the date you completed them on the "Did By" lines. Be sure to fill in "What I Did to Achieve My Goal(s)."

---

24   *Everyday Leadership*

	To Do By	Did By
○ I will help a friend or classmate on a project not because it necessarily interests me, but because he or she wants my help.		
○ I will discuss a controversial topic with someone who holds an opposing view without trying to convince him or her of my opinion.		
○ I will join a group or committee that needs more volunteers even though I tend to be nervous with new groups at first.		
○ I will tell my friends when I really need to be by myself, even though they may be disappointed or get mad at me for not doing something with the group.		

Other "Do Something About It" Ideas

○ _____

_____

What I Did to Achieve My Goal(s)

LEADERS AND FOLLOWERS

(PAGES 25–29 IN *EVERYDAY LEADERSHIP*)

GOALS

Participants will:

- examine how different types of people may work with different types of leaders

- discuss one theory of human behavior and how leaders can guide individual behavior within a group, both positively and negatively

MATERIALS NEEDED

- Set of colored rod and connector construction toys, such as Fiddlestix or Tinkertoys (available at educational or toy stores, or via the Internet)

- Table and five chairs

GETTING READY

Make sure your rod and connector construction set has the pieces listed below, plus another 10 pieces of any shape or color:

20 large circular discs	5 red sticks
5 green sticks	20 small circular discs
5 orange sticks	15 yellow sticks
5 end pieces	15 blue sticks
5 round, oblong, or tubular connector pieces	

Arrange a table and five chairs in the center or front of the room with enough surrounding space for people to stand nearby. Make a copy of each of the "Instructions for Try This" on pages 34 and 35–36. You may also want to make a copy of the "Find Out More About It: Leadership and Human Behavior" handout for everyone in the group (page 33).

Getting Started

Most people have a certain leadership style they prefer to use when leading a group. Depending on who's in the group, the leader's approach may not always be the most effective. Some group members may prefer very specific directions; others may favor more flexibility. In this session, teens explore how important it is for leaders to pay attention to who they're leading and if necessary, to adapt their leadership style.

To introduce the session, you might say:

Today, you will explore two things: the impact a leader has on a group as well as what type of person

you are within a group. Then you'll compare the outlook you have when you're a leader to your outlook when you're a group member. Everyone works better with a leader whose way of leading just fits. What you want and need from a leader may be different from what the person next to you wants and needs. To be an effective leader, it's important to understand how you treat people in your group to get things done. Before you choose how to lead, consider who are the people in your group and what they need from you to achieve specific goals.

Invite two volunteers to serve as leaders and 10 others to be members of two different groups of five following the leaders. Ask other participants in the session to observe what happens between each group and the two different leaders.

TEACH THIS

All Shapes and Sizes

Plan on about 20 to 25 minutes total for the two role plays. Review guidelines with participants for the role play if necessary (see page 4 in the "Introduction"). Designate two volunteers as Leader One and Leader Two. Give each the appropriate copy of instructions and ask them to read them silently. (You may choose to give the two teens the instructions prior to the session; if so, be sure to tell them not to share their roles with others in the group.) Explain to the two leaders what their roles are. Each will direct one of the groups to build a construction project using a rod and connector set.

Tell Leader One to present the guidelines on the instructions labeled "All Shapes and Sizes—Leader One" and encourage the group to work cooperatively and creatively. Leader One is to comment positively on the group's efforts and interact with the group yet maintain a leadership role.

Tell Leader Two to present the rules on the other set of instructions labeled "All Shapes and Sizes—Leader Two." This leader is to direct the group members to work independently of one another and do exactly as he or she says. Leader Two is to be directive and very explicit. For this leader, the structure of how the group operates is more important than the creativity of the project.

Ask five of the volunteers to sit at the table; direct the rest of the group to observe how the two leaders affect the group members individually and as a group. Give Leader One the rod and connector set and ask her or

him to begin. When the first group of volunteers finishes, have them leave their model or models on the table and join the others observing. Then ask the next group of five volunteers to sit at the table and prompt Leader Two to begin. Support both leaders' role-playing during the activity but avoid interfering.

Talk About It

To explore what the activity revealed, take 10 minutes for discussion. Ask:

- **What happened in the group with Leader One? with Leader Two?**
- **What was it like to be a member of the group with Leader One? with Leader Two?**
- **Which leadership style did you prefer?**
- **List and discuss the positives and negatives of both styles of leadership.**
- **Which of these styles of leadership appeals most to you as a leader? How about as a group member?**
- **What aspects of this role playing felt natural? What felt uncomfortable?**

Transition discussion to focus on Douglas McGregor's Theory Y and Theory X in "Find Out More About It" on page 26 in the teen books (page 33 in this book). Before they read, you might say:

> What you just experienced is based on the work of psychologist Douglas McGregor. He spent years studying how leaders lead, how leaders treat people in their groups, and how others follow. Although he mostly studied manager and employee roles, the ideas he wrote about and taught are now used in schools and community groups as well as in businesses. McGregor's ideas can be helpful as increasingly diverse groups look for ways to determine what people need to achieve goals.

As teens read the "Find Out More About It" page in their books, you may want to pass out the "Find Out More About It: Leadership and Human Behavior" handout to help fill in more information during discussion. Point out that according to McGregor's work, Leader One in the activity treated the group members according to Theory Y and Leader Two according to Theory X.

Wrapping Up

As teens complete "Think and Write About It" (pages 27–28 in *Everyday Leadership*), suggest that they think about different situations they've experienced with the same leader. Prompt them to consider whether those situations required different kinds of approaches depending on who was in the group at the time.

In "Do Something About It" (pages 28–29 in *Everyday Leadership*), encourage teens to keep in mind the specific needs of the people they're directing. Remind participants that in order to be most effective when working with different groups, they may need to adapt their preferred styles of leading.

Session 5: Leaders and Followers   27

Think and Write About It

While some leaders are group-centered and some leader-centered, most people in leadership roles generally use a combination of approaches to lead a group, depending on the situation. For example, if you are captain of a sports team that has been together for some time, you'll likely use more of a group-centered leadership style. You realize the group doesn't need much direction from you. If you're a camp leader training a new group of counselors, you're more likely to be directive and leader-centered to make sure the counselors are prepared to work with young kids. You recognize there's a lot of information they must learn, with little room for mistakes.

As you respond to the following questions and statements, keep in mind different situations you've experienced with the same leader. Consider whether the leader used different approaches in guiding the group, depending on who was in the group at the time.

Write about a leadership experience of your own or one you observed where you felt a group-centered leadership style was effective. Describe the situation, how people were treated in the group (as Ys or Xs), and why the style was effective.

Write about a leadership experience of your own or one you observed where you felt that a leader-centered leadership style was effective. Describe the situation, how people were treated in the group (as Ys or Xs), and why the style was effective.

---

28   Everyday Leadership

When you take the lead with groups, either in a formal role or under more everyday circumstances, do you tend to use a group-centered or a leader-centered leadership approach? Write your answer and explain why this approach is a natural fit for you or if it's a style you would like to change.

Based on what you learned about McGregor's Theory Y and Theory X (see page 26), write what you've discovered about how you treat people in groups (as Ys or Xs).

Do Something About It

Gaining awareness of how you treat others in a group as well as how you like to be treated in a group can help you fine-tune your leadership style. Doing this takes time and practice. You may discover that in one situation you act one way, and in another situation you act differently—this is human nature.

Check the goal(s) you will set to demonstrate your leadership abilities. If you have ideas of your own that you prefer, add them on the lines provided. Then write a date by which you plan to put your goal(s) into action on the "To Do By" lines and the date you completed them on the "Did By" lines. Be sure to fill in "What I Did to Achieve My Goal(s)."

	To Do By	Did By

○ I will offer to show a substitute teacher or new staff member around and help deal with new or difficult situations during a class or an activity.

Session 5: Leaders and Followers   29

	To Do By	Did By

○ I will be the first to volunteer in a situation that requires a group leader.

○ I will try to recruit someone new to help with a club or an organization project.

○ I will take time to listen to others' ideas and resist insisting that I know how to deal with a situation.

Other "Do Something About It" Ideas

○

○

What I Did to Achieve My Goal(s)

For future reference, you may want to put a check next to the questions you are assigning.

FIND OUT MORE ABOUT IT

Leadership and Human Behavior

Inspiring others to do more and become more is the key to being an effective leader. Uncovering exactly how to help people do their best, though, can take some figuring out. Thanks to psychologist Douglas McGregor, leaders have some very useful ideas to guide them.

In 1960, McGregor developed what is known as Theory Y and Theory X about human behavior.* He greatly changed the way leaders throughout the world, and far beyond just business settings, think about helping a group be as creative and productive as possible. Today, people still widely accept his Theory Y and Theory X.

In Theory Y, leaders believe that people in their group are very capable, highly self-motivated, and require little direction—these group members are seen as "Y" people. In Theory X, leaders believe people in their group are not as capable or self-motivated, need a lot of structure, and prefer to be told what to do—these group members are seen as "X" people.

Leaders themselves are neither Y nor X people; rather they are "group-centered" or "leader-centered" in how they lead the people in their group. Group-centered leaders depend heavily on the contributions of the group and guide members in a general or unobvious way. Leader-centered leaders direct members more specifically.

Neither group-centered nor leader-centered leadership is necessarily the best way to lead a group. What's important for an effective leader to recognize is his or her own behavior and how he or she views the individuals in the group.

For example, when group members are excited and motivated by what they are doing, they don't necessarily need a lot of direction or structure (they're Y people with a group-centered leader). With a different set of circumstances, however, these same people may be more productive if told what to do and how to do it (they're X people with a leader-centered leader).

Theory Y and Theory X influence how leaders choose what actions to take, and drive the way leaders and group members work together. There's nothing automatically wrong with being more direct or less direct as a leader. Nor with being a member of a group who needs a lot or little guidance.

Now that you know more about human behavior and leadership, ask yourself:

- How do you generally see yourself as a leader? How about as a follower?
- How do you tend to see the people in your group when you're the leader?
- What type of leader most motivates you when you're a member of a group?

To learn more about leaders and followers working together, see session 13 about team building.

*McGregor, Douglas, *The Human Side of Enterprise*, annotated ed. (New York: McGraw-Hill, 2006).

All Shapes and Sizes—Leader One

Your employer, a toy company, has assigned your work team to create a model using the company's signature toy, the rod and connector construction set, for a sculpture to be built in front of the new headquarters. You decide to give your team these guidelines to get started on building a model.

Place all the pieces from the rod and connector construction set on the table. Tell your five team members sitting at the table:

Our team has been assigned to create a model for a sculpture to be built in front of the new headquarters. We are to use the company's rod and connector set. Here are your directions:

✱ You may build anything you want.

✱ You may each build a model or you can build one together as a group.

✱ You can move around the table talking and interacting with one another as much as you want.

✱ You will have about 10 minutes to make your creations.

Interact with the group, encourage them to be creative, and give a lot of positive feedback. After about 10 minutes, ask them to explain what they have made.

All Shapes and Sizes—Leader Two

Be directive and tell the group members to take apart the model or models on the table from the previous group. Then say:

Our team has been assigned to create a model for a sculpture to be built in front of the new headquarters. We are to use the company's rod and connector construction set. I am going to tell you exactly how this project is to be done. Listen closely.

Number One: You must each stay seated and use only your own space.

Number Two: You are each to work on your own model.

Number Three: There is to be no talking with one another.

Number Four: I will be taking you through some specific steps to construct the model that you are to follow exactly.

Number Five: If you have a question, raise your hand and wait until I acknowledge you before speaking.

Read the "Steps for Construction Project" to the group. As the group is working, firmly correct anyone who makes a mistake, fails to follow directions, talks, or giggles. When everyone's finished, ask each group member to comment on the model.

Steps for Construction Project

1. **Pick up the large round disc with the hole in the center and holes around the rim.**

2. **Pick up the red stick and insert it in the hole in the center of the disc.**

3. **Pick up another round disc with the hole in the center and holes around the rim.**

4. **Insert the red stick into one of the holes in the rim of the disc.**

5. **Pick up a blue stick and insert it into the hole on the right side of the rim of the disc.**

6. **Pick up another blue stick and insert it into the hole on the left side of the rim of the disc.**

7. Pick up an orange stick and insert it into the hole at the top rim of the disc.

8. Pick up another round disc with the hole in the center and holes around the rim.

9. Attach the disc to the orange stick by inserting the orange stick into one of the holes on the rim of the disc.

10. Pick up a green stick and attach it to the disc by inserting it into the hole on the rim opposite from the orange stick.

11. Pick up a blue stick and insert it into the hole on the rim of the disc immediately to the right of the orange stick.

12. Pick up another round disc with the hole in the center and holes around the rim.

13. Attach the disc to the blue stick by inserting the stick into one of the holes on the rim of the disc.

14. Pick up a yellow stick and attach it to the disc by inserting it into the hole immediately to the left of the green stick.

15. Pick up a round, oblong, or tubular connector piece with a hole in the center and holes around the rim.

16. Attach the connector piece to the yellow stick by inserting the stick into one of the holes on the rim of the ball.

17. Pick up a yellow stick and attach it to the connector piece in the hole directly opposite the yellow stick which has already been attached on the left side of the green stick.

18. Pick up a yellow stick and attach it to the disc in the hole directly opposite the blue stick which has already been attached to the right side of the orange stick.

19. Pick up a button piece with a hole in only one end.

20. Attach the green stick to the button piece by inserting the stick into the hole.

(PAGES 30–36 IN *EVERYDAY LEADERSHIP*)

GOALS

Participants will:

- discuss types of power
- learn how different types of power can be used
- differentiate between power, influence, and authority

MATERIALS NEEDED

- Bag of candy (or snacks; take care to note if any participants have food allergies or health issues, or can't eat candy)
- Seven chairs
- Chart paper or whiteboard
- Markers for paper or whiteboard
- Masking tape
- Handout: "Find Out More About It: Making Things Happen"

GETTING READY

Arrange the seven chairs in the front of the room facing the group. Make two copies of the "Instructions for Try This" on page 44. If using chart paper, tape two sheets on the wall, bulletin board, or whiteboard.

Make enough copies of the "Find Out More About It: Making Things Happen" handout for everyone in the group. You may also want to copy the "Find Out More About It: What You Know or Who You Know?" handout.

Getting Started

Leaders are able to accomplish certain goals based upon the power they have with people who follow their lead. In this session, teens gain an awareness of different types of power and different ways of expressing that power with positive or negative effects.

To introduce teens to the concept of power and how it relates to leadership, you might say:

Power impacts all relationships in everyday life— how a parent treats a child, how a coach trains an athlete, how politicians get their bills passed, and more. Leaders are able to accomplish certain goals

based upon the power they have with their group. In some cases, informal leaders—those not in the official leadership position of the group—may have just as much or even more power than the official leader. Just as leadership is defined in many ways, so is power. There are many different types of power; we are going to investigate seven sample types.

TEACH THIS

Sweet Rewards

In this activity, participants demonstrate the types of power described in "What You Know or Who You Know?" on pages 31–33 in their books (pages 41–42 in this book). Wait to have teens read this background information until after facilitating the activity so as not to influence their behavior. Issues related to power are very familiar to teens. They often believe they are only the recipients of someone else's power, without recognizing how often they actually use their own power. This simulation allows them to experience first-hand the subtleties of power and gain greater awareness of how they use power daily.

Ask for seven volunteers to sit on the chairs at the front of the room facing everyone else. Select another volunteer and give him or her the bag of candy and a copy of "Instructions for Try This: Sweet Rewards" on page 44. Keep the other copy of the instructions for yourself.

Instruct the candy volunteer to read the dialogue for each type of power—but *not* to say what type of power it is. For each type of power, this volunteer is to select a different person among the seven seated and as indicated in the instructions to give or take away candy. As the volunteer selects different people, note the selected person's name on your copy of the instructions. You'll refer to these individuals during the discussion.

Ask the candy volunteer to stand to the side of the seated volunteers, so everyone can see all the facial expressions and nonverbal reactions. This activity takes about 10 minutes.

Have all the volunteers return to their original seats. Allowing about 5 minutes, ask everyone to read "What You Know or Who You Know?" on pages 31–33 in their books (pages 41–42 in this book). Ask teens to keep their books open to this section for group discussion.

Talk About It

Referring to the names you wrote down on your copy of the instructions, review briefly with teens which type of power was associated with each of the seven volunteers. Plan on group discussion for at least 10 minutes about the impact of power in everyday life and teens' relationships with authority figures. This is a hot topic for teens. Ask:

- Which of the power types demonstrated have you observed or experienced the most? Describe the situation. Were they used effectively? Why or why not?

- Which types of power do you think are most effective and why? Which types are ineffective and why?

- What other types of power not on this list have you observed or experienced?

- In what ways have you seen leaders use their power unfairly?

- How have you seen people respond to different types of power?

TEACH THIS

Influence and Authority

Pass out the "Find Out More About It: Making Things Happen" handout and give teens a few minutes to read it. Next ask for two volunteers to be recorders, using the whiteboard or chart paper. Designate one to write "Authority" and the other "Influence" at the top of each sheet of paper or on the board. For about 5 to 10 minutes, have the group brainstorm examples of authority and influence, including any that relate to the "Sweet Rewards" activity.

Talk About It

Discuss for about 5 to 10 minutes teens' perceptions of power, influence, and authority. Ask:

- When you're the leader, what style do you most often use: influence or authority?

- What style do you respond best to when you're following someone else's lead?

- In what ways can a leader have too much influence?

- Are you always aware of when you are responding to influence or authority? Why or why not?

- Share an example of when someone influenced you, but you didn't realize it until later.

Wrapping Up

Encourage teens to be specific in "Think and Write About It" (pages 33–34 in *Everyday Leadership*) when they write about leaders using power with positive or negative effects. For example, they can write, "Senator Howell shows she understands how to use power positively when she lobbies other senators," rather than make broad generalizations such as "Some politicians abuse their power."

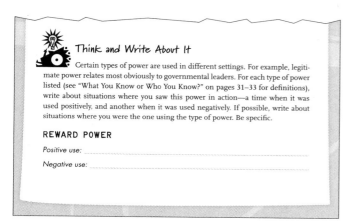

Think and Write About It

Certain types of power are used in different settings. For example, legitimate power relates most obviously to governmental leaders. For each type of power listed (see "What You Know or Who You Know?" on pages 31–33 for definitions), write about situations where you saw this power in action—a time when it was used positively, and another when it was used negatively. If possible, write about situations where you were the one using the type of power. Be specific.

REWARD POWER

Positive use: ....

Negative use: ....

34   *Everyday Leadership*

REFERENT POWER

Positive use: ....

Negative use: ....

LEGITIMATE POWER

Positive use: ....

Negative use: ....

INFORMATION POWER

Positive use: ....

Negative use: ....

EXPERT POWER

Positive use: ....

Negative use: ....

CONNECTION POWER

Positive use: ....

Negative use: ....

COERCIVE POWER

Positive use: ....

Negative use: ....

For future reference, you may want to put a check next to the questions you are assigning.

In reminding teens to select a goal or two from "Do Something About It" (pages 35–36 in *Everyday Leadership*), encourage them to think about what types of power they use consciously or subconsciously, and how it's expressed.

Do Something About It

To increase others' awareness of you as a leader, try expressing your personal power in different ways to see what works well when. For example, if you tend to use authority to get things done, try using influence. If you mostly use influence, try authority.

Check the goal(s) you will set to demonstrate your leadership abilities. If you have ideas of your own that you prefer, add them on the lines provided. Then write a date by which you plan to put your goal(s) into action on the "To Do By" lines and the date you completed them on the "Did By" lines. Be sure to fill in "What I Did to Achieve My Goal(s)."

	To Do By	Did By
○ I will survey others at school or in my community group to see if they will help me resolve an issue we've been complaining about.		
○ I will ask a friend to help me interview a teacher, coach, parent, trusted adult, or business or religious leader about his or her views on using power. I will write about what we learn and if possible share it with the group.		
○ I will contribute to the decision-making process with my friends as we plan to do something together. If I normally dominate decisions made with my friends, I will listen to or ask for their opinions. I will not push everyone just to do what I want. If I'm normally quiet and just agree to what others suggest, I'll voice my opinion.		
○ I will register to vote, if that is an option for me, and let others know why I think it is important to vote.		

	To Do By	Did By
Other "Do Something About It" Ideas		
○		
○		

What I Did to Achieve My Goal(s)

FIND OUT MORE ABOUT IT

What You Know or Who You Know?

Leaders are able to accomplish certain goals based upon the power they have with their group, and how they got it or use it. Here are seven types of power. Each one includes an example of how a leader can use that power and possible positive or negative results. An effective leader seeks to use different types of power positively, rather than one particular style exclusively.

Reward Power is based on a leader's ability to give rewards and positive consequences if people do what is asked of them.

Example: While shopping at the grocery store, a father promises his daughter a candy bar if she will be quiet until they are done.

- *Positive effect:* The potential for a reward motivates the daughter to be quiet.
- *Negative effect:* Once the daughter realizes her father's strategy, she may only be quiet if she gets candy. She also won't learn the basic value of proper behavior.

Referent Power is based on a leader's likeability. People often are willing to do as the leader asks because they like or want to be like this person.

Example: An admired friend encourages you to do well academically.

- *Positive effect:* A person's admiration for someone who offers encouragement inspires the person to do well.
- *Negative effect:* Admiration for another person and "encouragement" from that person in the form of peer pressure can also inspire making poor choices, such as cheating in order to get a better grade.

Legitimate Power is based on a leader's position. People see the position as one that gives the leader power.

Example: Political figures, government officers, police, teachers, principals, student council members, youth group leaders, or athletic team captains are all leaders whose positions represent legitimate power.

- *Positive effect:* While someone holds a certain position, people respect and respond to him or her in that position.
- *Negative effect:* Just because an individual holds a leadership position doesn't mean the person is an effective or admirable leader.

Information Power is based on a leader's control of or access to information that is perceived as valuable.

Example: The adult advisor to a youth group knows what other adult decision makers in the organization would support or disapprove of regarding possible youth activities.

- *Positive effect:* This person can share information with the youth group to help propose some activities rather than have the group spend a lot of time strategizing for something that is not likely to get approved.

MORE

✻ *Negative effect:* This person could inappropriately share other decision makers' preferences with the youth group. Or this person could prevent sharing information from the youth group with the other decision makers.

Expert Power is based on a leader's expertise, skill, and knowledge. People respect the leader's expertise and are influenced by it.

Example: Doctors, scientists, lawyers, professors, athletes, or anyone who has a great deal of experience in a particular field, activity, or hobby.

✻ *Positive effect:* People can get the best and most accurate information from people who are considered experts.

✻ *Negative effect:* An expert could take advantage of someone by providing incomplete or misleading information. This may influence a person to make a decision that he or she might not make otherwise with the right information.

Connection Power is based on who a leader knows. People see the leader as having power because of his or her connections to or relationships with influential or important people.

Example: A high school senior knows a parent who is an alumnus of a nearby private college. The alumnus can get the student an interview with the Admissions Office.

✻ *Positive effect:* Connections can help people obtain important things, such as a recommendation, a job, acceptance into a school or special program, tickets to a show, or passes backstage to meet a performer.

✻ *Negative effect:* Connections can mean some people get certain things without deserving them, or keep others from getting what they deserve.

Coercive Power is based on a leader's ability to invoke fear in people. The leader has the ability to take away privileges or punish those who do not cooperate.

Example: A parent who insists you complete a project exactly the way he or she says or else you can't do something you were hoping to do.

✻ *Positive effect:* Sometimes, setting specific rules is the only way to get a job done.

✻ *Negative effect:* Often, threatening punishment doesn't help people recognize the value of the project.

FIND OUT MORE ABOUT IT

Making Things Happen

To get things done and use their power, leaders apply different styles. Some draw on their *authority*, the process of insisting or demanding that others do a task; others use *influence*, a way of persuading that's less direct or obvious. Both styles are ways of expressing power, and leaders can use them with positive and negative effects. Consider the differences.

Authority

Authority is a leader's position or rank, such as president. That authority can be given or taken away by someone else or an organization. A leader uses his or her authority to:

* give directions and see that they are carried out.

* reassure the group that someone is in charge.

* state her or his preference, without offering anyone choices or opportunities to ask questions.

* Make others obey regardless of whether they agree with the request.

* oversee a project, but may not get involved in the actual work.

Influence

Influence is a quality some leaders allow others in the group to use; anyone may be able to motivate or inspire other members regardless of the position she or he holds. A leader uses her or his influence to:

* support others accomplishing things without threats.

* ask people to help achieve goals together, so sometimes the group doesn't even realize who's in charge.

* encourage cooperation, communication, and interaction to achieve the goals.

* allow people to ask questions for clarification.

* take the first steps toward getting things done.

* drive particular decisions, which could be positive or negative, such as taking a risk that may or may not be worthwhile.

Although authority and influence differ, there are times when you might use both. Especially depending on your position or role, or your relationship with a single person or a group. For example, as a lifeguard you have the authority to control what happens at the pool, but you may prefer to use influence when carrying out the rules. If you know one person in a group that's fooling around too much, you can use your relationship with that individual to get everyone in the group to follow the rules. Whatever your style of power is, when you use it positively, you can take the lead with success.

Sweet Rewards

Read aloud the script for each type of power below—but *don't* say what type of power it is. For each type of power, select a different person among the seven people seated to give or take away candy as indicated in the script. Each line in the script is numbered. Following the script is a key to identify each type of power. Stand to the side of the seated volunteers so everyone can see one another's facial expressions and nonverbal reactions.

Begin by telling the seven seated volunteers the following:

Thanks for volunteering for this activity. Don't be nervous about what we're going to do. Just remember, for the most part, I'm in charge. [Smile.] **No, seriously, I'm going to use this candy to demonstrate different ways leaders, including ourselves, get others to do things.**

Script

1. _____, since you have been so terrific in our sessions, here's a piece of candy.

2. _____, your leadership skills are admirable. If there is anything you need help with, you can count on me. It would be an honor if you would have a piece of my candy.

3. **Please take a minute or two as a group to select a leader.** Once the leader has been selected say, **Congratulations, _____, now that you're in charge, you can decide who gets the next piece of candy.**

4. **Who should I talk to to get the recipe for this candy?** Give a piece of candy to the person who provides you with information.

5. _____, you're an expert on candy; tell me everything you know about this type of candy. I'll even give you a piece of candy so you can explain in detail!

6. _____ should get the next piece of candy because she (or he) is a friend of the candy maker.

7. If you all do not pay attention for the rest of class, I am going to take back all of the candy I just gave you.

Key

1. Reward Power   2. Referent Power   3. Legitimate Power   4. Information Power   5. Expert Power   6. Connection Power   7. Coercive Power

COMMUNICATE WITH STYLE

(PAGES 37–42 IN *EVERYDAY LEADERSHIP*)

GOALS

Participants will:

- identify effective leadership skills for communicating with others
- improve individual listening and speaking skills to accomplish a group goal
- explore the impact of nonverbal cues and positive feedback

MATERIALS NEEDED

- Soft items of some weight (softball size or smaller, such as rubber or plastic balls, stuffed animals or bean bags; available at toy stores or large discount retail stores with "dollar" bins), one for each participant (these same items also are used in session 13)
- 5-gallon empty plastic paint tub or other large plastic bucket with a top
- Digital stopwatch or wristwatch with timer

GETTING READY

Collect the soft items and store them in the bucket. Move any tables, desks, and chairs to the sides to create a large open area (or ask teens to assist when you begin the session).

You may also want to make enough copies of the two "Find Out More About It" handouts for everyone in the group.

Getting Started

What people say and how they say it greatly affects their success as leaders. In this session, teens learn how effective communication skills make a difference in group members hearing what leaders mean to say—and vice versa.

For additional activities to build communication skills, see sessions 8 and 18.

As teens enter the meeting room, have them gather in a circle in the open area, approximately an arm's length apart from one another. To introduce the topic of communicating with style, you might say:

What you say and how you say it has a major impact on your success as a leader. Whether your goal is making a positive first impression or building a connection with others you lead, the specific

45

communication skills you use affect how well your message gets across. Often it's not so much about saying exactly "the right thing," but ensuring that you identify potential misunderstandings: What assumptions have I made? Are we all speaking the "same language"? How do I best give feedback to avoid turning someone off? What is someone not saying but showing? Today, we are going to look at these issues through a series of games.

TEACH THIS

Group Juggle to Warp Speed

This activity is a classic in getting groups to focus on a goal and communicate with one another. Participants learn they have to pay attention to communication and feedback, both verbal and nonverbal (eye contact or signals), if the group is to succeed. To set the guidelines, say:

> I am going to hand a ball (or other item) to one of you to be the Starter. The Starter will toss it to someone in the circle who is not directly next to him or her. The next person will do the same, tossing it to someone who hasn't yet received the ball, and so on, until everyone has tossed and received the ball once. The last person will toss it to the Starter. This will establish your pattern.
>
> The ball must remain in the air. If you bounce it toward a person or drop it, the group must restart. Before tossing the ball, state the name of the person you're tossing it to.

Ask the Starter to begin, and after two rounds to set the pattern, time a round, telling participants how fast they were. Have teens set a goal for how quickly they can get the ball around and time them a few more times to see if they can do it faster.

Next, challenge the group to do the same pattern with more balls, and let the group choose how many more. Once they've tossed around several balls a few times, conduct at least one timed pattern with the multiple balls. Then subtly add a few more balls up to the amount of people there are in the group to reach "warp speed!" Keep timing to see how well they can do before the game turns into hilarious chaos! Facilitate this game for about 10 to 15 minutes before taking 5 minutes to talk about it. Collect the balls or other items when done.

Talk About It

To relate the game to communication and leadership efforts, ask:

- What was necessary for the group to succeed?
- What was important to communicate with each other and what communication skills did you rely on?
- What makes a person an effective communicator?
- How long did it take for everyone to realize what you needed to do as individuals so the group could succeed, given no one was designated as a leader?
- How did you feel if you had difficulty tossing or catching the ball, or dropped it? How did the group react?
- What, if any, nonverbal responses or examples of feedback or comments from others did you notice?
- How did timing the group affect group communication?

TEACH THIS

Birthday Lineup

Tell teens they are going to play another game to achieve a group goal, but they will use different communication skills. This time they are not allowed to speak. Addressing nonverbal skills in the context of a communication lesson reminds teens they don't need to be terrific speakers to get their message across. Practicing nonverbal skills also guides participants to tap into other skills necessary for leaders to be good communicators such as listening and connecting with others.

Depending on the size of your group, this activity can take 5 to 10 minutes. To set the guidelines, say:

> In this game, you may ask me questions for clarification before you begin, but you may not strategize or speak with one another at any time. Nor can you use any other resources around the room or on your body, such as a calendar, driver's license, student ID, paper, or pen. Your goal is to line yourselves up in order of birthdays, by month and day. It's up to you as a group to convey a nonverbal agreement (for example, by nodding your heads) that the line is correct.

Take a few minutes to answer any questions. Remind the group not to talk with one another during the activity. Instruct them to begin. Once they agree they've got the line correct, ask each person to state his or her birthday, beginning with the end of the line designated as January.

Talk About It

Even if the group does not line up correctly, the process raises a number of issues. These include: how the group overcomes obstacles to reach a goal, how often they overlook the power of communicating without speaking, how they can learn new ideas from people who usually don't talk in the group, and if they hurried through the task, what they might have achieved had they slowed down. To address these issues in discussion, ask:

- **What was necessary for the group to succeed?**
- **How did you begin to know what to do?**
- **Did you develop a common language? Describe it.**
- **What specific roles did you take? Did a leader emerge? How and why?**
- **What did you learn about the type of communication you most often rely upon?**
- **When are some times leaders might need to give feedback?**
- **Has someone ever given you helpful feedback? Describe.**
- **What makes feedback effective in everyday conversation as well as when you're the leader?**

Ask teens to turn to "What You *Don't* Say Can Say It All" and "How You Say It" on pages 38 and 39 to learn more about nonverbal communication and feedback. As they read through this information, you may want to pass out the corresponding "Find Out More About It" handouts. Then discuss positive and negative examples of nonverbal cues and feedback.

Wrapping Up

Reflection in "Think and Write About It" (pages 39–41 in *Everyday Leadership*) this session asks teens to rate themselves on a number of statements about how they communicate. Self-rating helps teens gain greater awareness of their own communication skills. Encourage teens to think about a variety of circumstances for each statement to determine a realistic rating.

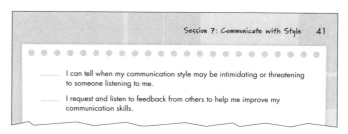

Think and Write About It

To give and receive feedback successfully, consider how you communicate with others whether speaking, listening, or sending nonverbal messages. For each of the following statements, rate yourself on a scale from 1 to 5, with 1 indicating you do it well and 5 meaning you need to improve in this area. Write the

---

40   *Everyday Leadership*

number on the blank line next to each statement. Think of a variety of circumstances for each statement to determine a realistic rating.

It's easier to boost your leadership talents and to communicate with style when you're more aware of your communication skills. Keep in mind the statements you rated as lower and try to improve them. You can practice them in everyday conversations, when you take on leadership roles, an in upcoming sessions.

_____ I can influence or help others when I communicate as well as be open to others' comments when they communicate with me.

_____ I stay aware of my prejudices and values so I am able to listen, empathize, and understand others' viewpoints as well as avoid misspeaking.

_____ I accept that it is my responsibility to clarify what I am saying if others don't understand me.

_____ I listen because I know I'm learning little if I keep talking and don't let anyone else say anything.

_____ I make sure I understand what others are saying.

_____ I pay attention to nonverbal messages and try to notice the feelings or motives behind people's words, even though I can't know exactly what someone else is thinking or feeling.

_____ I am an attentive listener and let the person speaking know I'm listening by nodding, using direct eye contact, or other nonverbal gestures.

_____ I make a special attempt to listen carefully when I disagree with what someone else is saying.

_____ I realize being a good listener doesn't mean I must agree with what another person is saying.

_____ I try to stay calm and not overreact to emotionally charged words or comments.

_____ I consider who's giving the feedback, how she or he is saying it, and the situation in which it's being told. I do this when messages either support or contradict something else I have heard.

Session 7: Communicate with Style   41

_____ I can tell when my communication style may be intimidating or threatening to someone listening to me.

_____ I request and listen to feedback from others to help me improve my communication skills.

For future reference, you may want to put a check next to the questions you are assigning.

Before participants choose their actions from "Do Something About It" (pages 41–42 in *Everyday*

Leadership), suggest they think about statements they ranked lower in "Think and Write About It" or areas they'd like to improve. As teens learn more about their unique communication strengths and style, they'll gain greater awareness in new situations to challenge old behaviors and practice new ones.

Do Something About It

Whatever your natural strengths may be when communicating and connecting with others, select actions from the following list that inspire you to challenge old behaviors and practice new ones. Consider which statements you ranked lower on pages 40–41. Improving your communication skills helps you take the lead more effectively when new situations arise.

Check the goal(s) you will set to demonstrate your leadership abilities. If you have ideas of your own that you prefer, add them on the lines provided. Then write a date by which you plan to put your goal(s) into action on the "To Do By" lines and the date you completed them on the "Did By" lines. Be sure to fill in "What I Did to Achieve My Goal(s)."

	To Do By	Did By
○ I will choose at least two of the statements on pages 40–41 that I rated as needing improvement and will practice those communication skills for at least one week.		
○ I will observe two people who I think communicate well and record ways they give effective feedback and nonverbal messages.		
○ I will resist getting into an argument with anyone, even if I believe my way is the right way to do something. I will listen to others' ideas rather than only think of how I want to handle the situation.		

	To Do By	Did By
○ I will ask for feedback about my leadership potential from someone I respect. I will write down the feedback for future reference.		

Other "Do Something About It" Ideas

○ _____

○ _____

What I Did to Achieve My Goal(s)

FIND OUT MORE ABOUT IT

What You <u>Don't</u> Say Can Say It All

Nonverbal responses—what our bodies, eyes, and faces express when we are talking or listening to others—are important to communicating successfully. What you say and what others hear, or vice versa, involves more than words. Whether you're trying to get a message across or let someone know you're hearing what they're saying, you often send nonverbal messages about what you're thinking. The same is true when giving helpful feedback (comments) about what someone said.

Several factors make up nonverbal cues. Some you can control. Others may occur as subconscious reactions. The more aware you are of what you're saying nonverbally, both as a speaker and a listener, the stronger your communication skills will be. As you talk with others, keep in mind the following ways in which you may be "speaking" to others.

Posture

How and where you stand can have meaning. Standing above someone who is sitting often indicates control over that person. Leaning forward generally implies interest in the person or topic of discussion, slouching implies boredom or disinterest. Crossing your arms over your chest may mean you believe you are better than the other person.

Voice

Your tone of voice can significantly change what you say. A person listening to you may interpret what you're saying based on how loudly (volume) and clearly (enunciation) you speak, as well as on how high (pitch) or with what style (for example, excited, monotone, dramatic). Sometimes, vocal qualities can suggest an underlying message, rather than the one you're saying out loud.

Gestures

Ideally, gestures match your verbal messages, although they can make whoever's listening react in certain ways. A clenched fist often suggests anger, a pointed finger asserts authority, and fidgety hands show nervousness. Gesturing of the head—a nod of approval or a shake of rejection—also can deliver a particular message.

Eye Contact

Eye contact can help show and maintain attention and interest. But a blank stare or glaring may suggest tuning out, superiority, or anger; avoiding eye contact can indicate discomfort, shyness, or lack of preparation on the topic. Looking away or to the side when you are speaking may also demonstrate lack of interest or that you are not telling the truth.

Facial Expressions

Facial expressions are both the easiest *and* most difficult nonverbal cues to control. They can send a message before you even say anything. You may at first unconsciously grimace or frown, and then try to say something with a smile. Some people use facial expressions to mask the true intent of their message (for example, smiling when angry), but it is important to strive for facial expressions that match what you're saying and feeling.

Appearance

The clothes you wear and how you style your hair are expressions of your individuality. But when making a presentation or representing a school or community group, it's important to consider your audience and show respect for a group. To help your message get heard, make choices regarding your appearance appropriate for your audience.

For more about communication skills, see "Find Out More About It" in sessions 8 and 19.

FIND OUT MORE ABOUT IT

How You Say It

Sometimes what you mean to say is not what people hear. And sometimes what you hear is not what others meant to say. People can be strong leaders when they communicate clearly and give effective feedback (comments). While unexpected feedback can make people defensive, remarks supported by concern and acceptance are tremendously useful. Giving or getting constructive feedback often helps people make decisions and take action. The following guidelines offer tips for *giving* helpful feedback; they also provide guidance on what to look for when asking others to give you feedback.

✱ Focus on a particular statement or behavior, rather than on the person, who may feel a need to defend himself or herself.

Unhelpful feedback: "No one could follow what you were trying to say. You were jumping from one detail to the next. You were confusing everyone."

Helpful feedback: "Think about the most important points you want to make in your presentation and state those at the beginning. Then you can go into the details. This will help everyone know exactly what you're going to cover."

✱ Provide information that is valuable, not because it feels good to say what you're really thinking.

Unhelpful feedback: "You're not a good public speaker. If you'd taken the time to practice your presentation, maybe it would have been better."

Helpful feedback: "Consider practicing your presentation in front of others next time. This could be very useful, and I'd be happy to be your audience."

✱ Seek clarification on what was said, instead of reacting to why you think the person said what she or he said. By offering descriptions rather than judgments, you can avoid making assumptions about another person's intent or motivation.

Unhelpful feedback: "Why would you say something like that? You just want everyone to do it your way."

Helpful feedback: "I may have heard you wrong. Did you say the people leading our team aren't very thoughtful? As one of the leaders, it will help me a lot if you can explain more clearly what you mean."

✱ Create an opportunity to share and suggest ideas, rather than tell someone specifically what to do. Seek possible choices rather than just look for a single solution.

Unhelpful feedback: "Since you haven't been able to resolve the issue yourself as head of the committee, it'll be quicker and easier if I as team leader just make the decision that we all will follow."

Helpful feedback: "As head of the committee, you may want to ask everyone to brainstorm some ideas as a group. This could be more helpful to you in the long run instead of relying on me as the team leader to figure out what to do about the issue."

- Avoid overloading a person with too much information at once. Suggest you talk about other points at another time.

  Unhelpful feedback: "You've got to create a stronger campaign given all the comments you're getting from current council members and the general student body. You need to focus on the schedule, your speech, what student council leaders think of you, how you can reach new students, and how to get teacher support."

  Helpful feedback: "I know hearing a lot of different comments from people while you've been working hard on the student council president campaign can be confusing. So let's focus first on what current council members are saying. Then let's meet again tomorrow to talk about appealing to the general student body."

- Focus on the current situation or conversation rather than past circumstances.

  Unhelpful feedback: "We planned themed events in the past just like you've suggested and no one ever came."

  Helpful feedback: "How about taking a survey of teens at the rec center to see what kind of theme they would like for this year's event?"

- Choose an appropriate time to give (or request) feedback. If a person is busy or distracted, he or she may easily misconstrue well-intended positive feedback.

  Unhelpful feedback: "I can't believe we lost. If everyone had made it to every practice this week, we probably wouldn't have made as many mistakes as a team."

  Helpful feedback: "We should talk about why we lost today, but the game just ended and we're pretty emotional right now. Let's get together before practice tomorrow and talk more about how we can work better as a team."

For more about communication skills, see "Find Out More About It" in sessions 8 and 19.

HEAR, THERE, EVERYWHERE:
ACTIVE LISTENING

(PAGES 43–50 IN *EVERYDAY LEADERSHIP*)

GOALS

Participants will:

- learn what it means to use active listening
- observe how passive listening can distort messages
- gain awareness of blocks that prevent active listening
- learn techniques for improving active listening

MATERIALS NEEDED

- Stopwatch or digital watch

GETTING READY

Make one copy of "The Accident" on page 59 for the "Accidental Witness" activity. Make enough copies of the "Mad Hatter's Questions" on page 60 for the "Mad Hatter's Tea Party" activity for half the number of teens in the group. You may also want to make enough copies of the "Find Out More About It: Now I Hear You!" handout for everyone in the group.

Getting Started

Being actively engaged in hearing what others are saying is a critical leadership skill. In this session, teens learn what can block and what can improve their listening. Practicing active listening skills is key to being an effective communicator and leader.

To introduce the topic of active listening to teens, you might say:

An important aspect of being an effective communicator involves how well you can listen. Although being a good listener is a necessary leadership skill, people often overlook its significance. For example, you may *hear* someone in a group you're leading present information to you, but because you aren't actively engaged in what's being said, you aren't really *listening* and don't realize what the other person is saying. While some people use the words

hearing and *listening* interchangeably, being an *active* listener takes practice and awareness of what can block versus what can improve communication. To learn more about active listening in developing your leadership skills, we'll need four volunteers for today's activity that involves some role playing. The rest of you will quietly observe what takes place over the next 10 minutes.

TEACH THIS

Accidental Witness

Preparing people to be active listeners requires helping them shift their typical listening behavior in everyday situations by imagining that everything they hear is equally important. This activity, which reinforces the value of listening fully during interactions, is based on the familiar "Telephone" game, also known as "Pass It Down." In "Telephone," one player secretly repeats to another a phrase or sentence that typically gets altered in transit by the time the last player says it out loud to all the players. In contrast, in "Accidental Witness," each volunteer, prior to listening to the story, is *not* told they will need to repeat what is being said.

If necessary, first explain or remind participants about ground rules for role playing (see page 4 in the "Introduction"). Then select four volunteers and ask one to stay in the room. Send the other three to a nearby location (or just outside the room with the door closed) where they cannot hear or see what is happening in the room. Next follow these steps:

① The first volunteer will be the witness. Inform the witness that he or she has just seen a terrible accident and distribute the copy of "The Accident" from page 59. Allow the witness time to silently read "The Accident." Tell the witness he or she must tell a police officer *exactly* what happened and to explain the details based on the story.

② Bring the second volunteer into the room and assign him or her the role of a police officer who has just arrived at the scene of the accident. Prompt the witness to tell the police officer the story.

③ Next retrieve the third volunteer and assign him or her the role of a medical professional who has arrived at the scene. Ask the police officer to tell the story to the medical professional.

④ Finally, bring the fourth volunteer into the room, and give him or her the role of a news reporter. Direct the medical professional to tell the story. Then ask the news reporter to repeat the details for the evening broadcast.

⑤ Ask the witness to reread the original story for all to hear.

Talk About It

To guide the group in discussing what occurred during this activity, first ask the observers:

- **What happened with each retelling of the story?**
- **What did you think as you heard each person tell his or her version of the accident?**

Then ask the volunteers who took part in the role play:

- **What was it like to be told the story and then asked to repeat it to someone else?**
- **Would it have made a difference if you knew before being told the story that you would have to repeat it? Why?**
- **How well do you feel you listened as you were being told the story? What helped or interfered with your listening?**

Before directing questions to everyone in the group, ask teens to read "Find Out More About It: Listening Blocks" on pages 44–45 in their books (page 57 in this book) over the next few minutes. Take an additional 5 minutes to discuss this information. For each "listening block" described, ask participants to give an example.

Direct these last questions about the activity to everyone in the group:

- **How did the activity show that being an active listener is a necessary leadership skill?**
- **How would you describe your usual listening style?**
- **What inspires you to pay attention and actively listen to what is being said?**

TEACH THIS

Mad Hatter's Tea Party

This activity is a fun way to practice focused listening. Because the activity requires half the group to be speaking at the same time, the room can sound a bit chaotic, like the Mad Hatter's tea party in *Alice in Wonderland*. Even so, when half the participants are speaking, the other half is probably listening better than in a quieter setting. Those listening are purposely not to repeat what they hear in order to focus strictly on listening. Group discussion helps teens gain further awareness of what it means to actively listen (asking questions or responding verbally in some way).

Split the group in two, with an equal number of teens in each group. If you have more than 20 participants, divide the group in four. Have the two groups sit a short distance across from each other on the floor. Tell teens which side will be the "Talkers" and which side the "Listeners." Explain what they're to do by saying:

> **Here is a list of questions for the Listeners** [distribute a copy to each Listener]. **Do not share it with the Talkers.** Listeners, you are to ask the Talker across from you one question on the list and then listen to what he or she says. You can choose any question you want, but don't list all the questions for the Talker to choose from. Talkers, you are to respond to the selected question for 1 minute. Listeners, don't interrupt or respond to what the Talker says. Be silent and concentrate on listening and offering encouraging nonverbal cues to the Talker.
>
> When a minute is up, Listeners and Talkers shift one seat to your right, so that everyone has a new partner. Those at the end of each row can rotate to the other row—a Talker becomes a Listener, and a Listener a Talker. Talkers, it's fine to tell a Listener to ask a different question if you've already answered the one selected. But it's possible that you may end up answering the same question more than once. Let's begin.

Continue timing and prompting teens to move every minute until everyone has had an opportunity to be both Listener and Talker. Monitor the group to make sure Listeners ask only one question and are listening rather than prompting Talkers further. Plan on at least 10 to 15 minutes for this activity and group discussion.

Talk About It

To help teens gain awareness about what it means to actively listen, ask:

- **What are some things you discovered about another person that surprised or interested you?**

- **Which role was more difficult for you, being a Listener or a Talker? Why?**

- **When you were listening, what differences did you notice in your behavior compared to listening to everyday conversations? Explain.**

- **As a Listener, what was it like not to be able to ask the Talker questions? As a Talker, what was it like to have to speak about a topic for a minute without being interrupted by questions?**

- **Talkers, did you ever wish the Listener would encourage you by asking a question? Listeners, did you ever want to help the Talker along? When and why?**

- **Talkers, did you find any of the questions more interesting? Why? For example, was it the way the person asked the question or your own reaction about the topic? What does your reason tell you about how to improve active listening in everyday conversation, in school and other activities, or as a leader, no matter what the topic is?**

- **Describe a time when you couldn't make a decision or take action on a project in a group or on your own because people didn't or wouldn't listen to what you were asking.**

Pass out the "Find Out More About It: Now I Hear You!" handout and have teens read it (or have them read that section on pages 45–46 in their books). Take an additional few minutes to discuss this information. For each approach described to improve active listening, ask teens to share examples.

For additional activities to build communication skills, see sessions 7 and 19.

Wrapping Up

In "Think and Write About It" (pages 46–48 in *Everyday Leadership*), teens reflect on specific scenarios and on how well they actively listen during these situations, what "listening blocks" get in the way, and what they might do to remove those blocks.

Think and Write About It

How actively you listen often depends on who's talking and what, if anything, the person speaking may want. But active listening in a leadership role requires a leadership attitude, no matter who's talking or what the person's asking or telling you. Complete the following sentences by describing how well you think you listen in each situation.

When someone in my family asks me to do something for her or him, I generally:

_____

When a teacher or group leader presents new information, I generally:

_____

When a friend invites me to do something with him or her, I generally:

_____

---

48   Everyday Leadership

For these same situations, describe what you can try to do to remove the listening blocks.

When someone in my family asks me to do something for her or him, I can:

_____

When a teacher or group leader presents new information, I can:

_____

When a friend invites me to do something with him or her, I can:

_____

When someone tells me about a problem or expresses strong feelings, I can:

_____

Session 8: Hear, There, Everywhere: Active Listening   47

When someone tells me about a problem or expresses strong feelings, I generally:

_____

Now reread "Listening Blocks" on pages 44–45 and put a star next to the listening blocks that most often hinder your active listening. Referring to the listening blocks you just marked, describe which ones get in the way during the same general situations you just wrote about. Explain why you think those listening blocks prevent more active listening.

When someone in my family asks me to do something for her or him, I generally:

_____

When a teacher or group leader presents new information, I generally:

_____

When a friend invites me to do something with him or her, I generally:

_____

When someone tells me about a problem or expresses strong feelings, I generally:

_____

For future reference, you may want to put a check next to the questions you are assigning.

The goals in "Do Something About It" (pages 48–50 in *Everyday Leadership*) offer participants a chance to put their active listening skills to the test and focus on getting the most from what others are saying.

Do Something About It

To be an active listener, it's important to focus on what others are saying and "turning off" or "tuning out" what else is going on in your head. Put your active listening skills to the test and try the following actions.

Check the goal(s) you will set to demonstrate your leadership abilities. If you have ideas of your own that you prefer, add them on the lines provided. Then write a date by which you plan to put your goal(s) into action on the "To Do By" lines and the date you completed them on the "Did By" lines. Be sure to fill in "What I Did to Achieve My Goal(s)."

	To Do By	Did By
○ I will select one of the techniques for active listening I've learned and commit to using this approach in at least five conversations. I will track how these conversations are different from others.		
○ I will not watch TV, talk on my cell phone, listen to a personal music player, or play video or computer games while others are talking to me in order to genuinely pay attention to them. I will do this for at least three days.		
○ I will ask for and listen to my friend's opinions when we plan to do something and not focus only on what I want to do.		
○ I will listen at least three times to a positive talk radio program instead of watching a regular TV program. I will record my observations about how well the talk show host listens.		
○ I will spend a day with an elder, either a grandparent or volunteering at a home for seniors, to practice my active listening skills. I will record what listening blocks sometimes get in the way of me being a good listener.		

	To Do By	Did By
Other "Do Something About It" Ideas		
○		
○		

What I Did to Achieve My Goal(s)

FIND OUT MORE ABOUT IT

Listening Blocks

What's the first thing you notice when someone talks to you? How often do you hear someone speak but then realize you're not sure what the person just said? If you are doing something other than focusing on what someone is saying (for example, silently thinking about something else), you create blocks that interfere with effective or active listening. The following "listening blocks" explain how you may appear to be listening but in fact are doing something else that prevents you from taking in what the person is saying. As you read the descriptions, think about what "listening blocks" can get in the way when you're in a leadership role.

Rehearsing

If while someone is talking you are busy silently rehearsing or planning a reply, it's harder to concentrate on what the person actually is saying.

Judging

If you're focused on how a person is dressed, looks, or talks, you may prejudge the person and dismiss the idea he or she is describing as unimportant or uninformed.

Identifying

If you're occupied thinking about your own experience and launch into a story before the person even finishes telling his or her story, you may lose sight of what the other person was trying to communicate.

Advising

If you're intent on offering just the right advice for someone's problems before the person is done talking, you might not fully understand the individual's situation.

Sparring

If you're focused on disagreeing with what someone else is saying, you're probably not giving the other person a chance to express himself or herself.

Put-Downs

If you're using sarcastic comments to put down another person's point of view, you could draw the other person into an argumentative conversation in which no one hears anything.

Being Right

If you're intent on proving your point or not admitting any wrongdoing, you may end up twisting the facts, shouting, making excuses, or even arguing the opposite of what you initially said. This may confuse and upset both you and the other person.

Derailing

If you suddenly change the subject or joke about what is being said, you're likely to weaken a speaker's trust in you and your ability to show understanding.

Smoothing Over

If you dislike conflict or want others to like you, you may appear to be supportive but not really fully engaged in the conversation.

Day Dreaming

If you tune out while someone's talking, drifting about in your own fantasies and thoughts, you're not likely to hear a word the other person says.

For more about communication skills, see "Find Out More About It" in sessions 7 and 19.

Now I Hear You!

When you focus on what others are saying, you can be a more effective and active listener. With active listening, you can:

- encourage a speaker to say more and reinforce your relationship with her or him.

- let a speaker know what you're hearing and ask questions if you don't understand.

- dig deeper for information from the speaker because you are paying complete attention to the conversation and want to understand more about what's going on.

- demonstrate your respect for a speaker by acknowledging her or his feelings so emotion doesn't become an obstacle.

- guide a speaker to organize and express his or her thoughts clearly.

Use the following techniques to fine-tune your listening skills as you take on more leadership roles and in your everyday communication. These approaches can help you keep whoever is talking on track, too.

Prodding or Encouraging

Gently persuade a person talking to tell you more by using eye contact (such as raising eyebrows), friendly facial expressions (such as smiling), and a relaxed body posture (such as nodding your head in agreement). Also say, "I see" or "Yes, I understand."

Probing

Ask probing questions: "How so?" "In what way?" "What makes you say that?" "Tell me more." This encourages a speaker to give additional information.

Echoing

Echoing is a form of probing where you repeat in a questioning tone a phrase or word another person just said. This invites the person to expand on what he or she is saying. So if the person says, "I was distracted," you can ask "Distracted? Why?"

Paraphrasing

Summarizing in your own words key thoughts a person just said can help you make sure you've understood his or her point. This also gives the speaker an idea of how clearly he or she is delivering a message.

Reflecting

When someone expresses a highly emotional message, respond with statements that reflect the emotion or situation described. For example, instead of, "I hear what you're saying," try statements that show your connection to the conversation and the person talking: "Sounds like you're upset because . . ." "Sounds like you're overwhelmed because . . ." Or "I sense that you disagree because . . ."

Acknowledging

When you notice the feelings behind what another person is saying, you can help the person put aside the emotion and get on with solving a problem. Acknowledge feelings by using statements such as "I understand how busy you feel you've been." Your acknowledgment doesn't necessarily mean you agree with what the person is expressing, but instead shows your empathy and that you care.

For more about communication skills, see "Find Out More About It" in sessions 7 and 19.

TRY THIS

SESSION · SESSION
8
SESSION · SESSION

The Accident

You have been selected to role-play the witness of a terrible accident. Below are the details of what happened. When the person role-playing the police officer arrives on the scene (enters the room), read what happened (but try not to sound as if you're reading). Speak expressively to convey your concern and what you saw or know. Do not give the copy of these details to the police officer.

A red two-door sports car was driving west on Leadership Avenue at noon today when a large St. Bernard dog ran across the lawn of a blue house and into the street in hot pursuit of a ball. The driver slammed on the brakes, sending the car into a 180° spin in front of oncoming traffic. The tail of the sports car smashed into a silver old-model station wagon. The driver of the station wagon was a 50-year-old man with two poodles in the front seat. When pedestrians assisted the man from the vehicle, the poodles leaped out and ran after the St. Bernard. The man fainted in the center turn lane, so one of the pedestrians called an ambulance. One of the poodles suffered minor bite injuries on the right leg from the St. Bernard. A passing motorcycle fatally injured the other poodle. Two teens playing baseball at the time of the accident swear that the driver of the red car was going faster than the 25-mph speed limit.

Mad Hatter's Questions

Ask the person sitting across from you one of the following questions. Listen to what he or she says in response. You can choose any question you want, but don't list or share all the questions for the other person to choose from. Don't interrupt or respond verbally to the other person while he or she is speaking for 1 minute. Be silent and concentrate on listening. You may offer encouraging nonverbal cues.

1. What's the greatest vacation you've ever had and why?

2. In the past six months, what do you consider your greatest accomplishment?

3. In the next six months, what do you consider to be your greatest challenge?

4. If you could live anywhere in the world, where would it be and why?

5. If you had one hour to speak with any major world leader (dead or alive), who would it be and what would you say?

6. If you were given a surprise day off in the middle of the week, what would you do?

7. If you could change the world in some way, what would you change?

8. How do you feel about competition?

9. Complete the statement: "My favorite band, performer, movie, or game is . . . because . . ."

10. What are the characteristics of a good friend?

(PAGES 51–55 IN *EVERYDAY LEADERSHIP*)

GOALS

Participants will:

- think about personal values related to leadership situations

- understand the role of personal values in decision making

- explore how values impact behavior in a group and as a leader

MATERIALS NEEDED

- Three large sheets of paper labeled "Important," "Not Important," and "Sometimes Important"

- Masking tape

GETTING READY

Place a long strip of masking tape on the floor to divide the room in half. Post the "Important" sign on one side of the room, the "Not Important" sign on the other, and the "Sometimes Important" sign even with the tape dividing the room.

Getting Started

Because personal values naturally influence decisions, leaders must continually strive to clarify what is important to them. In this session, teens gain an understanding of a leader's responsibility to balance personal values with what's necessary for the greater good of the group.

To introduce the topic of values, begin a brief discussion by asking:

- **What in life is important to you?**

- **How do you know when something is important to you—that you value it?**

- **When you say one thing, but do another, what does that tell people about your values?**

- **What do values have to do with leadership?**

TEACH THIS

What Makes Me Who I Am

In this first activity, teens take steps to identify some of their values and why it's important for a leader to know her or his values. Ask teens to turn to page 52 in their books and read through "What Makes Me Who I Am."

Allow about 10 minutes for participants to respond in the appropriate areas regarding core values and value conflict. Ask if teens have any questions about the reading and invite those interested to share their responses. Ethics is briefly mentioned in "What Makes Me Who I Am" but is fully addressed in session 10.

TEACH THIS
What I Value

In this next activity, teens *show* instead of merely *tell* others that something is important. Showing helps teens clarify for themselves the significance of each value. Seeing where others stand also increases awareness of what others value—something leaders often have to consider or manage, especially if group members say one thing but do another.

Ask teens to stand. Tell them that you are going to read a series of value statements (see "Value Statements" on page 63). Explain further by saying:

Some of these values are personal, and some relate to your role in a leadership position. After I read each statement, move near the sign that most closely expresses how you feel about the statement: "Important," "Not Important," or "Sometimes Important."

Point to where the signs are located in the room. Continue by saying:

Wherever you stand, be prepared to explain your choice. Notice where others stand. If you recall having dealt with a value conflict after hearing a certain statement, please share your story.

As you read each value statement and teens pick which sign to stand near or share their examples, you may also want to ask some of the questions in "Talk About It." Alternatively, you can wait to ask all the questions until after reading all the statements and the activity is completed. Teens may struggle to pick which sign to stand near and need a little time to decide. The activity can take about 30 minutes if you incorporate the questions, depending on the size of your group. If you wait until after the activity to ask the questions, plan on at least 10 minutes for discussion.

TRY THIS

What Makes Me Who I Am

Do you know what's really important to you? Can you explain why? Each of us has our own set of values that helps determine our way of life. You probably share many similar values with the people you spend the most time with. As you get older, meet new people, and try new activities, your values are likely to change over time.

CORE VALUES are absolute values—these values tend to be unchanging, even as you grow in years and experience. Some people use the phrase *core values* interchangeably with *morals*. Morals are an individual's principles or standards with respect to right or wrong. Typically, moral standards of right and wrong come from a person's personal and cultural upbringing.

Examples of core values include: treating others as you would like to be treated, putting family first, not stealing, and telling the truth. For some people, core values are tied to specific religious or spiritual views. (Ethics, in comparison, typically are *society's* standards of right and wrong. They are tied to social norms and expectations. You'll explore ethics in session 10.)

VALUE CONFLICT occurs when you aren't sure about what you believe or want. It may also occur when you aren't clear which of your values is more critical in a situation. It's important to recognize value conflict when you are a leader because it can sway decisions you make for or on behalf of your group.

The clearer your values are to you and the more you can recognize and respect what others value, the easier it is to deal with conflict. As you complete the following statements on the lines provided, think about what's important to you and what that says about who you are.

Core values that are important to me include _____

_____

because _____

_____

The greatest influence (who or what) on the *core values* in my life includes _____

_____

because _____

_____

A value conflict I have dealt with is _____

_____

I handled it by _____

_____

A value conflict I have faced (or could face) as a leader is _____

_____

I handled (or would handle) it by _____

Value Statements

Being happy with who I am

Having a family of my own

Having lots of money

Having freedom to do what I want to do

Being good at my job

Having at least one close friend

Choosing a career that interests me

Becoming famous

Going to college

Being a leader

Having lots of friends

Being happy with my job or career

Knowing others believe in me

Being good at sports

Having my own car

Being able to make a difference

Choosing a career that pays well

Choosing a career that serves others

Being recognized for what I know

Being a role model for others

Being religious or spiritual

Getting good grades

Having good health

Believing in myself

Serving in the military

Being popular and well liked

Being able to reach goals I set

Being able to continue despite difficulties

Talk About It

- For which statements was it easy to decide where to stand? Which statements were more difficult? Why?

- Were you surprised at how others ranked some of the values? Why or why not?

- What do you do when your values differ from your friends' values?

- Do you hold a particular value because it is important to your family? Which ones and why?

- Do you think your values change over time? Why or why not?

- Have you ever disregarded someone else's values when making a decision? What did you do? What was his or her reaction?

- How does knowing your values help you become a better leader?

- How did your ranking of values in the activity support being an effective leader? Explain.

- As a leader, how can you balance the values of all the members of your group?

Wrapping Up

The reflection questions in "Think and Write About It" (pages 53–54 in *Everyday Leadership*) prompt teens to think about their attitudes toward people whose values differ from their own. Participants also can explore how as leaders they approach conflict between personal values and group needs.

Think and Write About It

Values are very personal in nature. In a leadership position, you may experience conflicts with your values. Sometimes being a leader requires compromising one value in order to honor another that is more important. Similarly, you may need to guide those you're leading to give and take so the group can move forward. Respond to the following questions and statements on the lines provided.

How do you determine what to do when your individual beliefs conflict with what the group you are leading needs you to do?

54   *Everyday Leadership*

Describe a situation when you felt you had to minimize your values to be accepted in a group (such as a team, a group of friends, on the street), or when you asked someone to put aside his or her values to be accepted in your group.

Are there any situations when a leader must set aside his or her values? Explain why or why not and describe the situations.

For future reference, you may want to put a check next to the questions you are assigning.

Seeking and acknowledging ways values are intertwined in daily behaviors is the theme of the goals in "Do Something About It" (pages 54–55 in *Everyday Leadership*). Because some of the actions are tied to observation, consider asking teens to share their experiences with the group during a later session.

Do Something About It

Noticing and respecting others' values can increase your own awareness of what matters to you. Showing others what it is that is important to you demonstrates your true values.

Check the goal(s) you will set to demonstrate your leadership abilities. If you have ideas of your own that you prefer, add them on the lines provided. Then write a date by which you plan to put your goal(s) into action on the "To Do By" lines and the date you completed them on the "Did By" lines. Be sure to fill in "What I Did to Achieve My Goal(s)."

	To Do By	Did By
○ I will observe and make a list of all the places where I see values openly expressed, such as on school or rec center bulletin boards, or in television commercials, community group newsletters, or stores.		

	To Do By	Did By
○ I will talk with someone I respect about a time when her or his values were tested or challenged by others.		
○ I will create a personal honor code and apply it to how I behave for at least a week.		
○ I will ask a leader in the community whose values I admire to meet others in my group and say a few words at our next meeting.		

Other "Do Something About It" Ideas

○ _____

○ _____

What I Did to Achieve My Goal(s)

_____
_____
_____
_____

DOING THE RIGHT THING

(PAGES 56–61 IN *EVERYDAY LEADERSHIP*)

GOALS

Participants will:

- learn factors to consider when making decisions about ethical situations

- evaluate and practice making ethical decisions in personal and leadership situations

MATERIALS NEEDED

- Chart paper
- Markers
- Tape

GETTING READY

Copy "Daily Dilemmas" on pages 71–72. Cut out as many of the dilemmas as needed to assign one per group (depending on how many groups of three to four you can form for the activity "What Would You Do?"). You may want to make enough copies of the "Find Out More About It: You're Doing What?!" handout for everyone in the group.

Getting Started

Feeling confident about making decisions, even in difficult situations, is important for teens in developing effective leadership skills. This session helps them recognize how frequently they face ethical situations and guides them in answering the question, "How do I make an ethical decision?"

To introduce the topic of ethics and ethical decision making, you might say:

We all experience moments when we have to make difficult choices. As a leader or when you're in a leadership role, making a decision often calls for balancing your personal ethics with the needs of your group. Ethics is deciding what is right—or most right—in any situation, especially when there's no clear answer.

Making ethical decisions as a leader is easier when you act consistently with who you want to be in life. If you are uncomfortable after making a decision, you may have acted unethically. Decisions grounded in ethics keep you from using excuses for your behavior.

Sometimes making a decision that involves ethics means making a choice that isn't fully satisfactory but is better than any other choice. Such situations, or dilemmas, happen often. When facing an ethical dilemma, the decision you make can depend on or affect your leadership position and how others see you as a leader.

When making a decision, you probably don't ask yourself "Is what I'm about to do ethical?" But, you may have a feeling about whether you've made a good decision. Let's practice and learn more about making ethical leadership decisions.

TEACH THIS
What Would You Do?

Ask teens to form groups of three or four with people they haven't previously worked with, or have worked with only minimally. If necessary, have them count off by threes or fours. Hand out chart paper, markers, and a different dilemma (previously copied and cut out from "Daily Dilemmas" on pages 71–72) to each group. If you have more groups than dilemmas, you may have to assign the same dilemma to more than one group. (See "Resources and Additional Reading" on page 210 for additional ethical case studies and resources.) Instruct teens as follows, allowing 15 to 20 minutes for them to complete the activity:

In your small groups, discuss the ethical leadership dilemma on your slip of paper. Talk about different issues to consider and different outcomes depending on what course of action you choose. On the chart paper, write alternative choices you identify, factors you considered to make your final decision, and your final decision.

Post each group's chart paper where it's visible to all. For the next 10 to 15 minutes, ask a spokesperson from each group to read their dilemma and explain their final decision.

Following the presentations, pass out the "Find Out More About It: You're Doing What?!" handout (or have them turn to page 57 in their books) and give teens 5 minutes to read it. Check if they have any questions. Discuss how this information and the suggested

questions to consider when facing ethical decisions provide practical steps to take in everyday life or in a leadership position.

Talk About It

Take 5 minutes to discuss in what ways the dilemmas were challenging. Also ask:

- **What are some ethical dilemmas you have faced?**
- **When dealing with ethical decisions in the past, how have you made your choices?**
- **How often do you trust your intuition—your gut—when facing dilemmas or making ethical decisions?**
- **Think of a dilemma you faced alone that you wish you had handled differently. If you had had a clearer ethical compass in mind—such as asking the questions recommended in the background reading—would that have changed how you made your choice? What about a group dilemma? Would a clear ethical compass have helped the group work together to make a better choice?**
- **How can using your ethical compass help you as a leader?**
- Remind teens of one of the daily dilemmas from the activity. Then ask: **If two groups had dealt with this dilemma differently, what do their actions tell you about ethics?**
- **In what ways will you approach ethical dilemmas differently after today's session?**
- **Based on your leadership experiences, describe some daily dilemmas different from those in the activity.**

Wrapping Up

Several additional dilemmas in "Think and Write About It" (pages 57–60 in *Everyday Leadership*) give teens a chance to weigh both personal and leadership-based factors and to test their own ethical compass in making decisions.

Think and Write About It

Read the following dilemmas. Using your ethical compass, decide what you would do; sometimes your choice may feel less than ideal. Write your responses on the lines provided.

GOOD GRADES

During your first semester of high school, you become friends with Kaden, whose academic skills impress you. You ask to study together for an upcoming biology test, your worst subject. When you meet at the library, Kaden hands you a copy of the upcoming test, which he admits he took from the teacher but hasn't shared with anyone else. The biology test is the first exam of the year, and your parents expect you to get good grades. If you *don't* take the copy and you tell the teacher what Kaden has done, you may lose a new friend. It also will mean a new test for everyone—one that could be harder than the first.

What choices do you have?

What will you do?

AFTER THE GAME

Your mom is gone for the weekend and you're staying with your best friend. Your friend's mom, Mrs. Reese, is like a second mom to you and your mom trusts her. Mrs. Reese plans to pick up you and your friend after a basketball game at the community center Friday night. When Mrs. Reese arrives, it's obvious she's been drinking. You don't feel comfortable getting into the car. Your friend also notices the drunken behavior but tells you not to say anything when you quietly protest accepting the ride. A few other kids are waiting for rides, but you don't recognize anyone to ask for help. Even if you did see someone, you can't stay with your friend after refusing to ride with Mrs. Reese, and you're also not supposed to stay

home alone all weekend. If you don't get in the car, you may lose your friendship. Mrs. Reese is urging you to get into the car and your friend starts getting in.

What choices do you have?

What will you do?

PARTYING

You're having a blast with friends at a party your dad has no idea you are at. The parents of the friend hosting the party are out of town. A few friends ask you to follow them into the garage to show you something. Once you get there, it's obvious several groups of kids are smoking pot. You're confused because your friends know you aren't interested in using drugs and don't respect others who do. As you turn to leave, Sam, an older kid you really admire, asks you to join the group. Assuming Sam is going to tell everyone to leave you alone, you're surprised when Sam takes a turn at smoking. Even though you don't have permission to be at the party, you know your dad will pick you up if you call him. But you also know if you call him, not only will you be in trouble, so will everyone at the party.

What choices do you have?

What will you do?

For future reference, you may want to put a check next to the questions you are assigning.

Practicing ethical leadership can present further challenges when teens step away from peer pressure and make decisions that contradict a group. Actions to commit to in "Do Something About It" (pages 60–61 in *Everyday Leadership*) include options for contemplating "moral or ethical independence" and "group think" while acting ethically.

Do Something About It

Practicing ethical leadership can be challenging when you have to confront peer pressure and make decisions that contradict a group. This is called *ethical independence*. In contrast, thinking and acting as a group is referred to as *group think*. Although group think can be powerful and successfully produce positive results in some situations, it also can cause negative effects. Keep group think and ethical independence in mind when applying your ethical compass.

Check the goal(s) you will set to demonstrate your leadership abilities. If you have ideas of your own that you prefer, add them on the lines provided. Then write a date by which you plan to put your goal(s) into action on the "To Do By" lines and the date you completed them on the "Did By" lines. Be sure to fill in "What I Did to Achieve My Goal(s)."

	To Do By	Did By
○ I will stand up for someone who is being picked on, teased, or otherwise taken advantage of, even if it means confronting my friends.		
○ I will read a biography or other book about a person or a group of people who confronted the unethical behavior of others. I will ask my teacher, a librarian, or another adult whose ethical behavior I admire for suggestions.		

	To Do By	Did By
○ I will identify a conflict in my life that I need to address and use my ethical compass to make a decision.		
○ I will talk with an adult I respect about an ethical decision he or she made that was a turning point in his or her life.		

Other "Do Something About It" Ideas

○ _____

○ _____

What I Did to Achieve My Goal(s)

_____

_____

_____

_____

FIND OUT MORE ABOUT IT

You're Doing What?!

Facing an ethical dilemma—whether personal or as leader of a group—is never easy. At first, you may feel you don't have a clue what to do. Or you may want to act on the first thought that comes to mind, regardless of how wise it may be. But if you take time to think about what's going on and what issues are involved, you'll probably find you do know what is the most right thing to do.

As a leader, making ethical decisions calls for balancing your personal values with the needs of your group. It means respecting everyone's values and acting with integrity while still doing what's best for the group.

Knowing when a decision feels right doesn't require special powers. Everyone has internal checks and balances or a "compass" for making ethical decisions. Encouraging others on your team to think or act ethically shows that you expect them to consider their own internal compasses as well, instead of reacting emotionally or automatically.

Your ethical compass doesn't always give you an exact decision. When facing a leadership dilemma—one that requires you to make a choice between less-than-desirable alternatives—your ethical compass helps *guide* you in the best direction.

In some situations, you may find that your best choice feels uncomfortable. Here are a couple examples:

* As leader of a youth group, you get to pick three people to attend a leadership conference. One of the three could be you. You've attended this conference once before, but no one else in the group has. This year's keynote speaker, who also is leading a workshop, is someone you've always admired and wanted to meet.

* You offer to throw a party for a friend who's moving out of town in a few weeks. Two other friends offer to help you. Figuring out when to have the party gets tricky with everyone's busy schedules. It turns out that the only evening that works is good for everyone except you.

Ask yourself the following "compass" questions when you have to make a leadership or personal ethical decision:

* If a friend of mine did what I am about to do, how would I feel?

* Will I be breaking the law?

* Will this decision result in a win-win situation for everyone?

* Will I have to lie in making this decision?

* If the newspaper writes an article on what I am about to do, how will I feel?

* If my mom, dad, or other important adult in my life were watching me while making this decision, how would I feel?

* Do I have to keep my decision a secret from anyone?

* What do I feel in my gut are the possible outcomes of my decision?

* What does my conscience say?

Karen Kitchener, an educator and researcher in the field of ethics, believes you must take into consideration the following questions to support a well-thought-out ethical decision:

* How will my decision respect my rights and the rights of others? Will my actions interfere with others' lives?

* Will my decision minimize harming others? Will my actions show my compassion for others?

* How will my decision make things better for others? What am I willing to sacrifice?

* How will my decision show my commitment to treat others or all groups fairly? Will my decision respect a particular group's needs while still promoting equality with other groups?

* How will my decision show that I am trustworthy and have no hidden plan? Will my choice show that I keep promises, tell the truth, act loyally, and follow through on agreements I make?

When you use ethics to consider choices, you distinguish yourself from leaders who take advantage of people or engage in uncertain behavior. Decisions grounded in ethics also keep you from using excuses for your behavior. By paying attention to how and why you make a decision, you—and others who may be affected by your choice—are more likely to be satisfied with what you choose.

Take a few moments now and go back to the example about choosing who gets to go to a leadership conference. Imagine you're the youth group leader and apply the "compass" questions as well as those suggested by Kitchener to help make a decision. Who would you choose to attend the conference?

Adapted from Kitchener, Karen S., Ph.D., Foundations of Ethical Practice, Research, and Teaching in Psychology (Mahwah, NJ: Lawrence Earlbaum, 2000) and Beauchamp, T. L. and Childress, J. F., Principles of Biomedical Ethics (Oxford: Oxford University Press, 1989). Used with permission.

TRY THIS

Daily Dilemmas

Copy and cut out each of the following dilemmas for use in the "What Would You Do?" activity.

You recently found out you're going to receive an "Outstanding Graduate" award at graduation in a few weeks. The principal asked you to keep this information confidential until graduation. Friday is Senior Day, which traditionally many students celebrate by skipping classes and heading to the beach. Of course, administration doesn't approve. Your friends are making plans and waiting for you to decide if you're going and if you can be one of the drivers. What do you do?

On Halloween, a popular skate park in your city hosts a party for younger teens with bands and food. After the party ends and the adults leave, several of your friends are hanging out and decide to graffiti the ramps and walls. You are known in your circle as a great artist and you could make it look really cool. Plus about a hundred people were at the party so it's not like anyone would know who did it. Do you help your friends with your artistic talents?

You are a DJ for your school's radio station. Nearly 10 times a day, someone calls in to request a popular song that promotes violence against police officers. Other school DJs have played it. What will you do when someone calls in while you are spinning and asks you to play the song? Does it make a difference if your parent is a police officer?

Your older sister sneaks out regularly to go to parties and you've promised to keep her secret. One night, when your mom finds your sister gone, she starts asking you what you know. Since most of the time you don't really know exactly where your sister goes and what she does, what do you tell your mom?

Your dad is short of cash to cover fees for your weekly community sports meet. To be eligible to play, you have to pay your coach today. You've already borrowed from him several times recently and you feel embarrassed to ask again. You're a member of the sophomore student council and you have access to its petty cash fund. You know you can repay the money by next week's student council meeting since you get paid for your part-time job before then. Do you borrow money from the account?

For as long as you can remember, you've always wanted a job at the nearby veterinarian's office. You've just been offered a position to check dogs and cats in and out of the boarding kennel, but at least once a weekend you'll need to work until 9 p.m. Working that late is legal for someone your age in your state. Your driver's license, however, limits you from driving after dark. Your mom is okay with you doing it and has given you permission to do so, but if you're caught by the police or highway patrol, it could mean waiting another six months to get your full license. It's only a couple of miles between work and home. What do you do?

A local recruiter has explained to you how the military can help pay for you to go to college. Both your parents served in the armed forces and paying for college could be a huge financial burden for your family. You only have to serve in the military for four years after college, so you decide it may be worth it to sign up. As you walk up to the recruiter's office, students against war are protesting. What do you do?

Additional Daily Dilemmas

Your best friend is six months older than you and luckily, he'll get his driver's license before school starts. He asks if you want to ride to school with him. After driving together for a month, your friend begins arriving late to pick you up, texts while driving, and includes other people in the carpool, but only asks you to split the cost of gas. You *really* don't want to ride the bus because it picks up at 6:15 in the morning and takes 45 minutes, versus the 10-minute car ride. What do you do?

- -

You are a mentor at your school for students with special needs. You've developed a close bond with one of the students who, because of her special needs, has very few friends. You help her in the classroom as well as on the playground. Recently, she's been clinging too close, hugging you and wanting to sit on your lap during lunch. You feel guilty that it bothers you when she invades your personal "bubble," and feel like it makes you seem like the other kids who avoid her. How can you handle this?

- -

A text dings on your phone. You don't recognize the number but you definitely recognize the person in the picture included in the text. The photo shows him grinning while shoplifting a pair of jeans from a store at the mall. The kid is really popular and even grown-ups think he does nothing wrong. He's always got an explanation if caught in questionable situations and seems to avoid any consequences. What do you do?

- -

For a class project, your teacher assigns students to groups instead of letting everyone choose their own. Your team works well together at the beginning, but as the project goes on, only you and two other students of the six are doing all the work. The teacher announces that grades will be based on her observations, group feedback, and self-reported individual effort. You overhear the three slackers talking about how they plan to fill out their evaluations and realize they think they're doing what is necessary for the project. How do you handle this?

(PAGES 62–70 IN *EVERYDAY LEADERSHIP*)

GOALS

Participants will:

- discuss differences between sex and gender
- explore stereotypes about how males and females lead and work in groups
- evaluate personal leadership styles based on contemporary social behavior

MATERIALS NEEDED

- Chart paper
- Markers
- Tape
- Handout: "Find Out More About It: Traditional vs. Modern Leadership Styles"

GETTING READY

Make two copies of the instructions "Guidelines for Creating Your Ideal Company" on page 78 for the activity "Ideal Company, Inc." (Make more copies as needed if you designate participants into smaller groups of four or five people rather than two larger groups for the activity.) Put together two sets (or more as needed, one per group if using several smaller groups) of 10 sheets of chart paper and markers. Have additional chart paper available if needed. Make enough copies of the "Find Out More About It: Traditional vs. Modern Leadership Styles" handout for everyone in the group.

Getting Started

Gender bias is an issue in a variety of situations and can keep people from really knowing and understanding one another as unique individuals. To effectively confront biases, leaders need to understand how different values and stereotypes about sex and gender influence decision making. In this session, teens learn that behavior styles traditionally considered feminine or masculine are both valuable in leading and aren't automatically tied to gender.

Although teens may exhibit some initial discomfort or make stereotypical comments, this session generally inspires new freedom for them to make choices that ring truer to their personalities and feel more congruent with the individuals they are. *Please note:* Language regarding differences between what's male or female is used for purposes of general discussion only and is not intended to be authoritative or all-inclusive.

Depending on your group, you may find that discussion on this topic requires more than one 45-minute period. If possible, conduct the session with this in mind and plan accordingly.

Briefly introduce the topic of gender biases by clarifying the terms *gender* and *sex*. You might say:

People often use the terms gender and sex interchangeably, but they are different. Sex describes the biological differences of males and females—that is, you are born male or female. Gender, on the other hand, describes norms, stereotypes, and expectations typically associated with one sex. Based on social, cultural, religious, ethnic, and psychological values, expectations and stereotypes about gender are often influenced by your upbringing. Examples include: "boys don't cry" or "only girls collect dolls."

Ask teens for examples of other gender stereotypes. Continue by saying:

Gender identity refers to the gender you perceive yourself to be. How you lead depends in part on the role of gender in your life. While male and female leadership styles tend to differ, biases also can play out among group members who may have biases about others of the opposite sex or about male or female leaders.

When you set aside stereotypes or expectations, how you act and the choices you make don't have to be based on being male or female. And everyone, regardless of biological sex and gender identity, can learn to improve certain skills to lead more effectively. Today, you are going to work in single-sex groups to explore gender differences.

TEACH THIS

Ideal Company, Inc.

By working in same-sex groups in this activity, teens are deliberately exposed to gender-based attitudes and actions. In everyday situations, teens may jokingly say, "You do this because you're a girl," or "Of course you'd say that, you're a guy." This activity creates a setting where teens can focus on gender attitudes they demonstrate when interacting with one another, whether or not they realize they are. This activity also illuminates ways for teens to act and communicate beyond what society dictates, as well as to recognize how they may respond to leaders in their lives based on the leader's gender.

Divide participants into two groups: one all girls, the other all boys. If your group is only all girls or boys, proceed with two teams as well. You are still likely to see interesting differences and similarities. You may also consider forming smaller teams of five, with four girls and one boy or vice versa to see what happens. To set the scene, you might say:

Your team is starting what you believe to be an ideal company. You already have some money to get it started, but you need to create a general plan. Use the questions on this handout as a guide for creating your plan. (Distribute copies of "Guidelines for Creating Your Ideal Company" on page 78.) **Record your details on this paper.** (Distribute the sets of chart paper and markers.) **Do not interact with the other team. Select a spokesperson who will present your company to the whole group in about 20 to 25 minutes.**

Help keep both groups on task, answering questions and offering prompts. If they need help coming up with an idea, suggest a few ideas other teens have used, such as a T-shirt design shop, a bowling alley, or a snowboard manufacturer. After the allotted time, ask each spokesperson to display the team's chart paper and present the general company plan. Allow 5 to 10 minutes for each presentation.

Talk About It

To compare each group's different processes and results, ask:

- **What differences do you see between the teams' plans? Which differences might come from gender attitudes? Why?**

- **What similarities do you see? Why do you think these occurred?**

- **What was it like to work together on this project? What was easy? What was challenging?**

- What, if any, biases or stereotypes became evident from developing your plans? Explain. In what ways were any biases based on beliefs about gender? Or about other factors, such as previous experience or individual ideas and backgrounds?

- What might you change about how your team worked together if possible? Why?

- If you didn't agree with the direction your group was taking, did you speak up? Why or why not? How did the group react to you or others who made different suggestions?

- If two completely different groups of all boys or all girls were to undertake this same project, how similar or different do you think their results would be?

- If one group was boys and one group was girls, ask: **What if your group had both boys and girls? What do you think might be different about your company?**

- If both groups were the same sex, ask: **What if you had worked in groups of boys and girls together? What do you think might be different about your company?**

- If both groups had the majority of one sex and one person of the other sex, ask: **What if you had worked in groups of only boys and only girls? What do you think might be different about your company?**

Pass out the "Traditional vs. Modern Leadership Styles" handout and read through it together. Check if participants have any questions. Allowing at least 10 minutes to discuss this material, ask:

- **In what ways do you find yourself responding to others differently because they are male or female?**

- **What biases have you experienced from other people because of your sex and gender?**

- **Do you agree males and females tend to lead differently? Why or why not?**

- **Based on the different gender leadership styles, how much of your own behavior do you feel is because of your expectations about gender?**

- **What differences and similarities do you see between female and male leaders?**

- What differences and similarities have you experienced between male and female teachers, coaches, advisors, or other leaders?

- When people support gender stereotypes such as "guys don't talk about their feelings" or "girls are too emotional," what are some positive ways people could respond?

- What can you do to prevent stereotypes from getting in the way of choosing effective leaders, whether in school, the community, or beyond?

- In your circle of friends, do both the boys and the girls stereotype each other through what they say or their attitudes? What can you do in everyday situations to promote boys and girls being able to express themselves as unique individuals instead of trying to fit into "boys-only" or "girls-only" expectations?

For more about stereotypes, see session 12.

Wrapping Up

The questions in "Think and Write About It" (pages 65–69 in *Everyday Leadership*) ask teens to review the modern and traditional leadership styles and write about characteristics that describe their leadership style.

Think and Write About It

How you're raised, what you're expected to achieve, and who your role models are, all influence—or are influenced by—your views about gender. For each category heading from the "Traditional vs. Modern Leadership Styles" chart, identify which leadership style, modern or traditional, most *closely* matches your leadership attitudes and behavior. Remember, most people have traits from both traditional and modern leadership styles. Use the following questions to guide you as you think about your typical style. Instead of answering each question specifically, simply describe the style you choose and explain why.

GENERAL APPROACH

How would you describe your general style as a leader? Do you emphasize individual responsibilities or working together as a team? What's important for a team to succeed?

GROUP ORGANIZATION

As a leader, do you tend to assign group members specific roles or prefer to share control with everyone when getting things done?

EXPECTATIONS

How do you measure success? In competitive situations, which is more important: quality of your team's output or beating your competition?

TEAM PARTICIPATION

What do you consider effective team participation when you're the leader? How much is too much? When is it not enough?

PROBLEM SOLVING

Do you welcome finding new ways of solving a problem? If a group member suggests possible ideas, what do you do with his or her ideas? How comfortable are you as a leader when it comes to taking risks that may involve others?

CONFLICT MANAGEMENT

How do you prefer to tackle conflict? What role do others' opinions play when you are a leader dealing with conflict?

POWER

When you're the leader, how do you get group members to do what needs to be done?

RELATIONSHIPS WITH OTHERS

How do you prefer to interact with group members when you're the leader? Do you think it's okay to become friends with group members you're leading?

COMMUNICATION

When you communicate with group members, do you show what you're really feeling and thinking? Or are you likely to express things in a more matter-of-fact manner?

PITCHING IN

Do you believe it's more effective for you to lead by directing group members or working with them?

For future reference, you may want to put a check next to the questions you are assigning.

In addition to examining personal attitudes and reactions to being male or female, goals in "Do Something About It" (pages 69–70 in *Everyday Leadership*) prompt teens to explore stereotypes they may have about gender or about being male or female.

Do Something About It

By examining your attitudes about being male or female, you gain more understanding of judgments you make or support. Try choosing actions from the following goals that challenge your traditional thinking about gender and allow you to expand your mindset.

Check the goal(s) you will set to demonstrate your leadership abilities. If you have ideas of your own that you prefer, add them on the lines provided. Then write a date by which you plan to put your goal(s) into action on the "To Do By" lines and the date you completed them on the "Did By" lines. Be sure to fill in "What I Did to Achieve My Goal(s)."

	To Do By	Did By
○ I will imagine my life as if I were born the opposite sex and discuss my thoughts with someone of the opposite sex I trust.		
○ I will pick a category from the traditional vs. modern leadership styles chart and for one week, I'll try to lead a group using the style I typically don't use.		

---

70   *Everyday Leadership*

	To Do By	Did By
○ I will talk with two adults I respect, one female and the other male, about their beliefs and the impact sex and gender expectations have on their life choices.		
○ I will speak up if I feel someone treats me negatively based on gender and sex, or if someone makes jokes or comments that I consider critical or a put-down to either sex.		

Other "Do Something About It" Ideas

○ _____

○ _____

What I Did to Achieve My Goal(s)

_____
_____
_____
_____
_____

TRY THIS

Guidelines for Creating Your Ideal Company

You and your friends have decided to start your own business. You already have money to get it going, but you need to create a general plan. Use the following questions to help design your plan. Use the chart paper your group leader or teacher provides to describe and record your plan as you answer each of the questions.

1. What is your company's purpose? What product or service does it provide?

2. What is the name of your company?

3. What roles or positions does each member of your team have in the company? Who's in charge?

4. How does your company hire and fire people?

5. How will your company promote its business? How will you attract people to use your product or service? Where will you advertise?

6. What is the company culture (for example, serious, fun, friendly, hard-working, flexible)? Are there any unspoken rules for how important it is to fit into the company culture? If so, how do you do this?

7. What values does your company promote?

8. How will the company recognize employees' achievements?

9. What makes your company a special place to work? Why would someone want to work for your company as opposed to another business that offers the same or similar product or service?

FIND OUT MORE ABOUT IT

Traditional vs. Modern Leadership Styles

People often use the terms *gender* and *sex* interchangeably, but they are different.

- *Sex* describes the biological differences between male and female—that is, you are born male or female.

- *Gender* describes the norms, stereotypes, and expectations people typically associate with one sex. Based on social, cultural, religious, ethnic, and psychological values, expectations and stereotypes about gender often are influenced by your upbringing.

- *Gender identity* refers to the gender you perceive yourself to be.

To explore more about values, see session 9; for more about stereotypes, see session 12.

To say women and men have different leadership styles is a generalization. Both male and female leaders can have what are sometimes described as *masculine* traits, like taking risks, and *feminine* traits, like trusting a feeling (see the Traditional vs. Modern Leadership Styles chart). In the past, men generally were the only acceptable leaders. Today, people are becoming more accepting of both men and women leading—and leading in ways that reflect who they are as individuals instead of based only on gender.

Even so, gender continues to be a major factor in influencing leadership style. Understanding its effect can help clarify your actions as a leader and the decisions you make.

Did You Know?

- While many women have held or hold various leadership positions in their countries, from 1952 to 1997, only 3 women worldwide held the primary leadership position for a country.

- Since 1997, 25 additional women worldwide have held the primary leadership position for a country.*

*Worldwide Guide to Women in Leadership, www.guide2women leaders.com (May 1, 2015).

Emotional Intelligence

In the last several decades, society has seen not only greater equality for women to assume leadership roles but also appreciation for what's known as *emotional intelligence*. Defined by psychologist Daniel Goleman, Ph.D., emotional intelligence is the ability to focus on positive feelings (such as confidence) and control negative feelings (such as self-doubt).[1] According to Goleman, it takes more than traditional smarts to succeed. It's not just your IQ (intelligence quotient) that counts, it's also your EQ (emotional quotient).

According to studies, leaders who rise to the top of their fields aren't just good at their jobs. They're able to be friendly, recover quickly from problems, and remain optimistic. The studies indicate that typically women deal with issues of social

1. Goleman, Daniel, Ph.D., *Emotional Intelligence: Why It Can Matter More Than IQ* (New York: Bantam, 1997).

responsibility and understand another person's feelings better, and men are more able to handle stress and be self-confident.[2] But all people can develop techniques to manage stress and learn the importance of paying attention to others' feelings. Each of these skills is significant for effective leadership and teamwork.

The Way Women and Men Talk

The ways men and women tend to communicate and get along with each other is another factor that contributes to today's views of women and men in leadership roles. Deborah Tannen, Ph.D., a linguistics expert, uncovered behaviors that can get in the way when men and women talk with each other.[3] To be heard, get ahead, and get things done, she advises men and women to be flexible and consider different approaches if things aren't going well. For example, someone who tries to avoid admitting fault can see that the benefits of gaining a person's trust by saying "I'm sorry" outweigh personal pride.

Use a Style that Works

To avoid relating feminine traits only to girls and women and masculine traits only to boys and men, think of feminine and masculine leadership styles as *modern* and *traditional*. Each way of leading has its own advantages and limitations.

The person leading and the situation in which the person is leading also influence leadership style. While some girls and women may naturally use more modern styles, and some boys and men may naturally use more traditional styles, these statements are generalizations.

To support more positive and productive leadership, many women and men use a leadership style that mixes modern and traditional styles. As you consider the differences in the following chart,[4] think about your own style.

2. Murray, Bridget, "Does 'Emotional Intelligence' Matter in the Workplace?" *APA (American Psychological Association) Monitor* (Vol. 29, No. 7, July 1998); see also Stein, Steven, Ph.D., and Book, Howard E., *The EQ Edge: Emotional Intelligence and Your Success* (Toronto, Ontario: Stoddart, 2002).

3. Tannen, Deborah, Ph.D., *You Just Don't Understand: Women and Men in Conversation* (New York: Ballantine, 1990) and *Talking from 9 to 5: Women and Men at Work* (New York: HarperCollins, 1994).

4. Adapted and compiled from: Rhode, Deborah L., editor, *The Difference "Difference" Makes: Women and Leadership* (Palo Alto, CA: Stanford University Press, 2003); Evans, Gail, *Play Like a Man, Win Like a Woman* (New York: Broadway Books, 2001); Kabacoff, Robert, Ph.D., and Peters, Helen, M.A., *The Way Women and Men Lead— Different, but Equally Effective* (Portland, ME: Management Research Group, 1998), abridged results of the detailed research report "The Glass Ceiling Revisited: Gender and Perceptions of Competency" by Robert Kabacoff, Ph.D., available at www.mrg.com/uploads/PDFs /Glass_Ceiling_Revisited_2012.pdf; Norton, Dee, "Gender and Communication—Finding Common Ground," *The Leadership News: A Quarterly Newsletter on Leadership and Diversity in the Coast Guard* (Issue 7, Spring 1998, Web ed.), also available at www.au.af.mil/au /awc/awcgate/uscg/gender_communication.htm; Schaef, Anne Wilson, *Women's Reality* (San Francisco: Harper Collins, 1992).

Traditional vs. Modern Leadership Styles (continued)

	Traditional Leadership Style (masculine)	Modern Leadership Style (feminine)
General Approach	• Emphasizes competitiveness (plays to win) and individual responsibility • Relies on good planning and a vision to determine potential success in the future	• Emphasizes teamwork and shared responsibility • Relies on agreement and clear expectations • Follows up to make sure members meet group goals
Group Organization	• Uses hierarchy (ranks group members) • Maintains power • Expects each member to take a specific role	• Doesn't rank members • Shares power • Willing to negotiate roles
Expectations	• Strives to win, be number one • May compromise quality to achieve better bottom line	• Strives for quality results • Less interested in comparing the group to competitors
Power	• Is controlling (uses power over others) • Objectively directs members to do their job (not influenced by anyone's emotions or prejudices)	• Is collaborative (works with others) • Shows empathy (considers others' feelings) to influence team members to act
Relationships	• Views relationships as a means to an end • Doesn't socialize with people in the group or team	• Views relationships as important in and of themselves • Is comfortable socializing with people in the group or team

Traditional vs. Modern Leadership Styles (continued)

	Traditional Leadership Style (masculine)	Modern Leadership Style (feminine)
Communication	• Is low key, reserved, avoids expressing emotion • Uses language and low-key manner to persuade others' support	• Is enthusiastic, energetic, willing to express emotion • Builds on open, close relationships to inspire others' support
Team Participation	• Views increased participation as a breakdown of leadership influence, sometimes even a threat to group stability	• Encourages everyone to participate to support creativity and strengthen group productivity
Problem Solving	• Is rational, strategic, analytical • Is willing to take risks • Likes to review past results to determine future paths	• Is creative, seeks innovation • Is willing to trust intuition (a feeling) • Supports ideas that have no previous data
Conflict Management	• Prefers response that generally results in a win-lose situation (competition) • Also favors avoiding a conflict in hopes that it will go away	• Prefers response that results in a win-win situation • Also favors accommodating so things work for everyone
Pitching In	• Thinks helping out the team may damage image as a leader	• Usually willing to help out the team in any situation

(PAGES 71–78 IN *EVERYDAY LEADERSHIP*)

GOALS

Participants will:

- discuss common definitions related to tolerance

- investigate personal and societal stereotypes and prejudices and their significance in leadership

- engage in productive dialogue about why tolerance is important and how leaders can promote tolerance

MATERIALS NEEDED

- Empty shoebox
- Small notepaper or index cards
- Markers
- Chart paper
- Masking tape

GETTING READY

You may want to make enough copies of the "Declaration of Tolerance" handout (page 90) for everyone in the group, as well as the "Find Out More About It" handouts.

Getting Started

In this session, teens examine their prejudices and the impact these beliefs and other stereotypes may have on their roles as leaders. They explore the importance of tolerance in promoting respect for differences and enabling people to live without fear of violence for their beliefs or way of life.

Because tolerance and diversity are sensitive subjects, it is important to first establish common definitions for these and related terms. Ensuring everyone understands the meaning behind various terms sets the tone for the group to work together respectfully and discuss a variety of issues.

To introduce the topic, you might say:

> **Tolerance is respecting and valuing people who are different from you. Showing tolerance of others, no matter how different they may be from you, is important because everyone deserves to have their beliefs and live the way they want without fear of being hurt.**
>
> **Realize, though, that not all cultures or countries value tolerance in the same way.**
>
> **People often have trouble admitting they may have prejudices or acknowledging that they act in intolerant ways. When it comes to confronting stereotypes, prejudice, and discrimination, there are no easy answers. A willingness to look inside yourself is the first step to valuing tolerance daily in your life and when you take the lead.**

Ask teens to turn to "Speaking the Same Language" on pages 72–73 in their books (page 89 in this book) and read the sample definitions. Use 5 to 10 minutes to discuss and clarify the definitions and leadership-related examples. Next ask teens to consider these questions and briefly discuss:

- **Many people think of prejudices in terms of race, culture, religion, economic class, age, gender. What are other kinds of prejudices people hold?** (For example, toward people who are overweight, extremely shy, or homeless; have a physical or learning disability; or come from homes that are different from theirs.)

- **Why do you think it's important for leaders to be aware of their prejudices and stereotypes? Why do you think it's necessary for leaders to be tolerant of others?**

- **What prejudices or attitudes do you think you have toward people who are different from you? Is it difficult to admit your own prejudices? Why? If you aren't willing to acknowledge prejudices you have, how successful can you be as a leader?**

- **Some prejudices and attitudes can take years to change. Think of examples in school or the community. What role do adult leaders have in changing these? What role do teen leaders have?**

TEACH THIS

Prejudice Gallery

This activity can be challenging to conduct because it directly examines prejudice and stereotypes. Some teens may find the notion of tolerance unnecessary and forced; others may expect everyone to share the same opinions. Though this activity may evoke impassioned responses, it helps teens grasp difficult issues and practice how to address situations they may encounter in leadership positions. Let teens know this activity may stir up strong emotions and remind them of standards of respect and other ground rules established by your group.

For the first 5 minutes, begin by asking all participants to list names of groups that people have stereotypes or biases about. Remind teens to stick to impartial names of groups, such as athletes, teen parents, religious groups, girls, Asian people, rather than list offending stereotype labels. Write each group name on a piece of small notepaper or index card, and then fold and place the paper in the empty shoebox.

Next assign everyone into smaller groups of four or five, ideally diverse in makeup (for example, by age, culture, ethnicity, belief system, or gender). If your group is more homogenous, determine small groups by an objective descriptor such as clothing color (for example, lighter or darker socks or shirts). Have each small group select a spot in the room separate from the other groups. Pass out a sheet of chart paper and some markers to each group.

Because the emphasis of this activity is on promoting open and honest discussion regarding prejudice and stereotypes, offensive words will come up. If possible, avoid the temptation to exclude any words because they seem overly repugnant. However, use your own judgment and set limits on what can be expressed if you feel it is necessary. Begin explaining to teens what they are to do by saying:

> **One person in each group will select from this box a slip of paper with the name or description of a group you identified. Don't look at the paper until every group has selected a slip. Once someone in each group has a slip, show the name only to your group. Each group is to brainstorm words, phrases, stereotypes, or slang terms—both positive and negative—that come to mind when you think of what's written on your slip. As difficult as this may be, you are to speak the words out loud and write everything down on your sheet of chart paper.**

You may want to have participants write their names or initials on the bottom right corner of the chart paper. This directly confronts a tendency to hide behind modern-day anonymity (for example, blogs, radio call-ins, surveys) and reinforces that the words exist in today's language. If group members do identify themselves on the paper, discourage them from personally qualifying which words they *didn't* write during "Talk About It."

Acknowledging personal awareness of stereotypical words is difficult for people, so asking teens to write their names on the chart paper may cause them to feel uncomfortable. In this context, that's okay, since it can create a meaningful learning experience. Alternatively, during "Talk About It," ask each group of teens to raise hands as you point to their chart paper.

Instruct teens to write their names, if you choose to. Then continue explaining the directions by saying:

The words and names you hear, although you may not believe in them, often are learned at an early age. You continue to see and hear them all around you—in media, movies, books, history lessons, family teachings. In this activity, you may feel uncomfortable discussing negative stereotypes. Keep in mind that someone in your small group may identify with the group listed on the slip of paper. Or members of your small group may have very strong opinions about the group on your slip. Each person's own experience and views will affect your discussion.

Clarify your expectations with participants by saying:

It's important to realize that the goal of this activity is to openly and productively address attitudes that bring about intolerance. Although you end up saying and writing some offending terms for this activity, it's not permission to use any offensive and inappropriate terms outside this setting.

Help teens anticipate how to handle any heated moments, if necessary, by adding:

If your group is having difficulty, stop discussion immediately to let emotions cool down and raise your hand for help. Think about your attitude and how you're acting. Pay attention to how easily prejudices, biases, and stereotypes can affect how people interact and relate to each other.

Due to the personal nature of the topic, it's possible that disagreements may arise within the small groups. Some teens in the group may defend their stereotypical beliefs or express that their entire family feels this way

and that things aren't going to change because of a leadership activity. Also, if you work with groups that have gang members or others who hold their beliefs within a certain system or group culture, acknowledging and confronting stereotypes may be quite difficult. Depending on the differences between the teens in your group and your setting (say in a classroom or a weekend youth group meeting), you may want to draw on examples that help individuals connect personally to the impact of the prejudices. Here are some ways to respond to tense situations:

- **Learning about diversity and dealing with prejudice doesn't mean everyone has to look at things identically. Take a moment to step away from your group and think about what is making you most uncomfortable, angry, hurt, or any other emotion.**

- **Step back for a moment, think about how this activity may apply in your own day-to-day life, as a friend, brother or sister, tutor, baby-sitter, or other important leadership role. What would you do if your friend or sibling or the child you care for or teach, tells you someone called him or her a bad name because of his or her culture, religion, or gender? What would you tell this person who feels hurt?**

- **It's okay for each of you to express how you feel, but avoid forcing others in your group to agree with you. Even if you all say the same words, it doesn't mean everyone feels the same about the words. All the groups will talk about this distinction after the activity.**

- **Remember, prejudice is something people learn over time; unlearning prejudice also takes time. The point of this activity is not to change how you feel about things or to put down one another. Rather, it's to try to see how others may feel when you say or do things that put them down or threaten who they are.**

- **You may feel uncomfortable right now, but doing this activity may actually help you feel more comfortable to speak up in certain situations in the future. Practicing letting others know how you feel when they say or do things to put you down is important.**

Address any questions or comments teens may have, and let them know they have 10 minutes to brainstorm within their small group and fill out the sheet of chart paper.

After clarifying any concerns, let one teen from each small group pick a folded slip from the shoebox. Once each group has a slip, direct everyone to start brainstorming. Check in with each group to see how things are going. If groups are writing silently, remind them to say the words out loud. Speaking the terms and phrases makes the experience more powerful because people often don't want to acknowledge the stereotypes or biases they have been taught or may hold.

If any groups (or individuals) are struggling with an overly emotional atmosphere, encourage them to take a short break. Reemphasize the goal of the session and encourage them to stay focused on completing their chart paper and contribute to the overall group discussion after the activity. Express a general expectation that effective leaders are able to address controversial topics without letting emotion override rational, productive discussions. Intervene with groups, if necessary, that aren't able to get back on track on their own, using some of the responses mentioned earlier.

As each group finishes, tape the sheet of chart paper on the wall where the group met. Ask participants to return to their seats and wait until the other groups have finished.

When every group is done, explain to teens that the next part of the activity is to be done in silence. Tell them they will be walking around the room quietly, one at a time, to read each sheet of chart paper. When they finish reading all the sheets, they are to sit quietly until everyone is done.

Direct one person to begin. Wait until this individual moves to the next sheet of chart paper before starting another person to walk around the room. Maintain silence in the room, especially once several people are walking around viewing the gallery.

Talk About It

After the silent walk and before discussion, you may want to refocus the group by saying:

Most of you probably related to at least one thing said or written during the brainstorming, either from being treated a certain way or treating others a certain way. It took you only 10 minutes to come up with everything on the chart paper, but people have been using some of these words for years. Viewing the various groups' chart paper, much like being in a gallery, can open your eyes as everyday leaders to how others may feel, even if you don't feel the same. This awareness is an important step in choosing tolerance.

After refocusing the group, ask participants these questions:

- **What was your immediate reaction to the name on the slip of paper your group selected? Why do you think you had this reaction?**

- **Was it easier to think of positive or negative words and phrases about the group? Why do you think such stereotypes exist?**

- **What was it like to say and hear what was said in your group? What was it like to look at the different sheets of paper? How did you feel reading terms that describe your ethnicity, religion, culture, or a group you consider yourself a part of?**

- **Do you feel everyone in your group was truthful? Based on what you read on the other sheets of chart paper, do you feel people in the other groups were truthful?**

- **How truthful do you feel leaders should be or are about prejudices and stereotypes in daily behavior?**

- **What role do leaders have or should they have in challenging stereotypes? Do you think leaders consider these issues important? Why or why not?**

- **What steps would you take personally to change people's stereotypes about a group you identify with? How would your actions promote tolerance?**

- **In what ways can you take what you experienced today and use it to increase tolerance among your friends, family, or other groups where stereotypes get in the way of people working together respectfully and effectively?**

To help teens further understand the significance of promoting tolerance as a leader, ask them to read "Leading with Tolerance" on pages 73–74 in their books (page 91 in this book) before completing their reflection writing. Discuss examples or ways teens can practice the principles in "Leading with Tolerance," such as admitting not knowing or increasing awareness. You may want to talk about tolerance again after teens complete their writing so they can more deeply express their personal experiences and reactions to this session and the topic or ask any questions. Finally, pass out the "Declaration of Tolerance" handout and invite teens to fill it out if they wish.

For more about sex and gender stereotypes and biases, see session 11.

Wrapping Up

In the privacy of their guidebooks in "Think and Write About It" (pages 75–76 in *Everyday Leadership*), teens have the opportunity to reflect further on what tolerance means to them as leaders. Encourage them to keep in mind what they experienced during the "Prejudice Gallery" activity as they do the reflection writing.

If people of different backgrounds are in your group, what must you personally do to be an effective leader?

Identify a bias or prejudice you may have toward an individual (or group of people) that is interfering with your ability to be an effective leader. Explain how you came to have this bias or prejudice and how it affects your leadership behavior.

Think and Write About It

Think about past experiences as the leader or a member of a diverse group and how you may have reacted toward different members of the group. Keep those experiences as well as the session activity in mind as you write your responses to the following questions and statements.

How might showing intolerance toward others impact those looking to you for leadership?

Have you ever acted intolerantly as a leader? How did people react? Is this behavior something you want to change? Why or why not?

Think of any times when leaders have been (or are) intolerant and what they have done (or do) to justify their attitude or actions. Describe your reactions to their attitude or actions. Why do you think people sometimes accept, and in some cases support, the intolerance?

For future reference, you may want to put a check next to the questions you are assigning.

With such great diversity in today's world, it's increasingly possible to encounter people of a different background or culture daily. Teens are offered actions to strengthen their leadership skills in "Do Something About It" (pages 76–78 in *Everyday Leadership*) that involve honestly acknowledging their reactions to people who are different.

Do Something About It

If you've ever been excluded or treated prejudicially, you know what intolerance feels like. When you can be truthful with yourself and acknowledge your biases and prejudices toward people who are different from you, you can begin to strengthen your tolerance as a leader.

Check the goal(s) you will set to demonstrate your leadership abilities. If you have ideas of your own that you prefer, add them on the lines provided. Then write a date by which you plan to put your goal(s) into action on the "To Do By" lines and the date you completed them on the "Did By" lines. Be sure to fill in "What I Did to Achieve My Goal(s)."

---

78   Everyday Leadership

What I Did to Achieve My Goal(s)

Session 12: Choosing Tolerance   77

	To Do By	Did By
○ I will meet three new people who are different from me. I will talk openly with them to find out more about their background or culture.		
○ I will practice leadership that demonstrates my commitment to including others by asking a few of my friends to sit with me at lunch at school with people we generally don't sit with and get to know them.		
○ I will speak up when my friends or members of my club, team, or youth or community group make prejudicial or stereotypical comments about others.		
○ I will invite someone of a different background to join my family for a meal or a holiday; or I will attend an event with someone from a different culture.		

Other "Do Something About It" Ideas

○ _____

○ _____

Speaking the Same Language

Leaders who practice and expect tolerance take steps to set a positive tone with their team. When addressing sensitive racial issues, gender relations, and other concerns related to a diverse society, it helps to establish a common language. Failure to even talk about prejudices and stereotypes may negatively affect how others respect you as a leader. Following are some terms and examples to keep in mind as you talk about and confront difficult tolerance issues.

Diversity

Diversity refers to including or recognizing people of different races, cultures, and backgrounds in a group or an organization.

Example: A leader who supports diversity purposely selects people different from himself or herself and one another to create a team with broad perspectives.

Prejudice

A prejudice is an opinion a person holds despite facts that indicate otherwise. A prejudice may also be a preconceived idea, usually unfavorable, that a person uses to make decisions or choices.

Example: A leader who demonstrates a prejudice refuses to pick a man for her team because she believes men aren't as qualified as women.

Bias

A bias is a preference for one thing over another. A bias isn't necessarily a negative factor in a decision, except when it works against one group over another.

Example: A leader who shows a bias assigns more challenging responsibilities to older team members because he prefers using their greater experience.

Stereotype

A stereotype is an assumption, exaggerated belief, or distorted truth that all individuals who have certain characteristics or are from certain backgrounds are the same. Stereotypes represent an oversimplified description of something or someone.

Example: A manager promotes a stereotype by claiming teens are lazy and late to work, and limits a high school student's hours before seeing what she or he does.

Tolerance

Tolerance in general means respecting the background, beliefs, and practices of other people who don't share your same background, beliefs, or practices. For leaders, tolerance involves more than "just putting up with" people's differences. It's about acknowledging and accepting who a person is and not trying to change her or him.

Example: A leader who supports tolerance promotes a team talking openly about differences and accepting those differences, without requiring members to agree with each other's views.

Ism

Ism refers to a harsh or discriminatory belief or practice, such as racism (one race is better than another), sexism (one sex is better than the other), or ageism (people of certain ages are better than others). By practicing an ism, a person favors one characteristic—usually her or his own—over another.

Example: A leader who shows racism prevents people of a different race from being on the team based on their race rather than on their abilities.

To explore sex and gender stereotypes and biases, see session 11.

𝔇eclaration of 𝔗olerance

I will demonstrate my commitment to tolerance and including others, even if this feels uncomfortable to me, by signing my name to the Declaration of Tolerance pledge:

To fulfill my pledge, I _____ will

- **examine my own biases and work to overcome them**
- **set a positive example for my family and friends**
- **work for tolerance in my own community**
- **speak out against hate and injustice**

𝔚e 𝔖hare a 𝔚orld

For all our differences, we share one world. To be tolerant is to welcome the differences and delight in the sharing.

FIND OUT MORE ABOUT IT

Leading with Tolerance

The degree to which you show tolerance of other people every day is a choice—*your* choice.

Even though people *believe* they treat other people as equals, they don't realize they often don't treat them equally. According to studies reviewed by Tolerance.org, many people have prejudices they're not aware of and that influence how they act toward others.

Leaders who unknowingly show their biases and prejudices can lose the respect of group members and the support they need to make things happen. People look to leaders to do the right thing, whatever the issue may be. If leaders are unaware of their biases and prejudices, they can create an environment of distrust, blame, and negativity within their team.

Many people think of biases and prejudices in terms of race, culture, religion, economic class, age, gender. But people show bias and prejudice in other ways, often toward those who are overweight, extremely shy, homeless, have a physical disability, a learning disability, or come from a home that's different from theirs.

Broadening your horizons as a leader requires recognizing and admitting any personal prejudices and stereotypes. It can be hard to step out of your comfort zone, but the more you do it, the easier it gets. Practice and promote the following principles to strengthen your tolerance skills. Tolerant leaders realize not everyone embraces diversity. But with patience and commitment, you can create an atmosphere that values the differences everyone brings to your team.

Admit Not Knowing

Be willing to learn and understand people's differences by admitting when you don't know much about their cultural backgrounds. Inviting team members to teach you shows your respect for them and increases their respect for you.

Increase Awareness

If you don't know about someone's culture or beliefs, find out more by asking questions instead of making decisions based on stereotypes or assumptions. Encourage conversations and create opportunities in which everyone can comfortably learn more about each other.

Acknowledge and Promote Diversity

Recognize that the world is increasingly diverse. Support the idea that diversity is what can make groups strong instead of pulling people apart. Regularly tell group members this is your outlook.

Immerse and Appreciate

Find opportunities to learn about other cultures. Enjoy what's different and what's similar. Seek out new friendships, visit new places, attend cultural events and festivals, or learn a new language. When you're comfortable around people who are different from you, it shows.

Model Tolerance

Speak up when you hear slurs (insults) and let people know that saying those things is unacceptable. Make positive statements about others.

STRENGTH IN NUMBERS

(PAGES 79–84 IN *EVERYDAY LEADERSHIP*)

GOALS

Participants will:

- recognize the roles and responsibilities of leading a team

- compare how a group and a team function differently

- realize how group members' leadership attitudes can make a difference in how a team functions

- learn how leaders can inspire people to work together as a team

MATERIALS NEEDED

This session's activity requires more materials than typical, but they are all readily obtained.

- Bicycle inner tube, cut into at least four pieces of different lengths, ranging from 1 foot to 1¼ feet; use more pieces if desired

- Wooden dowels, ½ inch to 1 inch in diameter, cut into three or four lengths, ranging from 1 foot to 3 feet, or three to four wooden measuring sticks, ranging in length from 1 foot to 1 yard

- Two empty 5-gallon plastic paint tubs (lids are not necessary)

- Rope or webbing (available at outdoor climbing stores), at least four pieces of different lengths, ranging from 6 feet to 15 feet; use more pieces if desired

- Soft items of some weight (softball size or smaller, such as rubber or plastic balls, stuffed animals or bean bags; available at toy stores or large discount retail stores with "dollar bins"), one for each participant (These same items are used in session 7, so you need only collect them once.)

- Sturdy rope cut in two lengths, one 15 feet and another from 40 feet to 50 feet

GETTING READY

You may want to make enough copies of the "Find Out More About It: Working as 'Me' or as 'We'?" handout for everyone in the group.

Getting Organized

Push tables, desks, or chairs to the sides of the room to create a large open area. Create a circle in the middle of the open space with the 15-foot rope. Using the 40- to 50-foot rope, create another circle surrounding the smaller circle, with at least 5 feet to 6 feet between the two circles. In the center of the smaller circle, set the two 5-gallon tubs upright without their lids. In one, place the balls, stuffed animals, beanbags, and other small items. Outside the large circle, place the remaining materials, including the bicycle inner tubes, webbing, and wooden dowels or measuring sticks.

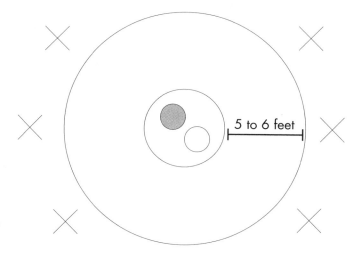

Getting Started

Leadership is essential to help a group of people move from just getting a job done to working together as a team. Today's session focuses on promoting an understanding of the importance of group members connecting effectively for a team to be a success.

To introduce the topic of teams and team building, you might say:

> **At one time or another, you've likely experienced being part of a team. What are some examples of teams you've been a member of or led?**

Allow for responses. If teens do not mention family and friends, note that these groups often function as teams as well. Point out also that everyone participating in these leadership sessions could be considered a team. Continue by asking:

> **What can a leader do to make people feel like they are part of a team as opposed to just being part of a group?**

Again allow for responses; then add:

> **Leaders can help members of a group feel as if they are connecting as a team by allowing members to use each other's strengths and develop trust in one another to do what they're supposed to do. Today, you're going to tackle an unusual task. Let's see how you can work together to be a team.**

TEACH THIS

Team Challenge

The object of this activity is for teens to transfer all the items from one tub to the other, using only the materials provided and following some specific rules. It's important to make sure teens follow the rules in order to help them recognize the relevance of overstepping boundaries, both literally and figuratively; in the activity, the ropes represent limits or boundaries in real life.

This task is challenging in a few ways. Often groups work well as a team starting out. Then frequently one or two people begin to think that it would just be easier to figure out the solution alone and forget about others in the group. Or a person may try to lead but poorly communicates her or his solution, which can make things frustrating for everyone. Ultimately, when all members of the group reconnect and stay connected, shifting their actions collectively from being just a bunch of individuals to working as a team, they will successfully complete this task.

So you know how the solution works (see "Sample Solution to Team Challenge" on page 96), you might want to do a practice run yourself with some colleagues, friends, or family. Or for fun, try it first without looking at the solution.

To begin the activity, ask teens to gather around the outside of the larger circle. To explain what everyone is to do, say:

> **In the next 30 minutes, you need to find a way to transfer all the items in one of the tubs to the other tub. To accomplish this, you can only use the materials you see lying outside the larger circle. You have to use the materials as they are; you may not cut, rip, or break them. You can tie knots. No one may**

step in the area between the two ropes or within the smaller circle, and the transfer of items must occur within the smaller circle. If you touch the area between the two ropes, you must sit silently for 30 seconds. The ropes represent limits or boundaries in real life, so it's important to take a few moments to think about the relevance of overstepping true limits, especially when you're part of a team.

If you've participated in a similar activity previously, please don't reveal the solution. Raise your hands to let me know.

Direct those who raise their hands to be observers and designate one to keep track of the time. (Track the time yourself, if no one raises a hand.) Ask participants if they have any questions and answer them, but avoid saying anything that may reveal the solution or hints to the solution. Check the time and ask teens to start. Intervene if anyone steps into or touches the off-limit areas or fails to follow the other instructions.

Checking in with the timekeeper, periodically state how much time is left. Some groups may need additional time. If necessary and possible, allow teens to negotiate with you for more time. Give more time in small increments (2 to 5 minutes at a time), so they can strive to complete the transfer as close to the original timeframe as possible. If teens finish, congratulate them. If teens do not figure out the solution in the time available, acknowledge their positive efforts and teamwork anyway and tell them the answer. During group discussion, address any interactions that may have prevented the group from solving the challenge.

Talk About It

To discuss what teens learned about working together as a team, ask participants and observers:

- **Overall how did the team share responsibility to solve this task? Did some people emerge as leaders? How did this happen?**

- If applicable, ask: **What did it take to get some individuals to work more with others? Do you feel the team would have accomplished this quicker or differently if the group worked more as a team? Why or why not?**

- **Would accomplishing this task have been different if the rules included picking a team leader first? Why or why not? What's different about**

what a leader does for a team compared to what a group of people working together does to finish a task?

- **When people made mistakes or overstepped boundaries, how did others respond? In what ways did the response support or interfere with team building?**

- For participants only, ask: **If there were any ideas that you felt others didn't listen to or that you felt you couldn't share, what was getting in the way of communicating openly?**

- **How can the attitude of members affect the atmosphere of a team? Is it possible for members whom others like to follow to affect how successful the team is at achieving its goals? Why or why not?**

- For participants only, if applicable, ask: **How did you feel about requesting additional time to complete the task? What could you have done differently so that more time wasn't necessary?**

- **What is the most important thing you learned from this activity that you would use as a team leader in a similar situation in the future?**

If time allows, ask teens to read "Working as 'Me' or as 'We'?" and "Tips for Building a Team" on pages 80–81 in the teen book (pages 97–98 and 99 in this book). You may also want to pass out the "Working as 'Me' or as 'We'?" handout, which has more information including a chart explaining what makes a group and a team. If you run out of time, ask teens to read these pages prior to completing "Think and Write About It" for this session.

Wrapping Up

When people feel as if they belong to a team, achieving goals seems much more possible. One option in "Think and Write About It" (pages 82–83 in *Everyday Leadership*) is to create a small poster to inspire a team attitude for a real or imaginary team. Consider facilitating another session to do this as a team project. Provide a large piece of banner paper and other art supplies, and a place to hang the finished product.

Encourage teens in "Do Something About It" (pages 83–84 in *Everyday Leadership*) to select actions that inspire teamwork and emphasize "we" instead of "me." Even those already active on teams or leading teams can take this opportunity to demonstrate new skills they've developed.

---

82   *Everyday Leadership*

Think and Write About It

When you're part of a successful team, as a member or a leader, you feel supported and understood, you share similar interests and goals, and you often accomplish things you never thought possible on your own. As you respond to the questions and statements that follow, think about your experiences on teams as a member or a leader. Use the lines provided to write your responses.

Describe a leader who has inspired a group you've been a member of to connect as a team. If you haven't experienced such a leader, describe specific things you would like a leader to do for your group to feel more like a team.

After leading a team that has been together for a long time, you notice that members are starting to seem disconnected as a team. What do you do?

When I am leading a team, members can count on me to lead by:

Session 13: Strength in Numbers   83

In the space below, create a design for a poster to motivate an existing or imaginary team. Have fun and be creative; show what you have learned about leading a group of people and helping them to develop a positive connection as a team. Transfer your design to a larger poster board to hang where your team and others can see it.

For future reference, you may want to put a check next to the questions you are assigning.

Do Something About It

When you model a team attitude as a leader and inspire a group of people to work together successfully, others are likely to want to join your team. As a leader, selecting actions that allow you to emphasize "we" instead of "me" helps you inspire group members to become a team.

Check the goal(s) you will set to demonstrate your leadership abilities. If you have ideas of your own that you prefer, add them on the lines provided. Then write a date by which you plan to put your goal(s) into action on the "To Do By" lines and the date you completed them on the "Did By" lines. Be sure to fill in "What I Did to Achieve My Goal(s)."

	To Do By	Did By
○ I will work with a group I lead to develop a motto, saying, or slogan to help solidify our connection as a team.		
○ I will research and lead a fun, interesting team-building activity for a group I'm part of (friends and family count!).		

---

84   *Everyday Leadership*

	To Do By	Did By
○ I will observe an adult I admire to see what strategies he or she uses to help a group work well together as a team.		
○ I will volunteer to organize and recruit people in a class, a community group, or my family to team up and do a service project.		

Other "Do Something About It" Ideas

○

○

What I Did to Achieve My Goal(s)

Sample Solution to Team Challenge

Teens can transfer the items from the one tub to the other according to the rules specified on pages 93–94 in a number of ways. Here is one possible solution.

Tie three lengths of inner tube together to form a rubber circle. Then tie three pieces of rope or webbing, one-third distance apart on the rubber circle. Next, three people position themselves one-third distance apart outside the large circle. Guided by the other participants, the three people positioned one-third distance apart outside the large circle pull the webbing to expand the rubber circle and lower it to surround the full tub. Releasing the tension of the rubber circle after it is around the full tub allows it to "grip" the tub. The three people pulling the webbing can then use the contraption within the smaller circle to lift the full tub and dump the items into the empty tub.

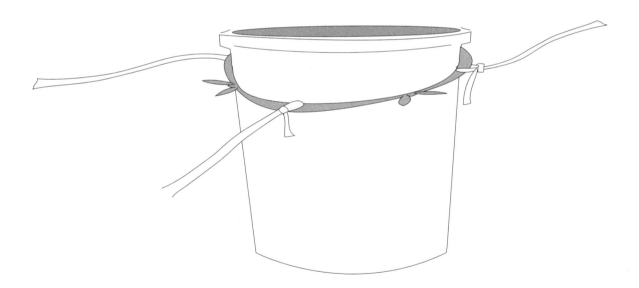

Note: The wooden dowels or measuring sticks, and any additional lengths of inner tubing and pieces of webbing, are decoys. Typically, they don't contribute to a solution—although you never know, people are resourceful! The minimum number of inner tubes and pieces of webbing indicated in "Materials Needed" on page 92 are necessary resources for most solutions.

FIND OUT MORE ABOUT IT

Working as "Me" or as "We"?

 Inspiring leadership is essential to help a group of people move from just getting a job done to working together as a team. When people truly feel part of a team, the sense of belonging affects attitudes and actions greatly; members believe they can accomplish things they never thought possible on their own.

You know what it's like being "in a group"—sitting in a class on the first day with a new teacher is a good example. But maybe you've also participated in a service project where you don't know anyone, or worked in a part-time job where the manager didn't inspire people on the same shift to do more than show up on time. Each of these scenarios presents the leader with an opportunity to encourage the group to become a team. The teacher might start a new class with a game or other type of icebreaker. The service project leader might partner members to complete the project. The manager might create incentives for shift workers and reward those who achieve certain goals together.

If you are a member of a team rather than the leader, your leadership attitude still makes a difference in how other members feel about the team. Informal leadership in any group—team members whom others like to follow—can make or break the team as much as the formal leader. Acknowledging other team members' skills provides good opportunities to encourage them to take the lead or deal with a particular situation. Recognizing members' abilities also reinforces the belief that everyone on the team is important, whether you're the leader or not. Similarly, one of the greatest leadership roles you can take as a team member is supporting the person in charge.

As a leader or a member of a group, it's important to realize how a group and a team function differently. To help understand what it takes to inspire a group to become a team, compare the distinctions in the following chart. Think about your leadership roles and if you and others act as a group or a team.

Working as "Me" or as "We"? (continued)

What Makes a Group	What Makes a Team
Members may feel obligated or forced to be part of the group (as in a class or job)	Members want or choose to be part of the team and are proud of their membership
Members aren't always aware of the group's goals	Members share a common vision and goal
Members share responsibilities but may also do things themselves because they aren't sure they can count on others	Members are comfortable sharing duties because they know they can count on others
Members may not fully trust others because they have different reasons for being part of the group	Members trust others to do what they say they will because they're committed to the team
Members may not trust their leader	Members trust their leader
Trust is not that important to why the group exists	Trust is important to members so the team can continue to succeed
Members may question why others are doing certain things and fail to learn what others' talents are	Members are valued for what they bring to the team and their talents are used to strengthen the team; they're interested in how they can interact with one another
Members don't expect their leader to look to them for help and prefer not to take on leadership roles if necessary	Members know their leader is comfortable asking them for help or to take on a leadership role if necessary
Members view moving forward as less important than just getting a job done	Members are active and look for opportunities to move forward; they want to examine how decisions are made and put into action
Members see conflict and mistakes as opportunities to complain about others or about ineffective leadership	Members see conflict and mistakes as opportunities to learn and grow
Members may not always realize the group's full potential because they work separately as individuals	Members realize their power and influence as individuals and as a team

FIND OUT MORE ABOUT IT

Tips for Building a Team

To help motivate your group to form a team identity, it's important for you as a leader to connect with everyone involved and identify what is needed to bring everyone together. Once you figure out what's keeping individuals from connecting as a team, you can make changes that encourage them to shift from "me" to "we" thinking. To help your group be a team, keep the following tips in mind.

Use Team-Building Activities

Team-building activities can help group members feel more comfortable with one another. If members enjoy an activity and learn something from it to apply in real situations, they are more likely to develop interest in how they interact with one another. Encourage valuing similarities and differences as well. Look to work in different small groups or alternate partners to uncover unique talents.

Build Commitment

Clearly express what you expect and why. When you communicate openly, members know what their responsibilities are and for what purpose, and everyone can share in how decisions are made and put into action. With open communication, it's easier for individual members to support goals and commit to you and everyone else.

Instill Confidence

An effective team leader is part of the solution, not part of the problem. Recognize what individual members bring to the team. And to help improve their skills, encourage them and respectfully provide constructive feedback. If one person is draining the team's energy and momentum, speak to that person alone. Take care not to let gossip and rumor negatively affect the team's attitude and ability to achieve success. (For more about positive feedback, see session 7.)

Inspire Trust

Underlying all of these efforts is how you can inspire members of the team to trust one another and to trust you, their leader. When you act reliably (such as show up on time, do as promised, keep committed), team members know that you keep your word. They can count on you to tell the truth and on your loyalty to the team. As a result of trusting you, they are more receptive to trusting everyone else on the team. And because they feel you always have the team's best interests in mind, they are willing to make changes to achieve success together. Trust increases everyone's energy, involvement, and positive team attitude and identity.

Empower Others

The ancient Chinese philosopher Lao-tzu once said, "When the best leader's work is done, the people say, 'We did it ourselves!'" Enabling your team to successfully "do it themselves" shows how well you've built your team. When informal and formal leaders are all willingly on the same page, there's no need to worry about anyone sabotaging or interfering with efforts. And if you feel comfortable that individuals on your team are capable of guiding members toward the necessary goals, then you can step back and let them take the lead. To help achieve team success, members can use the same positive leadership attitudes you've upheld, whether or not you're around.

SESSION · SESSION · SESSION · SESSION · SESSION ·

14

TURNING CONFLICT INTO COOPERATION

(PAGES 85–92 IN EVERYDAY LEADERSHIP)

GOALS

Participants will:

- identify their personal approach to dealing with conflict

- consider different styles people use to manage conflict

- learn techniques to resolve team conflict productively

GETTING READY

You may want to make enough copies of the "Find Out More About It" handouts for everyone in the group.

Getting Started

To be an effective leader, it's important to learn how to help a team resolve conflict productively and satisfactorily for all members of the team. This session focuses on helping teens gain awareness of their style of dealing with disagreements as well as other people's styles.

To introduce the topic of positive conflict resolution, you might say:

Everyone deals with conflict differently. Although people generally want to resolve conflict positively, some may try to avoid it altogether in hopes it will

go away. Others may continue it for personal reasons. As a leader, it helps to view conflict as an opportunity to inspire new ideas or ways of doing things rather than as a burden or something to avoid. Whether big or small, conflict often indicates some dissatisfaction with how things are and that a change could likely benefit everyone involved.

How you deal with conflict typically is influenced by previous experiences or habits. The way your parents or other important adults in your life deal with conflict has a big impact as well. As a leader, if you can identify the best method for helping any individuals at odds with one another to resolve their situation, the outcome is more likely to be positive for everyone. **The attitudes and actions you take to resolve conflict can make all the difference in how others regard your leadership.**

TEACH THIS

Managing Conflict: What's My Style?

Ask teens to turn to "Managing Conflict: What's My Style?" on pages 86–87 in their books. Direct them to read the instructions, complete the quiz, determine their score, and identify how they typically deal with conflict. Gaining awareness of how teens manage disagreements can help them increase their sensitivity to other people's styles and what's needed to resolve team conflict. Allow about 10 minutes.

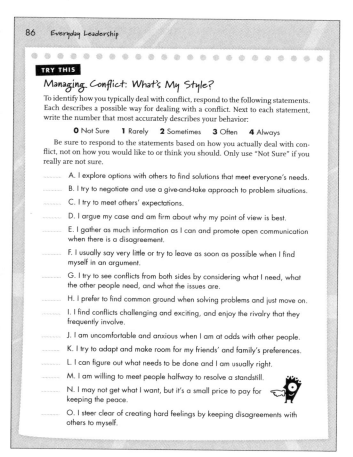

86   *Everyday Leadership*

TRY THIS

Managing Conflict: What's My Style?

To identify how you typically deal with conflict, respond to the following statements. Each describes a possible way for dealing with a conflict. Next to each statement, write the number that most accurately describes your behavior:

0 Not Sure   **1** Rarely   **2** Sometimes   **3** Often   **4** Always

Be sure to respond to the statements based on how you actually deal with conflict, not on how you would like to or think you should. Only use "Not Sure" if you really are not sure.

_____ A. I explore options with others to find solutions that meet everyone's needs.

_____ B. I try to negotiate and use a give-and-take approach to problem situations.

_____ C. I try to meet others' expectations.

_____ D. I argue my case and am firm about why my point of view is best.

_____ E. I gather as much information as I can and promote open communication when there is a disagreement.

_____ F. I usually say very little or try to leave as soon as possible when I find myself in an argument.

_____ G. I try to see conflicts from both sides by considering what I need, what the other people need, and what the issues are.

_____ H. I prefer to find common ground when solving problems and just move on.

_____ I. I find conflicts challenging and exciting, and enjoy the rivalry that they frequently involve.

_____ J. I am uncomfortable and anxious when I am at odds with other people.

_____ K. I try to adapt and make room for my friends' and family's preferences.

_____ L. I can figure out what needs to be done and I am usually right.

_____ M. I am willing to meet people halfway to resolve a standstill.

_____ N. I may not get what I want, but it's a small price to pay for keeping the peace.

_____ O. I steer clear of creating hard feelings by keeping disagreements with others to myself.

Session 14: Turning Conflict into Cooperation   87

To figure your score, total the numbers you wrote down for each group of statements with the letters associated with the following five styles of dealing with conflict:

Accommodating: C, K, N   **Avoiding:** F, J, O   **Collaborating:** A, E, G

Competing: D, I, L   **Compromising:** B, H, M

For example, if you put 1, 3, and 4 for statements C, K, and N, your total for "Accommodating" would be 8. If you put 1, 1, and 1 for statements F, J, and O, your total for "Avoiding" would be 3. The style with the highest total is the approach you use most frequently; the style with the lowest total is the approach you are least likely to use. Write down your highest total and style and lowest total and style.

Highest Total and Style _____

Lowest Total and Style _____

To learn more about dealing with conflict, read the following "Managing Conflict: What Helps When?"

As participants finish their scoring, invite volunteers to share any comments. Then go over "Managing Conflict: What Helps When?" on pages 87–88 in their books. You may want to pass out the "Find Out More About It: Managing Conflict: What Helps When?" handout to help teens learn more about the five different styles of dealing with conflict.

Talk About It

To help teens consider ways to use the information they identified from the quiz in the activity and read about in "Managing Conflict: What Helps When?" ask:

- **Do you feel the quiz results accurately describe how you deal with conflict? If not, how do you differ?**

- **How do you think knowing your style for dealing with conflict can help in the future? How will you use this knowledge?**

- **How do you think knowing how others in the group (or in general) deal with conflict can help in the future? How will you use this knowledge?**

- **What style do most people you interact with use to resolve conflict? In what ways does this style work for you (and the others) and in what ways doesn't it?**

- **If you were leading a team that had diverse styles for dealing with conflict, what could you do to resolve the conflict successfully?**

TEACH THIS

Promoting Team Resolution

Have teens first read "Tips for Resolving Conflict" on pages 88–89 in their books (page 105 in this book). Answer any questions and encourage them to keep these strategies in mind during the activity. In this activity, participants get a chance to explore how effective their natural style for dealing with conflict may or may not be in a certain situation. Depending on the size of your group, have teens count off by threes to form groups. Then say:

> You are part of a team in the middle of a project to sort through donated clothes for washing or tossing at a shelter. Half of the team isn't helping because they don't like the idea of handling unwashed clothes. The other half of the team is working enthusiastically, saying it feels great to know they're helping people. They're trying to encourage the other half of the team but also are getting increasingly annoyed that they're not helping. Take turns over the next 10 to 15 minutes to be the leader or a representative of either team half. As a leader or team member, consider whether your natural style for dealing with the team's conflict works or if you need to adopt a different style.

While helping shelters is a common project, some teens in your group may either receive or have received services from a shelter. Others may shop at secondhand stores. Be sensitive to this possibility and focus teens on working respectfully as a team. You might say:

> Remember that some issues leaders and groups deal with can be very personal. Focus on working together respectfully to accomplish your task. Use the tips you just read about to discuss the project.

Talk About It

To help teens further address how they can guide a team to resolve conflict positively, ask:

- As the leader, were you able to guide the team to a positive resolution? Why or why not?

- If you used your natural style, as identified in the quiz, for trying to resolve the conflict, were you successful? Why or why not?

- If you adopted a different style than your natural style, were you successful? Why or why not?

- How did the tips to promote productive conflict resolution help you?

- In guiding the team to resolve the conflict, what, if any, new solution or strategy did you work out?

To continue exploration of conflict resolution at another time, consider having participants complete the *Thomas-Kilmann Conflict Mode Instrument (TKI)*, a widely used tool for assessing conflict styles, skills, and behavior (see "Resources and Additional Reading" on page 212).

Wrapping Up

"Think and Write About It" (pages 89–90 in *Everyday Leadership*) this session inspires teens to reflect further about how to manage reactions, their own and other people's, when conflict arises and help everyone resolve the issues successfully.

> ### Think and Write About It
> Gaining awareness of how you deal with conflict can help increase your sensitivity to other people's styles. Often, the way you respond to or help resolve team members' disagreements is influenced by previous experiences or habits. How your mom, dad, or other important adults in your life deal with conflict has a big impact as well. Keep the knowledge you gained about yourself in the session activity—as well as others' styles you've experienced—in mind while responding to the following questions and statements.
>
> In what ways will you use your knowledge of different styles of dealing with conflict as situations arise with your friends and family?

Think about a conflict you experienced as a team member that you wish had been resolved differently. What would you have done if you had been the leader?

Think about a conflict you experienced as a leader that you wish you could have helped resolve differently. What would you have done instead?

Think about an ongoing conflict you've been struggling with as a leader. What steps can you take to achieve a meaningful outcome now?

Do Something About It

Helping a team resolve conflict productively and satisfactorily for all members takes practice. As you choose from the following goals, think about your natural style for managing conflict and what new approaches you can try.

Check the goal(s) you will set to demonstrate your leadership abilities. If you have ideas of your own that you prefer, add them on the lines provided. Then write a date by which you plan to put your goal(s) into action on the "To Do By" lines and the date you completed them on the "Did By" lines. Be sure to fill in "What I Did to Achieve My Goal(s)."

	To Do By	Did By
○ I will take my time when dealing with a team conflict to carefully consider all the issues rather than jump to conclusions about what the outcome should be.		
○ I will watch two TV shows and observe how the characters deal with conflict. I will write about how successful the approaches were or alternative ways they could have managed the conflict better. (Alternatively, I will watch the shows with a few friends and lead a discussion about our observations.)		
○ I will ask for feedback about my style of dealing with conflict from someone I respect. I will make notes about the feedback to keep for future reference.		
○ I will test a different approach from my preferred style for managing conflict the next time a team conflict arises.		

For future reference, you may want to put a check next to the questions you are assigning.

The actions in "Do Something About It" (pages 91–92 in *Everyday Leadership*) provide additional opportunities for teens to explore various approaches to resolving conflict positively.

	To Do By	Did By
Other "Do Something About It" Ideas		
○		
○		

What I Did to Achieve My Goal(s)

FIND OUT MORE ABOUT IT

Managing Conflict: What Helps When?

People may deal with conflict in all kinds of ways, but often they're unaware of how they're acting. As a leader, help manage the different ways team members react to a disagreement, whether or not they realize what they're saying or doing. Then you can better guide them to resolve the situation. Below are five styles* people use when dealing with conflict. Each has pros and cons, depending on the situation, the personalities involved, the timeframe in which you are trying to resolve the issue, and how you tend to deal with conflict.

Competing

Objective: Deal with the conflict one way, my way.

A leader who uses a competing or controlling style is aiming to achieve her or his solution. This style works best when a situation requires a quick decision, or a leader needs to control others who may take advantage of the situation. It can, however, create a win-lose scenario that leads to resentment.

Avoiding

Objective: Stay quiet and remain neutral.

A leader who uses this style withdraws from conflict. The leader aims to maintain a relationship rather than to engage in a disagreement. This style is best used when confrontation may result in worse conflict. Sometimes, avoiding conflict allows time for people to settle down or get more information. Avoiding conflict also can mean that problems remain unresolved, relationships fall apart, or others may try to take advantage of the situation.

Accommodating

Objective: Minimize conflict or treat it as no big deal.

A leader who readily accommodates or seeks harmony when there's conflict emphasizes relationships. They matter more than anything else. An accommodating leader decreases everyone's discomfort. Or creates the impression that the conflict isn't that important. Sometimes, however, a few individuals may take advantage of this softer approach or become resentful or bitter because an important issue is forgotten or minimized.

Compromising

Objective: Meet others in the middle.

A leader who compromises identifies which goals are worth keeping or sacrificing. This style is effective when the issues are complicated and time is short. While everyone's interests get considered, too much compromising can mean that no one is satisfied or the solution is less than ideal.

Collaborating

Objective: Creating a win-win situation for everyone.

A leader who collaborates when there's conflict tries to resolve the issue fairly. To collaborate means to work together. This style builds on qualities such as honesty, respect, trust, and clear communication. By avoiding negative feelings, collaborating leaders encourage everyone to commit to a solution. But because this style can require lengthy discussion, dealing with the conflict can take a lot of time. Time isn't always an option.

---

*The headings for these styles are commonly used in conflict resolution quizzes or tools. Similar terms are originally attributed to Kenneth W. Thomas, Ph.D., and Ralph H. Kilmann, Ph.D., authors of *Thomas Kilmann Conflict Mode Instrument (TKI)* (Mountain View, CA: CPP, Inc., 2002).

FIND OUT MORE ABOUT IT

Tips for Resolving Conflict

Whatever style you use as a leader to help a team manage a conflict, the following basic tips are helpful in any situation. Keep them in mind as you continue to take on more leadership roles.

Understand the Conflict

Consider the circumstances with an open mind. Be sure you know what all the issues are.

Separate the People from the Conflict

Focus on the particular issues involved, rather than on the individuals, who may feel a need to defend themselves.

Be Specific

Clearly state what needs to change rather than offer vague requests. This helps everyone involved understand what is expected.

Be Flexible

Even though you may tend to deal with conflict a certain way, try developing other styles and approaches. As new situations arise, you'll be better prepared to take the lead.

Seek Advice

Even the best leaders can benefit from an outsider's perspective to manage an issue. Some people are specially trained to help resolve conflict. For example, in your school or community program, you may have peer mediators who can offer guidance. Parents or guardians, adult relatives, teachers, coaches, community leaders, or other trustworthy adults may also be able to help you resolve difficult situations objectively.

(PAGES 93–99 IN *EVERYDAY LEADERSHIP*)

GOALS

Participants will:

- understand and practice majority rule decision making
- explore the effectiveness of majority rule in certain situations
- gain knowledge about group dynamics related to decision making
- learn tips to guide a group discussion prior to taking a vote using majority rule

MATERIALS NEEDED

- Whiteboard or dry erase board (preferred), or chart paper
- Dry erase markers or regular markers
- Masking tape (if using chart paper)
- Handout: "Find Out More About It: Majority Rule: Putting It to a Vote"

GETTING READY

If using chart paper, tape at least five sheets on a wall where they're easily visible. Make enough copies of the "Find Out More About It: Majority Rule: Putting It to a Vote" handout for everyone in the group.

Getting Started

Leaders often use different approaches to guide groups to make a decision, depending on the situation and who's in the group. Majority rule is one approach. Teens learn in this session about its benefits and limitations.

You can present another approach to decision making, consensus rule, in session 16.

For the first 5 to 10 minutes, get teens thinking about group decision making in general and the role leaders can play. You might say:

Groups often use different approaches to make a decision, depending on the situation. Think of a time you helped a group, whether it was with friends or family or a youth group or athletic team—any group—to make a decision, solve a problem, or come to an agreement. Did you just vote on people's preferences, or did you talk until everyone could agree on a particular option?

Allow for responses. Then ask participants to explain their understanding of majority rule. Supply additional information if necessary. You might say:

When a group uses majority rule to make a decision, each person gets to vote for or against a particular issue or for one choice among several. Whatever the majority decides, the entire group must follow. With majority rule, groups can make a decision quickly. Majority rule is one approach you're going to explore.

TEACH THIS

The Island

(pages 94–95 in *Everyday Leadership*)

In this activity, teens use their own survival as a motivating factor for choosing five people they'd most want to help them on a deserted island, first independently of one another and then together as a group. Some teens may make their individual choices based on whimsical reasons; others will think carefully about who could help them survive. When members of the group negotiate together for the final five, overall priorities tend to shift and the group usually eliminates people who don't have the necessary skills. This shift reinforces how effective majority rule can be, especially after allowing for discussion. It helps the group achieve a result that generally reflects the fundamental needs for individual survival. It also encourages teens to continually focus on what the group's true goal is (survival)—or in other situations, for example, choosing a service project or theme for a homecoming float—and connect this goal with the steps necessary to make decisions that meet this goal.

Ask teens to turn to the "The Island" activity on page 94 in their books. Allowing 5 minutes, direct them to each identify five well-known people who would help them survive being stranded on an island and briefly explain why. Ask for a volunteer to record all the names (not the reasons) on the board or chart paper as each participant shares his or her picks and reasons.

---

94 *Everyday Leadership*

TRY THIS

The Island

If you were stranded on a remote island, what five well-known people (no family members or friends) would you choose to be with to help survive? Write your choices (the well-known people may be dead or alive) and explain why you chose these individuals. Wait to discuss your choices until everyone in your group has finished writing.

MY CHOICES

1. Name: _____

Why: _____

_____

_____

2. Name: _____

Why: _____

_____

_____

3. Name: _____

Why: _____

_____

_____

4. Name: _____

Why: _____

Session 15: All in Favor, Say "Aye" 95

5. Name: _____

Why: _____

_____

_____

Share your individual choices with the rest of the group.

Now as a group, identify five people everyone in the group would want to help you all survive on the island. Record the group's five choices and reasons why.

Next ask for two new volunteers, one to serve as leader to guide the group in choosing the five best people to include from all of the names recorded, and the other to record the final decisions. If necessary, help direct the leader to maintain order, keep the group on task, and encourage everyone to speak up. Explain to teens that they are to continue their deliberations for no more than 20 minutes. With about 5 minutes to go, they are to finalize their decision using majority rule and have the volunteer record the winning names on the board or chart paper and why the group picked those names.

Talk About It

Take 5 to 10 minutes to discuss what teens thought of using majority rule in "The Island" activity and ask:

- **What reasons became most important to you as the group debated the different choices? What reasons became most important to the group?**

- **Do you feel that others heard your voice? Why or why not?**

- **Did other people's choices and reasons change your mind about your choices? Why or why not?**

- **In voting, did you feel you had to compromise your choices to help make a group decision? Why or why not?**

- **Do you think using majority rule worked well in this situation? Why or why not?**

Ask teens to turn to "Majority Rule: Putting It to a Vote" on pages 95–96 in their books. Pass out the "Find Out More About It: Majority Rule: Putting It to a Vote" handout. Give them 5 minutes to read the information. Ask teens if they have any questions and to list other examples of situations in which they believe majority rule is the most effective decision-making approach.

Wrapping Up

"Think and Write About It" (pages 96–97 in *Everyday Leadership*) offers teens a chance to explore the effectiveness of majority rule in different personal situations and in current events.

Think and Write About It

When a group takes time to discuss various issues before agreeing to a majority rule vote, new information or other attitudes can potentially change one member's point of view. Talking also can open the possibility for finding a better solution than one originally proposed. Eventually, though, majority rule puts the issue to a vote. This leads to a decision, even if some group members may "lose."

Describe a group experience at home, at school, with friends, at work, at camp, or somewhere else in which you *effectively* used majority rule. Explain what made this method effective in this situation?

Describe a current events issue, locally or nationally, in which majority rule was *effective*. Explain what made this method effective in this situation?

Describe a group experience at home, at school, with friends, at work, at camp, or somewhere else in which majority rule was *not effective*. What made this method ineffective in this situation? How else could the decision been made?

Describe a current events issue, locally or nationally, in which majority rule was *not effective*. What made this method ineffective in this situation? How else could the decision been made?

For future reference, you may want to put a check next to the questions you are assigning.

Voting in different real-life circumstances enables teens to understand firsthand the impact of majority rule. The goals in "Do Something About It" (pages 98–99 in *Everyday Leadership*) suggest some specific actions to take.

---

98   *Everyday Leadership*

Do Something About It

To learn more about different approaches to making decisions in groups, including majority rule vote, challenge yourself to observe or participate in situations where different decision-making strategies may be in action. Consider the standard way you approach getting things done in a group, especially when you're the leader and in a position to help a group make better decisions most effectively.

Check the goal(s) you will set to demonstrate your leadership abilities. If you have ideas of your own that you prefer, add them on the lines provided. Then write a date by which you plan to put your goal(s) into action on the "To Do By" lines and the date you completed them on the "Did By" lines. Be sure to fill in "What I Did to Achieve My Goal(s)."

	To Do By	Did By
○ I will lead a discussion with my family about changing a rule at home or proposing a new one and suggest that we use majority rule vote to decide.		
○ I will create a survey on an issue that I feel strongly about, such as recycling, and ask my friends to fill it out. Even if the majority does not support my concerns, I will see if those who do, want to help me take some action.		
○ I will participate in the next voting process to select youth leaders in a community, school, or youth group program, or other teen club or team.		
○ I will interview a community leader (such as a school board president, mayor, community college president, city human rights council member) regarding how he or she most effectively leads group decision-making processes. I will share what I learn with this group.		

Other "Do Something About It" Ideas	To Do By	Did By
○		
○		

What I Did to Achieve My Goal(s)

Majority Rule: Putting It to a Vote

One of the more challenging roles for a leader is guiding the group when making a decision. In an ideal world, you would snap your fingers and everyone in the group would agree on a single choice. But that's not realistic.

Even when everyone in the group knows one another well, making a group decision is often no easy task. It can be stressful and may or may not take into account everyone's opinion.

Every situation involves different issues, people, and goals. The reason for making a decision, whom it will affect, and how much time you have to make it also are important. To pick an option that satisfies the entire group, leaders can choose between different approaches for making the decision. One approach is *majority rule*.

When to Use Majority Rule

The following factors in different situations and examples point to whether or not using majority rule to make a decision would be most effective or appropriate.

Good Times to Use Majority Rule

Situation: Group members have been informed of the options, which are clear-cut and not likely to be misinterpreted.
Example: Selecting new student council members after time has been allowed for campaigning at school and informing students of the candidates' platforms.

Situation: The group has discussed an issue at length, but can't come to a common agreement.
Example: Choosing a name for a sports team or a theme for an event.

Situation: The group has a limited time frame to make a decision.
Example: Deciding how to use some grant money by a certain date or before the funding is withdrawn.

Situation: Power in the group is somewhat balanced, so all members' "voices" are heard equally.
Example: Selecting what band should play at an annual carnival by a diverse group, where no one individual or group of individuals (for example, one culture) dominates.

Not-So-Good Times to Use Majority Rule

Just as there are situations where using majority rule is very effective, there are instances when using it wouldn't be particularly effective. Generally, this is because these situations have one or more of the following factors:

* The leader realizes that if everyone doesn't agree on the same outcome, the decision will not be successful or people will try to get around it.

* Group members feel strongly about conflicting issues and believe a vote would minimize the importance of certain issues.

* The time available to make the decision is unlimited, as long as everyone agrees with the final choice.

Power in the group is unevenly distributed and cliques in the group could easily sway a vote.

For situations like these, you would want to use another approach to decision making called *consensus rule*. You can explore consensus rule and why it would be more effective in these types of circumstances in session 16.

Tips for Guiding Discussion

While majority rule can help groups reach a decision efficiently, it's helpful as the leader to give people a chance to debate or discuss the issues prior to voting. The final decision then represents an *informed* majority opinion, even if some members voted differently.

How you help direct group discussion prior to taking a vote using majority rule will make a difference in how effectively the group arrives at—and supports—a decision. Your behavior as a leader sets the tone. Group members also will be watching what you say and how you guide the decision-making process to see if you have a hidden agenda. To successfully guide group debate of the issues behind a decision, keep the following tips in mind:

✴ **Encourage open discussion** so options are laid out clearly for everyone in the group to consider.

✴ **Offer realistic scenarios** for the possible decisions—if the choice is "A," then "X" happens, if the choice is "B," then "Y" happens. By talking through various alternatives, you can avoid confusion and help group members fully understand the impact of different choices. Also, members are less likely to complain that they were misled during the decision-making process.

✴ **Work hard to involve all members** so everyone hears all the pros and cons, all the hopes and concerns. Doing so likely will increase support once the final vote is counted.

✴ **Avoid offering your personal opinion** about the way you want a vote to go. If members perceive you're trying to influence the decision for personal gain, they may doubt your sincerity as a leader whenever new issues arise.

✴ **Cut off any bullying**, such as teasing other members or making fun of or putting down their ideas. Make it clear that is not acceptable behavior for your team. This helps create an inclusive atmosphere so members feel valued and are comfortable expressing their opinions.

✴ **Maintain balance in group power**, especially if cliques are a concern, by ensuring that the voting is confidential. With a written vote, people can make their own choice instead of just doing whatever their friends do.

✴ **Motivate all members to vote** by reminding them that voting is a way to influence group goals and accomplishments. If people are uninterested in voting, explain that you won't be open to complaints from people who choose not to vote.

By encouraging your team to use majority rule when making a group decision in appropriate situations, you reinforce that the opinions of all members matter to you. Putting into practice a decision that comes about through discussion and a final vote also demonstrates that as a leader, you are determined to keep the team moving forward successfully.

ALL FOR ONE AND ONE FOR ALL

(PAGES 100–104 IN *EVERYDAY LEADERSHIP*)

GOALS

Participants will:

- understand and practice consensus rule decision making

- explore the effectiveness of consensus rule in certain situations

- gain knowledge about group dynamics related to decision making

- learn tips to guide the group process when using consensus rule

MATERIALS NEEDED

- One large envelope (9" x 12") and two business-sized envelopes

- Scissors, tape

- 16 chairs (or fewer depending on group size; optional)

- Handout: "Find Out More About It: Consensus Rule: Talking It Through"

GETTING READY

If using chairs, arrange them in a circle. (Or participants can sit on the floor to form a circle instead.) For groups with more than 16, plan on additional teens observing outside the circle.

Make enough copies of the "Find Out More About It: Consensus Rule: Talking It Through" handout (pages 119–120) for everyone in the group.

Make a copy of "Labels for Choose a Color" on page 116. Make a copy on colored paper of "Roles for Choose a Color" on pages 117–118. To prepare all three envelopes for use in the activity, cut and tape the appropriate labels and insert the role slips as follows:

1. Cut out the label "General Instructions," which includes the directions below the title. Tape the label and instructions to the outside of the large (9" x 12") envelope.

2a. Cut out and tape the label "Envelope I" to the outside of one of the business-sized envelopes.

2b. Cut out and place the directions for Envelope I inside Envelope I.

3a. Cut out and tape the label for "Envelope II" to the outside of the other business-sized envelope.

3b. Cut out and place the directions for Envelope II inside Envelope II.

3c. Cut out the 16 role plays into slips. Fold and insert them into Envelope II. For groups with fewer than 16, exclude the observer roles first and then any additional roles that are least necessary for your group's experience. Some roles are deliberately repeated to mimic typical behavior, conflict, and competition that may arise when a group is trying to make a decision.

4. Place Envelopes I and II in the large envelope labeled "General Instructions."

Getting Started

Depending on the situation and who's in the group, leaders often use different approaches to guide a group to make a decision. Consensus rule is one effective approach. Teens learn in this session about its benefits and limitations. You can present another approach to decision making, majority rule, in session 15.

To introduce the topic of decision making in general and the role leaders can play, you might say:

Flipping a coin or cutting a deck of playing cards is often an easy way to make a decision when only one or two people are involved. But how about when you're part of a group? Which do you think is more important for a group: The actual decision a group makes in a situation, or the process the group goes through to make the decision?

Allow for responses. Then ask participants to explain their understanding of consensus rule. Supply additional information if necessary. You might say:

When a group uses consensus rule to make a decision, everyone in the group gets to express their opinion. But everyone must also agree to the same decision or course of action. In contrast, when a group uses majority rule and everyone gets a vote, the majority preference wins. With consensus rule, groups can make a decision that promotes a win-win atmosphere. Consensus rule is one approach that you're going to explore now.

TEACH THIS

Choose a Color

In this activity, teens strive to reach a consensus twice. Selecting a leader, as directed in Envelope I, allows the participants to experience the natural process of consensus without having specific roles assigned. It also offers teens an opportunity to think about their personal investment in a situation, especially when compromise plays a role. During this first task, if teens want things to move forward, they discover they can push to be the leader or encourage someone else to take that role. Once the group moves onto Envelope II, specific roles are assigned to create conflict and imitate behaviors that can exist in groups trying to make a decision. Both decisions reinforce the need when using consensus rule for everyone to agree before the group can move forward. Generally, the first decision is made quickly and easily because members don't approach the process with conflicting motives. While selecting the team flag color, participants gain more awareness of what's necessary for a leader to build group consensus when members play different roles that support or block consensus (including members who aren't satisfied with how a leader is guiding the process). Because the observers aren't involved in the role playing taking place, they can provide feedback and insight afterword about consensus in action, including commenting on how conflict can derail consensus.

Depending on your group size, identify those teens who will participate and those who will observe. Ask participants to sit on the chairs in a circle (or on the floor), and observers to sit to the side. Review guidelines with participants for role playing if necessary (see page 4 in the "Introduction").

Place the large envelope with the label "General Instructions" in the center of the participants' circle. Briefly explain they must carefully read the instructions taped on the outside of the large envelope. The instructions will direct them to the two envelopes inside, beginning with Envelope I. They will have 5 minutes to respond to the instructions inside Envelope I. Then they are to open Envelope II and respond to those instructions. Reinforce that they are not to share with anyone what's written on the colored slips of paper inside Envelope II.

Instruct the observers to silently watch the participants and ask one of them to be timekeeper. Inform the timekeeper that the participants have 5 minutes to respond to the directions in Envelope I and 15 minutes for those in Envelope II. Ask the timekeeper to give the participants a warning when 1 minute is left for each part of the activity. If the group is demonstrating difficulty coming to a decision, you might ask:

With where the group is now, is it possible for you to reach a decision if you are given 2 additional minutes?

If the answer to this question is "yes," allow the team another 2 minutes to discuss a decision before beginning "Talk About It." If the answer is "no," end the activity and begin "Talk About It." A "no" answer indicates the group is at a stalemate, something that can happen in nonscripted consensus decision making, which you can address during discussion.

Whenever the activity ends and before beginning group discussion, have all of the participants read their role slips to the group before you collect the envelopes and instructions. This allows the group to see how the dynamics were set up from the beginning. Teens also enjoy laughing and commenting about how on target everyone's role playing was.

Talk About It

To lead a group discussion about the activity, ask participants and observers the following:

- **When instructed to select a leader, did you want to be chosen or did you want the leader to be someone else? How do you balance pushing for what you want or think should happen in your group, while knowing you may need to compromise to reach agreement with everyone else?**

- **Was the group atmosphere while choosing a leader and acting as yourselves different from when trying to choose a team flag color and role playing? Explain why or why not.**

- If applicable, ask: **In picking a leader, how did the group manage any conflict or if someone refused to compromise or negotiate?**

- **Were the roles played in choosing a team flag color accurate examples of behaviors that can arise when any type of group is attempting to use consensus rule? Why or why not?**

- **In trying to reach consensus, how can a leader manage any conflict or guide someone who refuses to compromise or negotiate?**

- **Why do you think time limits were set? How did everyone respond to these limits?**

- **Is using consensus rule for a group to choose a flag color an effective decision-making approach? Why or why not?**

- **What factors are important to consider when choosing the strategy a group wants to use for making decisions?**

Ask teens to turn to "Consensus Rule: Talking It Through" on pages 101–102 in their books (pages 119–120 in this book). Pass out the "Find Out More About It: Consensus Rule: Thinking It Through" handout. Give them about 5 minutes to read the material. Ask teens if they have any questions and to list other examples of situations in which they believe consensus rule is the most effective decision-making approach.

Wrapping Up

"Think and Write About It" (pages 102–103 in *Everyday Leadership*) presents three different situations that offer teens an opportunity to further apply an understanding of the possibilities and challenges consensus rule presents. Teens must describe what steps they will take to build a group consensus in each situation.

Think and Write About It

Achieving consensus as a group can be challenging. It isn't unusual for groups to give up trying to reach agreement and just take a vote. Success in using consensus as a leader begins with creating an environment where everyone feels comfortable expressing his or her opinions. And when group members who often disagree can discover common interests or common ground, it is more likely everyone will support a decision.

Each of the following scenarios describes a situation in which a group needs to deal with a difficult issue. Imagine you are the group leader or well-respected team member. What steps will you take to help the group build consensus and resolve the problem?

During a youth group meeting, someone expresses that the group never does anything new and every meeting is boring. Others disagree and feel the group is doing fine.

At the neighborhood community center where you lead tutoring activities for younger kids, one of the best-liked kids, who also tends to be a bit lazy, won't participate. Now other kids are losing interest, too.

Do Something About It

To learn more about consensus rule, challenge yourself to take on more decision-making roles. Think about your various circles of influence—with friends, family, a school club or youth group, an athletic team—and the role consensus can play in decision making among these groups as an alternative strategy to voting.

Check the goal(s) you will set to demonstrate your leadership abilities. If you have ideas of your own that you prefer, add them on the lines provided. Then write a date by which you plan to put your goal(s) into action on the "To Do By" lines and the date you completed them on the "Did By" lines. Be sure to fill in "What I Did to Achieve My Goal(s)."

	To Do By	Did By
○ I will plan a teen and adult meeting with others in my community youth program or school group to discuss and agree on activities, policies, or steps to take that support a teen-friendly environment.		

During your team's last game, players were distracted and not playing their best because the captain kept making jokes when the coach gave instructions. The team lost the game and now some are angry with the coach, while others blame the captain.

For future reference, you may want to put a check next to the questions you are assigning.

In "Do Something About It" (pages 103–104 in *Everyday Leadership*), the goals offer teens some group opportunities to practice consensus decision making. Encourage teens to identify ways in which their family and friends regularly make decisions. These situations may provide alternative opportunities to use consensus rule to make a group decision.

104   Everyday Leadership

	To Do By	Did By
○ When my peers complain about something they do not like or know about, I will help them find information about that issue and guide a discussion to agree on what to do.		
○ I will run for a position on a student advisory board or student council, an athletic team, or other school or community club or organization to increase my opportunities to practice my leadership and consensus-building skills.		

Other "Do Something About It" Ideas

○ --

○ --

What I Did to Achieve My Goal(s)

 **TRY THIS**

Labels for Choose a Color

Make a copy of the following labels and directions and cut them out on the dotted lines.

General Instructions

Enclosed you will find two envelopes that contain directions for this activity.
Open Envelope I at once. Follow the time line and open Envelope II as instructed.

Envelope I

Envelope I Directions

Time Allowed: 5 minutes

Task: Choose a group leader using consensus rule. You may not make your decision by taking a vote. Wait to open Envelope II until after you have chosen a group leader. When it's time, your new leader is to open Envelope II and read the instructions on the white paper first. Don't look at the colored slips of paper until instructed to do so.

Envelope II

Envelope II Directions

Time Allowed: 15 minutes

Task: Choose a color for a team flag using consensus rule guided by your new leader. Before making a decision as a group, each member, except your new leader, is to take one of the small colored slips of paper from this envelope and follow the individual instructions. Don't let anyone see your instructions or tell anyone what they say.

TRY THIS

Roles for Choose a Color

Make a copy on colored paper of the following roles. Then cut out the roles needed and insert them into Envelope II.

Throughout this activity, act according to this description:

You believe everyone has an opinion and deserves an opportunity to express it. Make sure everyone gives some input throughout the decision process. You support choosing the color *blue.*

Throughout this activity, act according to this description:

You believe it's important to relieve tension and keep the process moving. When people disagree, suggest a new color option.

Throughout this activity, act according to this description:

You tend to ask a lot of questions during group activities. Sometimes you even bring up unrelated topics to keep things lively. You support choosing the color *red.*

Throughout this activity, act according to this description:

You easily share your opinion with others in an effort to be helpful. You also like asking questions. You are willing to have any color except *red.*

Throughout this activity, act according to this description:

You like to be different and unique, and prefer more creative options. Introduce unusual colors, such as neon green or bright blue. Refuse to accept any traditional colors (red, blue, yellow, etc.), but support *green* if it is suggested.

Throughout this activity, act according to this description:

You are a follower and tend to agree with anyone. You prefer *yellow,* but will support any shade of *green* if it is introduced. You are against *red.*

Throughout this activity, act according to this description:

You continually give your opinion; in fact, you talk all of the time! You are against *blue.*

Throughout this activity, act according to this description:

You are very much a team player and have no preference for a particular color, though *green* is your *least* favorite. When it sounds as if a decision is made, you try to wrap up the conversation.

Throughout this activity, act according to this description:

You have no faith that anything can get done in a group. You prefer doing things yourself or relying on past ways of doing things. Whenever anyone presents new information, you find something wrong with it.

- -

Throughout this activity, act according to this description:

Although the group selected a leader, you are to behave in such a manner that shows you think you would be a better leader. For example, interrupt the leader or point out how your ideas are better.

- -

Throughout this activity, act according to this description:

Although the group selected a leader, you are to behave in such a manner that shows you think you would be a better leader. For example, interrupt the leader or point out how your ideas are better.

- -

Throughout this activity, act according to this description:

You strongly dislike or are extremely uncomfortable with disagreement in a group and tend not to voice your opinion. When people seem to be butting heads, you jump in to prevent it from continuing. The only time you speak up to disagree is if someone suggests your least favorite color, *black.*

- -

Throughout this activity, act according to this description:

You don't like any color in particular, say yes to everyone's ideas, and joke about the group's goal. You kid around so much people don't take you seriously.

- -

Throughout this activity, act according to this description:

You're an observer. You watch what everyone in the group does. Don't speak with the others. If anyone asks for your opinion, avoid giving one.

- -

Throughout this activity, act according to this description:

You're an observer. You watch what everyone in the group does. Don't speak with the others. If anyone asks for your opinion, avoid giving one.

- -

Throughout this activity, act according to this description:

You're an observer. You watch what everyone in the group does. Don't speak with the others. If anyone asks for your opinion, avoid giving one.

FIND OUT MORE ABOUT IT

Consensus Rule: Talking It Through

When it's just you and one or two other people, it's often easy to make a group decision by flipping a coin or cutting a deck of playing cards. But when a larger number of people are concerned, those methods aren't necessarily appealing or satisfying for everybody.

Larger groups often use different approaches to make a decision more effectively, depending on the situation. One approach is *consensus rule.* You can explore another approach to group decision making called *majority rule* in session 15. In that session, you can learn why majority rule is more effective in certain circumstances, as well as some general information about making a group decision.

When to Use Consensus Rule

The following factors in different situations point to whether using consensus rule to make a decision would be most effective or appropriate.

Good Times to Use Consensus Rule

Situation: The leader realizes everyone must agree on the same outcome for the decision to be successful.

Example: Selecting where or how many times your service project team wants to volunteer or fundraise over the next year.

Situation: Group members feel strongly about conflicting issues and believe a vote would minimize the importance of certain issues.

Example: Determining whether your school-funded club should participate in a parade hosted by a local activist group that the City Council doesn't support.

Situation: The time available to make the decision is unlimited, as long as everyone agrees with the final choice.

Example: Helping your city youth commission decide where to build a skate park and drop-in teen technology center.

Situation: Power in the group is unevenly distributed and cliques in the group could easily sway a decision if determined only by having everyone vote.

Example: Deciding whether the only high school in town should change its mascot because certain groups in the community consider it offensive.

Not-So-Good Times to Use Consensus Rule

Just as there are situations where using consensus rule is very effective, there are instances when using it wouldn't be particularly effective. Generally, this is because these situations have one or more of the following factors going on. When these factors exist, using majority rule would be preferable.

* The group has a limited time frame to make a decision.

* The group doesn't have a limited time frame, but the time it would take the group to reach consensus could be more wisely used doing something else.

✻ The group can make a decision easily since there's no controversy.

✻ The group has been informed of the options, which are clear-cut and not likely to be misinterpreted.

✻ The group has discussed an issue at length but can't come to a common agreement and a vote is necessary to move the group forward.

✻ The group is very large and getting everyone's input wouldn't be easy or necessarily change the outcome if a vote were requested.

✻ The group is relatively balanced in terms of power, so the "voice" of any members in the minority won't be excluded.

Guiding Discussion

When you use consensus rule as a leader, having everyone agree on the outcome outweighs any other factor to reach a decision. Even so, aim for guiding discussion for only so long without a decision. By setting a time limit for discussion, you can help avoid members getting fed up or frustrated.

To keep people concentrating on the specific issues at hand, offer realistic scenarios and play out various alternatives. With focused discussion, members also are less likely to complain that they were misled during the decision-making process. Discussion that's well guided also helps decrease the time needed for the team to reach final agreement.

For additional specific tips on how to guide group discussion productively, see the handout "Find Out More About It: Majority Rule: Putting It to a Vote" from session 15. Whether you're using consensus rule or majority rule, following these tips will make a difference in how successfully your group reaches consensus and supports a final decision.

TAKING CHANCES

(PAGES 105–110 IN *EVERYDAY LEADERSHIP*)

GOALS

Participants will:

- pursue a risk-taking challenge as a team

- explore factors leaders need to consider to take appropriate risks

- discuss leaders' responsibilities when taking risks or encouraging others to take risks

MATERIALS NEEDED

- 9' x 12' (unless 6' x 9' is available) plastic painter's tarp (found at painter's supply or hardware store)

- 1"-wide masking tape

- Stopwatch or wristwatch with second hand or timer

- Pen or pencil

- Chair or stool (sturdy to stand on)

- Party horn, noisemaker, or whistle (optional)

- Handout: "Find Out More About It: Risk Taking: I Dare You To!"

GETTING READY

Make enough copies of "Find Out More About It: Risk Taking: I Dare You To!" handout for everyone in the group.

Make a copy of the "Zapping Maze Key" on page 126. The darker boxes and arrows on the key show the correct path to get from the start to the end of the maze.

Make room to create and tape down a tic-tac-toe-like maze for the activity by pushing any tables, desks, or chairs (except one, unless using a stool) to the side. To make the maze, fold the 9' x 12' tarp in half along the 12-foot length and cut along the fold to create two 6' x 9' tarps. Set one aside for another use; take the other and starting on one of the 6-foot edges, measure 1 foot from the edge and lay a piece of tape straight across from one end to the other. Continuing along the 6-foot edge, at 1-foot increments, place four more lines of tape from end to end to create six rows. Repeating the process along the 9-foot edges, lay eight pieces of tape to create nine rows and 54 boxes covering the tarp. Orient the maze on the floor such that one of the 6-foot edges is the starting edge. Tape the corners of the maze to the floor so the tarp doesn't slip. Place a chair (or a stool) at the other 6-foot edge, which will be the end of the maze where everyone steps off. Make sure there's enough space around the maze for teens to step on and off and to gather as a group.

6 feet

finish

9 feet

start

Getting Started

Risk taking and leadership go hand in hand. Teen leaders face risks daily—deciding how to present new ideas to their team, deciding whether to participate in a certain club or group activity, or even choosing who to sit next to during lunch. Teen leaders also face risks when trying to guide their group to put on an event that has never been done before or taking on positions that put them in the spotlight. In this session, teens explore what risks are appropriate to take on behalf of a group, as well as how and when to inspire others to take risks. Even though teens relate easily to the topic of taking risks in their everyday life, making the connection between risk taking and leadership may be a new concept.

Rather than begin the session by introducing the topic of risk taking, start with the activity. Telling teens they will be experimenting with taking risks may give away much of what comes naturally from participating in the activity. As soon as teens arrive, ask them to gather at the starting edge of the maze.

TEACH THIS

Zapping Maze

In this timed activity, teens attempt to solve a group task that can't be done unless people take risks. The risk involves figuring out which squares everyone needs to step on to get from one side of the maze to the other without getting "electrified" or "zapped" and losing time.

With a pen or pencil and a copy of the "Zapping Maze Key" in hand, begin the activity. Ask teens to gather around the starting side of the maze. To explain what everyone is to do, say:

Pretend the maze in front of you is "electrified" or "zapped" and from where you're standing to the other side there is only one correct path. Your goal is to figure out as a team what that path is without getting "zapped." To do this, you will follow some specific rules. Before anyone moves or says anything, though, listen to the rules.

You have 25 minutes for everyone to get through the maze, one at a time, following the same path. Use as much time as you want to strategize, but once the first person steps on the maze, whether purposely or accidentally, you can no longer verbally communicate with one another. If anyone speaks after the first person has stepped on the maze, you will lose a minute.

You also will lose a minute if someone gets "zapped," which can occur in several ways. If you touch the tape marking the squares on the maze or take a wrong step, you will be "zapped." You must

keep your feet inside the squares. If you take a wrong step, you must also retrace your path back off the maze. If you make a mistake retracing your steps, you'll get "zapped" again and lose another minute. I'll make this noise (beep horn, blow whistle, or say "beep") whenever someone gets "zapped."

Only one person can be on the maze at a time. You can move in any direction, sideways, forward, backward, or diagonally, although each step of the path is connected to the next. You may not leave any clues to your path on the maze or write them down. To guide whoever's on the maze, you may point to particular squares, but you may not touch the maze or say anything. If you do, you'll also get "zapped" and the group will lose another minute. Everyone must try to go through the maze once before trying again. Keep the same order the second go-through.

You may ask questions now, but if any of you begin strategizing when others are asking me questions, your 25 minutes will begin.

Allow time for questions, paying attention to side conversations and people possibly touching the maze. Once teens begin strategizing or have no more questions, start tracking the time. Stand on the chair or stool, if you prefer, so you can clearly see participants' steps on the maze. Also pay attention to what others around the maze are doing. Initially, teens will stay at the starting end to watch whoever is on the maze, but as they get further through the maze, they will move around the edges and to the other end as they guide each other.

Each time someone breaks a rule or takes a wrong step, use your voice or whatever noisemaker you chose to make a loud "beep" signifying getting "zapped." Be sure to subtract a minute each time. Just as you beep, some participants may insist they were just "testing" a box (it wasn't a full step) or look at you but say nothing. Make eye contact with the person and say, "We'll talk about that later." Address during group discussion the importance of maintaining integrity when taking risks, whether in everyday situations or leadership roles.

It may be helpful to record on the key to the maze a hatch mark for every minute lost, as well as the wrong squares the group repeatedly steps on the most. During group discussion, you may want to show teens how often they took the same path, even though it was wrong. Reiterate to teens that risk taking is about trying new paths, instead of doing the same thing with unsuccessful results.

If time is running out, and it's possible, allow the group to negotiate for more time, ideally in increments of 2 to 3 minutes. Keeping additional minutes to a minimum, especially if the group is close to solving the path, helps the group stay focused.

Being timed reinforces a common issue involved in taking risks—that time is of the essence—and by stalling or using too much time to plan, some opportunities may slip away. Losing a minute whenever participants make a mistake relates to the consequences that can arise when trying new paths or even when someone really knows better (for example, if participants misstep when having to retrace their paths, they also lose a minute). Participants often lose the most time retracing their steps off the maze.

At the same time, if your group is one that might benefit from not being timed, eliminate this aspect of the activity. The experience of working together through this challenging process remains equally meaningful. If you choose not to time, simply exclude debriefing questions related to the topic.

To successfully complete this activity, teens have to quickly learn how to rely on one another without speaking. This requirement relates to how people don't always know how others' actions may impact the outcome of a risk. For example, the person on the maze may not pay attention to what those standing around the maze silently recommend. Since the person isn't paying attention, they don't know what step he'll take and whether it'll be correct.

Teens also learn about what they can or can't control when taking risks. The five different ways they can be "zapped" and lose time are all things they can control as individuals and as a group (to speak, misstep forward, step on the tape, misstep backward, or touch the maze when it's not your turn). To succeed requires focusing on what they can control (careful planning, paying attention, and making the most of mistakes along the way).

If everyone makes it through the maze, congratulate the group. If some participants don't figure out the correct path in the time available, acknowledge their positive efforts and willingness to take a risk and try, and show them the answer. You can ask why the group wasn't successful during group discussion, encouraging them to figure out what, if anything, they could have done differently. Sit in a circle to discuss the activity.

Talk About It

Before asking the following questions, present your observations about how much time was lost and the most common ways the team lost time. Point out the squares they incorrectly stepped on repeatedly and ask them why they think they did. Then ask:

- **Do you think you took too much or not enough time to strategize before someone started stepping on the maze? What does this tell you about taking risks as leaders?**

- **In what ways do you think you could have used your time more effectively?**

- **How different did the maze look when you stood in the middle of it compared to when you stood outside of it? Relate this to a leader *thinking* about taking a risk versus *taking* the risk.**

- **How do you think the group worked together? Where and how did you get stuck?**

- **How did people take on leadership roles? How did this help the team?**

- **Why do you think it is so difficult to take risks as a leader?**

- **As the leader of a team, how do you communicate to everyone that you want to take a risk on their behalf? How do you communicate that you want them to take a risk?**

- **What did this activity and our discussion teach you about ways leaders can use a team's failures and successes to take on new risks?**

- **When you are presented with a risk to take and know others are watching, are you more or less motivated to take it? Explain.**

- **Why do you think it's important to maintain integrity (being honest, supporting high standards) when taking risks?**

- **How do you think this activity will affect your willingness to take risks in the future as a leader?**

After discussion, ask the group to turn to "Risk Taking: I Dare You To!" on pages 106–107 in the teens' books. Pass out the "Find Out More About It: Risk Taking: I Dare You To!" handout. Give the group a few minutes to read the information. Ask teens if they have any questions or risk-taking leadership experiences to share.

Wrapping Up

By imaging themselves in different leadership roles and situations, teens have a chance to further evaluate their attitude toward risks in "Think and Write About It" (pages 107–108 in *Everyday Leadership*).

Think and Write About It

Read the following scenarios. Imagine first that you are *ready* to take the risk described. Then imagine that you will *take* the risk described. Write your answers to the following questions on the lines provided after each scenario:

- How do you know you are ready to take this risk?
- What emotions are you feeling inside? Fear, excitement, curiosity, hope, or something else?
- What are you thinking when taking the first steps?
- When you are done, how do you feel about having taken this risk?

You have never run for a leadership position but believe you're ready to try. You want to take the steps to become a candidate at school (or youth community program or advisory board, or other group) and go through the election.

A close friend has been using drugs and drinking. You're worried because he or she has admitted to going to school and other activities under the influence. You want to confront him or her and let an adult you trust know what is going on.

Last year, a significant number of immigrant families settled in the community. A lot of long-time residents treat them disrespectfully. Teens have even started fights with new kids at the rec center because they are different. You want to attend the next city council meeting to ask that something be done to change the situation.

You've been accepted to your first choice college, which is in another state. You'll be the first one in the family, including close relatives, to attend college. Your parents want you to be closer to home. With a scholarship and a part-time job already lined up so your parents won't have to pay, you believe the decision is yours. You're going to tell them you still plan to attend your first choice.

For future reference, you may want to put a check next to the questions you are assigning.

Teens are given choices in "Do Something About It" (pages 109–110 in *Everyday Leadership*) that allow them to test their tolerance for risk taking in a group setting, or by themselves. If some participants tend to take risks without considering the consequences, encourage them to identify specific goals of their own that require them to stop, think, and then act, instead of the other way around.

Do Something About It

Your comfort in taking risks may be very different in a group setting than by yourself. Perhaps it's easier to try new paths when you have group members' support. Or maybe it's easier to take risks when you're the only one involved. Either way, willingness to take appropriate risks can increase your confidence and enable you to make the most of new leadership experiences.

Check the goal(s) you will set to demonstrate your leadership abilities. If you prefer your own ideas, add them on the lines provided. Then write a date by which you plan to put your goal(s) into action on the "To Do By" lines and the date you completed them on the "Did By" lines. Be sure to fill in "What I Did to Achieve My Goal(s)."

	To Do By	Did By
○ I will sit with a new group at my community youth program or eat lunch at school with people I normally don't.		
○ I will speak up in class or at a group meeting where I usually don't or I will try a new activity I've been curious to learn.		
○ I will inspire my team to try something we've never done before, such as trying out for a competition or getting a new policy passed.		
○ I will lead my team to do a project or put on an event that is completely different from anything we've done before.		

Other "Do Something About It" Ideas	To Do By	Did By
○		
○		

What I Did to Achieve My Goal(s)

Zapping Maze Key

The blackened boxes and arrows show the correct path from the start to the end of the maze.

Finish

Start

Risk Taking: I Dare You To!

"I dare you to!" Ever since you were little, you've probably heard these words from friends or other kids. Maybe some grown-ups told you to ignore such challenges. In many cases, this is good advice. When you're a leader, though, taking risks may be necessary.

Taking risks means being open to the unknown—positive or negative. Speaking in front of a group or sharing a new idea with a group is a risk. These risks aren't physically dangerous, but if your speech doesn't go well, you may feel as if you're a failure; if people don't like your idea, you may lose confidence in yourself. A risk is *positive* if the outcome is likely to be successful, and *negative* if it's more likely to prevent success.

When you take positive risks, you show others your leadership attitude, as well as what you care about and your willingness to try new things. You also learn to set goals and face challenges. In the process, you'll learn more about yourself and others on your team.

For some people, trying something without knowing for certain the outcome is very unsettling. For others, the excitement of doing something new or different outweighs everything else, even if you feel like a bundle of nerves. If you're not comfortable taking risks, sticking with things as they are may be better. Yet, sometimes not taking a risk is the greater risk because you won't ever know what could have been possible.

Is the Risk Worth Taking?

As a leader, figuring out when to take a risk can be confusing. If you're not sure, it helps to first ask yourself why taking the risk is important and to realistically think about what the most likely outcome will be.

For example, you want to put a group member in charge of an important project. Your two best candidates both present some risks: a well-respected but disorganized group member or a less popular but organized and reliable group member. Who to pick is likely a struggle, but when you weigh possible outcomes, your choice becomes clearer. With the irresponsible member in charge, things might not get done as well as you'd like or on time, even though everyone likes him or her. With the responsible member in charge, things are more likely to

happen the way they need to, even if the person isn't everyone's favorite. Because the project is important, choosing the less popular but reliable member is a better risk to take.

To help decide if a risk is right for you or your team, here are some general questions to think about and a few specific examples.

■ Would trying something new help solve a problem or is it just something that might be fun to try?

Example:

Risk: Deciding to let someone new head up a busy team.

Why It's Risky: A new team leader might not do a good job. It's also possible that the current team leader won't want to give up the position.

Is It Right for You? Probably, although if there's no real need to switch, you'll want to talk with the current leader to provide a helpful explanation. One reason might be that changing leaders gives another person a chance to practice and learn new skills. You'll also need to be clear about your expectations with the new leader.

■ **Will taking this risk help or hurt anyone or anything?**

Example:
Risk: Getting rival cliques together to talk about increasing disrespectful behavior.

Why It's Risky: Without an organized plan and clear rules, the meeting could make things worse.

Is It Right for You? Possibly, depending on where and how the meeting is run. Gathering in a neutral location can reduce the risk involved. So, too, can having trained adults present to manage the situation, and clear rules to guide discussion.

■ **Will taking this risk support or break any laws or program or school policies?**

Example:
Risk: Organizing an end-of-year activity to honor the graduating class that people will attend during school hours.

Why It's Risky: Teachers may not support what students really want to do. And if the activity isn't cool enough, some kids may get bored and leave.

Is It Right for You? Probably, if class members provide a lot of input. The planning team can have students fill out a survey to collect ideas. Involving as many kids as possible in planning may also help increase interest and enthusiasm.

■ **Are there small steps you can take to try out the new idea before risking too much?**

Example:
Risk: Installing new fresh-food vending machines at school or the rec center.

Why It's Risky: It could cost the student council or youth group a lot of money to sign a vending contract before knowing if people will want or buy the new items.

Is It Right for You? Yes, if the vending service agrees to put some of the non-junk food items in the existing vending machines for a month before signing a contract.

■ **Are you willing not to take the risk if others prove or convince you that it isn't worth taking?**

Example:
Risk: Telling a good friend not to speak disrespectfully to her parents the next time it happens.

Why It's Risky: Telling her the moment she does it may embarrass her, and she may not want to be friends any more.

Is It Right for You? Yes, at the right time. Other friends, who respect your wanting to say something, suggest you speak to her privately after the next time it happens.

Be specific with yourself and your team when thinking about taking a risk. In taking a risk, you'll also want to consider a few final things, including:

✱ Can you identify steps to make it positive?

✱ Is it worth taking only at certain times or in particular situations?

✱ Will you uphold personal and group values without compromising ethics?

* Can you inspire the group to work together, through the ups and downs, even though you're not sure of the outcome?

* Could you fix or learn from any mistakes to become an even stronger leader?

Adventuring into the Unknown

Obviously, there may be times when you have to make quick decisions, both in everyday circumstances and in more formal leadership roles. In these situations, you'll have to rely on your instincts or gut reaction. But if you have time to weigh the pros and cons and still aren't sure what to do, talk to others about your thoughts and feelings. Speak with respected friends and trusted adults, such as a parent, teacher, school counselor, coach, or community program or congregational leader.

Being comfortable with taking risks, as an individual and as part of a group, develops over time with practice. While you hope for a great outcome, there's a chance that things won't turn out well. In spite of any setbacks, team members depend on you as a leader to make the best of a situation and to inspire and motivate them. If you do fail, the risk may have been worth it if you learned from the experience.

As a leader, taking a risk shows your commitment to think things through. It proves your ability to make decisions with your group's best interests in mind.

THINKING CREATIVELY

(PAGES 111–116 IN *EVERYDAY LEADERSHIP*)

GOALS

Participants will:

- think creatively to accomplish a group task
- discuss the value of creative thinking to solve problems
- investigate the necessity for creative thinking in leadership roles

MATERIALS NEEDED

- Raw eggs in the shell, 2 to 3 for each group of three
- Plastic straws (with or without paper wrapping), 20 for each group of three
- Masking tape, including one 30-inch piece for each group of three
- 2 to 4 large plastic garbage bags (or the unused half of the plastic painter's tarp from session 17)
- Chair or stepping stool
- Handout: "Find Out More About It: Be a Creative Thinker"

GETTING READY

Cut the seams of a couple garbage bags and lay them or the plastic tarp out on the floor underneath and around a chair or stepping stool. Tape the edges of the bags or the plastic tarp to the floor so they don't slip when someone steps on them. Place the chair or stool on top and in the middle of the bags or tarp.

Make enough copies of the "Find Out More About It: Be a Creative Thinker" handout on pages 135–137 for each group member.

Getting Started

Being creative and inspiring others to be creative is important for any leader. Creativity enables leaders and groups to cope with unusual tasks and situations as well as to find new solutions to old problems. In this session, teens explore the value of creative problem solving.

To introduce the topic to teens, you might ask:

What does it mean to think creatively? How many of you think you solve problems creatively? How many of you believe you don't really think creatively? Why or why not? What sorts of things help or keep you from thinking creatively?

Allow a few minutes for answers. Then explain:

Thinking creatively is being able to come up with new ideas or deal with problems in fresh ways. Although creative thinking doesn't always come naturally, it is a skill you can develop with practice. You can even make creative thinking a positive habit. People sometimes believe they aren't creative thinkers because they get stuck on the words creative or creativity. They think creativity means art, music, writing, and other particular talents. Creativity also is a talent leaders use to find unique ways to solve problems instead of doing things the same old way. Similar to taking risks, thinking creatively means a leader looks for other paths to achieve group success. Today, you'll explore how thinking creatively can help in leadership roles and when working as a team.

Pass out the "Find Out More About It: Be a Creative Thinker" handout. Read through the ways to overcome the ten "locks" that prevent creative thinking. Ask teens to share examples from their personal experiences.

TEACH THIS

Mission Impossible

Everyday situations provide chances to think creatively, yet people still tend to think uncreatively. During elementary and early middle school years, teachers and other adults stress creative thinking through classroom projects, puzzles, and games, as well as at summer camps and other activities outside of school. As children get older, adults often promote logic and reliability, sending creativity by the wayside.

Logic and reliability are essential leadership qualities, but so is thinking creatively. In this session, teens build an unusual contraption. This activity reinforces that serious things can be discovered in fun ways. In addition, the activity demonstrates that creative thinking can be successful despite restricted time and resources. Relating the activity to personal situations, teens also can see how using imagination can drive solutions to problems, even when they have to interact with others who aren't making progress.

Divide participants into teams of three, grouping teens who haven't previously worked together. Have each team find an area in the room to work undisrupted and uninfluenced by the other teams' ideas. Say:

A research company for space exploration is looking to hire a talented group to create a special contraption. This contraption is to enable an egg to reenter the atmosphere and land on earth without breaking. The contraption must be created around the egg, not as a target for the egg to land on. Each team will get a limited number of resources to create your contraption. You may not use any other materials or tools such as scissors, clippers, pens, pencils, hair bands, or keys.

In addition to creating your contraption, pick a team name and choose a spokesperson to promote your contraption to the research company. Then, to prove your contraption works, one representative from each team will drop it from about 6 feet off the ground (stand on the chair to illustrate), **where it must land without the egg breaking. If more than one contraption works, the respective teams will re-drop the contraptions from higher heights to determine which is most successful. You have 25 minutes to create your contraption. Be very careful because your resources are limited. Questions?**

Answer any questions, but avoid giving hints about ways to create a contraption. If teens ask if they can use their body in any way (for example, their teeth), simply restate the items they *can't* use and refrain from answering more specifically so as not to influence them in anyway. This allows them freedom to use their imagination and on-hand resources, which of course includes their body. Avoid implying or suggesting that there is one right method or design—there isn't. As long as teens follow the rules and the contraption works, whatever they come up with, is up to them. Some of the most peculiar contraptions are equally successful or unsuccessful. For one creative solution idea, see page 138.

Ask teens to tell you their understanding of brainstorming. If necessary, remind them that brainstorming means all ideas are considered.

Make sure the teams wait to begin until everyone has the materials and you begin timing. Pass out 1 egg (initially), 20 straws, and the 30-inch piece of masking tape to each team.

As you track the time, check in with each team and offer encouragement. If some groups get stuck, suggest one of the members read out loud the tips for unlocking thinking in the "Be a Creative Thinker" handout. Some teens may be tempted to spy on or copy what other teams are doing. If this is the case, remind teens that the goal of the activity is to think creatively. You might add:

Remember, the research company isn't looking for deliberate imitations or ideas "borrowed" from somewhere else. It wants to hire a team that can solve problems in ways that haven't been thought of before.

If any eggs break, allow each team at least one replacement. Emphasize that resources are limited and encourage participants to focus on keeping the egg from breaking.

After 25 minutes, give each group spokesperson 1 to 2 minutes to share the team name, promote the contraption, and stand on the chair or stepping stool to drop it. If the egg remains unbroken, have the group hold onto it until the others take their turns. If no other eggs make it without breaking, congratulate the winning team. If other eggs also make it in one piece, have the successful teams take additional turns dropping the contraptions from greater heights until only one remains. Congratulate the winning team before moving onto discussion. Use the extra plastic bags to discard the broken eggs and bags taped to the floor.

If none of the contraptions is successful, take 2 to 3 minutes to have the group brainstorm which features of each contraption could be combined to possibly create a successful contraption. You might say:

Creative thinking allowed you to approach this task in new ways, even though the contraptions weren't successful. Sometimes, you can reach your desired goal by putting your ideas together with other people's ideas. Even when creative thinking fails the first time, you aren't necessarily making a mistake. Your ideas may spark future, unexpected results.

If you've conducted session 17, connect the unsuccessful egg contraptions with how leaders deal with taking risks and having things go other than expected or hoped for.

Talk About It

To help relate the activity to teens' roles as leaders, ask:

- **Describe the steps your team took to create your contraption. What roles did people take on?**

- **Was the lack of specific directions and the expectation to use your imagination uncomfortable for you? Why or why not?**

- **Was it hard to get others to think creatively? Why or why not?**

- **How can you help a group see that problem solving can be fun and effective? Do limited resources or restrictive rules make a difference? Why or why not?**

- **How is it possible for two different groups to come up with the same new idea? How can a leader or group members encourage creative thinking?**

- If applicable: **A couple teams created different successful contraptions. In what ways does this influence your attitude about problem solving and thinking creatively in future situations?**

- **In what ways is creative thinking important to being an effective leader?**

Wrapping Up

"Think and Write About It" (pages 112–114 in *Everyday Leadership*) this session prompts teens to think further about what creativity means to them and the impact creative—and fun—thinking can have in problem solving.

Think and Write About It

To become personally comfortable thinking creatively, it's important to fine-tune your creative thinking attitude. Read the following situations and write your ideas for how you would think creatively. Use the example to jumpstart your thinking.

EXAMPLE

The Situation
The boys' lacrosse team needs new jerseys but didn't get money this year from the youth activity fund.

Thinking Creatively About It
One of the players suggests holding a car wash or bake sale to raise the money. Another player mentions how the nursing home near his neighborhood also needs to raise some money to get a new piano. The team decides to do a fun run and use some of the money raised for the uniforms and donate the rest to the nursing home. Doing a fundraiser with a nursing home gets

---

the team away from the standard car washes and bake sales, involves an intergenerational activity that doesn't take the players away from practice time, and also may attract a few more new fans from the nursing home.

The Situation
The first Saturday of every November, the middle school students hold Shelter Sleep Out, sleeping in the schoolyard in cardboard boxes, to raise money for a local homeless shelter. This year the weather is supposed to be bitterly cold, and you are finding it hard to motivate people to participate because of the expected weather. The shelter relies on this event to raise money for services they provide through the winter. As one of the co-leaders, what can you do to attract more participants?

Thinking Creatively About It

_____

_____

_____

The Situation
A group of regulars at the skate park, including you, want to hold an exhibition event. Getting permission requires a stamp of approval from the city council, which could take a long time. It's even possible they won't give their approval because some council members have made stereotyped comments about skateboarding teens. What ideas do you have for getting the event to take place soon and hopefully annually for the future?

Thinking Creatively About It

_____

_____

_____

The Situation
The after-school program has decided the entire inside of the building needs painting. As one of several graffiti artists who happen to participate in the program, you want to suggest that the teens in the program do the painting. How do you get the staff to agree to let you get the paint (more than just beige!) and have a go at the walls?

Thinking Creatively About It

_____

_____

_____

The Situation
Everyone says you can't be an effective leader because you messed up in middle school. But the younger kids at the rec center really look up to you, and your mentor has nominated you to be a youth coach at the center. The rec center director is hesitant, so what can you do to convince the director to pick you?

Thinking Creatively About It

_____

_____

_____

For future reference, you may want to put a check next to the questions you are assigning.

Encourage teens to find creative opportunities in daily activities in addition to choosing from the goals in "Do Something About It" (pages 114–116 in *Everyday Leadership*). Emphasize using their imagination and thinking creatively.

Do Something About It

Thinking creatively allows you and groups you lead to achieve more success. Strive to free up your thinking and be open to all kinds of possibilities.

Check the goal(s) you will set to demonstrate your leadership abilities. If you have ideas you prefer, add them on the lines provided. Then write a date by which you plan to put your goal(s) into action on the "To Do By" lines and the date you completed them on the "Did By" lines. Be sure to fill in "What I Did to Achieve My Goal(s)."

	To Do By	Did By
○ I will plan a fun and creative surprise activity for my group to blow off steam when working on a project or specific team goal.	....	....
○ I will let group members try to solve a problem using a brainstorming approach we have never tried before.	....	....
○ I will encourage friends, family, or people on my team who continually come up with excuses about why something won't work to instead be open to trying a new approach or idea.	....	....
○ I will participate in an activity I consider creative and normally wouldn't imagine myself doing.	....	....

Other "Do Something About It" Ideas

○ ....
....
....

○ ....
....
....

What I Did to Achieve My Goal(s)

....
....
....
....
....
....
....

FIND OUT MORE ABOUT IT

Be a Creative Thinker

Anyone can be a creative thinker. You don't need to be an artist or a musician. Thinking creatively means letting your mind wander to think about anything and everything. In fact, leaders who succeed over time use their imaginations in everyday circumstances, coming up with fresh ideas and encouraging others to do the same.

Lots of people depend on logic to solve problems. But being open-minded lets leaders—or anyone—discover amazing ideas that wouldn't have been tried had they stuck with tried-and-true ways.

Unlock Your Thinking

What can you do to boost your creative thinking? To start, put aside any attitudes and actions that could get in the way of using your imagination.

Roger von Oech, a well-known expert on creative thinking, identified 10 "locks"—or attitudes—that keep individuals and groups stuck and unable to think creatively. Here are von Oech's 10 locks to creativity,* followed by tips you can use to inspire creative thinking.

🔒 *The Lock:* Looking for the Right Answer

Trying to find the one *right* answer can keep you from looking beyond the obvious to explore other possibilities. To unlock your thinking:

* Look for the second and third "right" answers.

* Brainstorm to generate ideas at the beginning of a project. Once you've come up with one idea, keep going! Use your first idea as a springboard for other possibilities or solutions.

🔒 *The Lock:* Thinking Something Isn't Logical

Sometimes being logical is the way to go. But often, thinking illogically (not so straightforwardly)

allows you to put together two seemingly unconnected things for a great solution. To unlock your thinking:

* Create your own word games. Replace key words in statements or short stories with blanks. Have everyone fill in the blanks together with words that relate to the group task. The completed funny sentences can jumpstart your team's thinking.

* In your free time, play word games, brainteasers, and puzzles to stimulate your mind to look at things from different angles.

🔒 *The Lock:* Following the Rules

Sometimes rules can keep people from seeing possibilities outside of what they can't do. But you don't literally have to break the rules to be creative. To unlock your thinking:

* Think of things as they may be, not only of things as they are.

* Identify any rules or policies that are non-negotiable, such as there's only so much money available to spend on decorations for an event. Then highlight that everything else is up for consideration. If still stuck, imagine there aren't any rules. The new ideas that pop up, even if they're not completely realistic, may lead you in a new direction or toward a fresh mindset.

*Adapted from *A Whack on the Side of the Head: How You Can Be More Creative* by Roger von Oech (New York: Warner Business Books, 1998). Used with permission. For more information, visit www.creativethink.com.

🔒 *The Lock:* **Being Practical**

People often get caught up in doing only what they know will work. But just because something is impractical or not easily doable doesn't mean it can't be done. To unlock your thinking:

❋ Plan an "opposite" or "backward" meeting—ask team members to do everything opposite or in reverse of how they usually would. For example, say "yes" instead of "no." Toward the end of the meeting, reintroduce the issue your group was stuck on and see what new ideas come up.

❋ Look at alternative ideas that may not seem sensible at first, but are useful stepping-stones to possible solutions.

🔒 *The Lock:* **Avoiding Uncertainty**

Giving your team specific instructions and only one way to do things doesn't allow room for imagination. Accepting uncertainty and the unknown lets your group search for new ideas or solutions. To unlock your thinking:

❋ If possible, at the beginning of a project, present your team with no other guidance than what the end goal is. Explain the end goal as broadly as you can—for example, creating a new team logo—to free up the group and let them go from there.

❋ Try something new *without* the help of someone who has done it before and could influence you in a particular way.

🔒 *The Lock:* **Believing There's No Place for Mistakes**

Leaders who treat mistakes as if they are reasons for punishment can keep team members from taking worthy risks and trying new things. To unlock your thinking:

❋ Instead of hiding mistakes, be respectful and open about what's happened. A leader who accepts mistakes as learning opportunities shows that he or she is comfortable taking a path less traveled.

❋ Even if a mistake happens because of one person, avoid holding it against any one. Instead, bring your group together to talk about any new ideas that come about due to the mistake.

🔒 *The Lock:* **Thinking Playing Around Isn't Important**

People sometimes think that unless you're acting seriously, you're not taking the situation seriously. But some of the best ideas often come when people are having fun. To unlock your thinking:

❋ Create a relaxed, unstructured environment for your group where everyone is having a good time. For many, thinking creatively happens most easily when things are more easygoing.

❋ Introduce a fun activity at each regular meeting to stir things up. For example, ask members to share a favorite line from a movie they've recently seen.

🔒 *The Lock:* **Doing the Bare Minimum**

Refusing to go above and beyond what's normally expected or what you're supposed to do drains everyone's enthusiasm to think in new ways. Thinking creatively often comes when you're on the lookout for possibilities outside of your own responsibilities. To unlock your thinking:

❋ Create an "Above and Beyond" award to regularly recognize when people come up with ideas beyond the ordinary.

❋ Look for ways to lend a hand to others on the team. Or ask them if they could use some help.

🔒 *The Lock:* **Avoiding Foolishness**

Being sensible may seem like the only way to think, but outrageous ideas can spark creative thinking. One crazy notion may inspire another person to come up with a great idea that is realistic. To unlock your thinking:

✱ Suggest the silliest ideas you can think of, even if they are foolish.

✱ Remember the things you wouldn't have learned if you hadn't risked feeling awkward or ridiculous at first, such as learning to ride a bike or speak another language.

🔒 *The Lock:* **Thinking "I'm Not Creative"**

Believing you're not creative has a way of becoming true. But by believing in yourself and your creative potential, you can take risks, discover new ways of thinking, and develop original ideas. Along the way, you'll inspire others to think creatively, too. To unlock your thinking:

✱ Open a team meeting or brainstorming session by having everyone say, "I'm creative and together we're going to think creatively!" Sounds goofy, but when people say things out loud, they're more likely to believe what is said.

✱ Sign up for a class or an activity that requires you to be creative or use creative thinking to succeed. Ropes courses, which include real and imaginary obstacles to climb or move around, are a great stimulation for creative group thinking. They're designed to help you become less self-conscious. Everyone shares ideas about how to get through the course together.

Sample Solution to Mission Impossible

Here's a description and drawing of one possible design for "Mission Impossible" on pages 131–132. There is more than one solution to the activity.

Line up most of the straws like logs in a row. Tape at least one side of the straws to align and hold them together. Place the egg on top of the straws, and then roll the "straw mat" around the egg to form a cylindrical tube. Flatten the ends of the tube and fold over, using additional tape to secure or close the openings at either end of the tube. Tape three or four remaining straws around the width of the sealed tube, a quarter- to half-inch apart, to form a buffer for the contraption when it hits the floor.

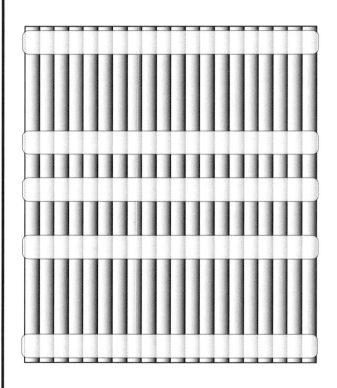

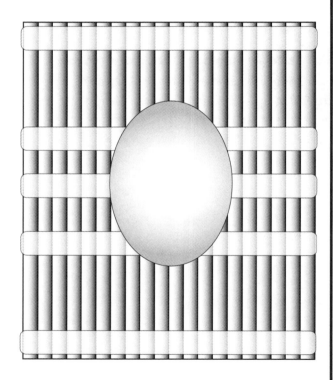

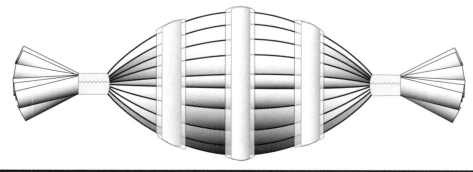

HAVING MY VOICE HEARD

(PAGES 117–122 IN *EVERYDAY LEADERSHIP*)

GOALS

Participants will:

- practice speaking in front of a small group
- receive feedback from peers to improve public speaking skills
- identify tips for organizing, preparing, and presenting information to an audience

MATERIALS NEEDED

- 5 paper lunch bags (or as many as needed, 1 for each group of 4 to 5 people)

- 50 small everyday items, such as tape, stickers, candy mints (in the boxes), paper clips, gum, erasers (10 items for each lunch bag); the more unique or funny, the better
- 5 small stacks of scrap paper
- 5 pencils

GETTING READY

Fill each of the lunch bags with 10 different items and roll over the tops so the items aren't visible. You may want to make enough copies of the "Find Out More About It: Getting the Point Across" handout on pages 143–144 for everyone in the group.

Getting Started

Teen leaders often are asked to make presentations to groups, and adult advisors or mentors spend a lot of time helping them get ready. Likewise, many informal situations arise where teens want to have their voices heard. Many times, though, teens aren't prepared to reply to on-the-spot questions when participating at meetings, especially when adults also are present. In this session, teens have a light-hearted opportunity to practice speaking skills and responding to unexpected questions in front of others.

Begin the session by taking 5 minutes to introduce the topic of public speaking. You might say:

Speaking comfortably with or in front of a group of people is a necessary skill for leaders. It's human nature to judge a speaker by how clearly and confidently the person speaks. If you want your voice to be heard, it's important to think about how you come across to your audience. When a leader uses poor language or is disorganized or overly nervous, people tend to notice the mistakes more than what the leader is trying to say. Or, if a speaker lacks energy and excitement about the topic, the audience can quickly become bored.

Think about what makes you listen when someone is speaking. What does the speaker do to keep your attention and get a message across. Consider using similar strategies for yourself. Even if you're shy, you learn how to express what you have to say so others hear it. Whether you're speaking to a small group of people you know or to a larger audience of strangers, first impressions can make a difference. Today, you get a chance to practice your speaking skills and get feedback from people you know.

TEACH THIS

Lunch Bag Speeches

While seemingly silly, this activity is one method for getting teens to practice on-the-spot speaking. Teens are to pick one of the items from the bags you prepared, and without showing the item to anyone, take 30 seconds to prepare and then deliver a 1½-minute speech to their small group. The others in the group are to listen quietly and then take a few minutes to give helpful feedback.

Using fun, everyday items in the bags increases teens' awareness of how often they are asked to speak to others, and how comfortable they are in doing so. Even though teens get very little time to prepare their speeches, the items to choose from in the bags are all familiar. Constructive feedback from peers helps teens improve their speaking skills. Even with the levity, it's important to help teens realize that organizing and clearly expressing their thoughts is a significant factor in having people actively listen to them.

Prior to the speeches, you may want to refer teens to the "How You Say It" handout from session 7 on pages 50–51 for tips on feedback. Ask teens if they have any questions about this information before beginning the activity.

To begin the activity, separate participants into groups of 4 to 5. Instruct each group to find an area of the room to work without being disrupted by the other groups. To explain the activity, say:

Each lunch bag is filled with a collection of random items. Each person is to pick an item from the bag and give a speech about it to your group. You will not pick an item until it's your turn to speak. So others in your group can't see your item, turn your back to them as you plan your speech. You get 30 seconds to prepare a 1½-minute speech. You can use this scrap paper to jot down your thoughts (distribute scrap paper and pencils). Take a few minutes to determine in what order group members will go.

Allow 1 to 2 minutes for the groups to decide and then continue with the directions:

When your 30 seconds of prep time are up, begin your speech. The rest of the group is to listen quietly. When the speaker is finished, take 3 to 5 minutes to give helpful feedback on the strengths of the presentation and areas to improve. Focus on the speaker's ability to organize her or his thoughts, not necessarily on what the person said. Also comment about style, nonverbal communication (such as posture, facial expression, eye contact, gestures), and delivery. Trade off who in your group is timing the speeches.

As you pass out the bags, discourage participants from showing the item they pick to others in their small group. This increases the spontaneity of each person's presentations, instead of having anyone suggest what to talk about. Once you've distributed all the bags, tell the groups to begin. Walk around the room, checking in with each group and offering assistance to any teens struggling. Depending upon the number of teens in each of the groups, and as long as everyone stays on task, the activity will take 30 to 35 minutes.

Talk About It

After everyone has given their speeches, bring all together to talk about their experiences. Ask:

- What strengths did you each observe in your smaller groups? In what ways did people struggle when giving their speeches?

- Who seemed most comfortable presenting in your group? What were each of you thinking about or focusing on while presenting?

- How did you use the 30 seconds of preparation time? Was this effective? Why or why not? In what ways could you have been more effective with this time?

- Had this been a real situation in which you were a leader delivering a message to a group, how effectively did you get your points across?

- In what ways was the feedback you received useful? If it wasn't, what would have been more helpful?

- In what ways will you use this experience for other on-the-spot situations where you want your voice to be heard?

Time allowing, have teens turn to "Getting the Point Across" on page 118 in their book (pages 143–144 in this book). You may also want to pass out the "Find Out More About It: Getting the Point Across" handout to provide more detailed information. Read together and clarify any of the tips before having teens complete "Think and Write About It." These tips are straightforward and helpful for when teens reflect on the situations in "Think and Write About It." If you run out of time, ask teens to read these pages on their own, and if needed, based on the ability of your group, allow time to discuss the information at your next session.

As an additional activity, have teens watch a speech or presentation on TV to critique the presenter's style and skills and discuss later as a group.

Wrapping Up

In "Think and Write About It" (pages 118–120 in *Everyday Leadership*), teens imagine themselves in various situations where they are speaking to others or in front of a group. Each situation is designed for teens to reflect on what it will take for them to communicate so their voice and opinion will be heard by their audience, large or small.

Think and Write About It

To have your voice heard doesn't mean you have to stand in front of a large crowd or shout into a megaphone. But being prepared to express yourself well in different situations will carry your voice far. Presenting in small groups or one-to-one are terrific ways to strengthen your speaking skills for larger settings.

Read the following descriptions of different opportunities to speak up. Think about what's important to you in each situation and what you'd like to say. How can you organize and express your thoughts? Consider possible questions listeners may ask and how you can respond. Explain your detailed thoughts on the lines provided.

You're one of twelve students invited to attend a youth forum hosted by a candidate for a government office. You'd really like to ask the candidate about her interest in requiring all teens to take a driver's education class before they can get their license. Where you live, the class is optional to get your driver's license, but taking it allows you to get your license at a younger age. The candidate is proposing a fee-based class with no scholarships. Many of your friends wouldn't be able to afford the class. Describe how you'll prepare your thoughts, introduce the topic at the forum, and keep the candidate focused on the important issues.

You're co-leader for planning an upcoming annual weeklong camping trip. Because you're extremely shy, you usually let the other co-leader run group meetings. Next week, the co-leader will be out of town. You have to give an update to the three adult advisors about the camping trip and what the teens have planned and organized. Two of the adults tend to doubt the ability of your group to prepare properly and are likely to have a lot of questions. Explain how you'll get your report ready during the next week, which should include travel information, food, and a budget. Also describe ideas for what you can do if you get really nervous during the meeting.

After returning from a group counseling session, you overhear another member of the group talking loudly and laughing about something that was shared confidentially at the session. The person talking is respected by others, but also tends to bully people. When the person is finally alone, you decide you want to say something about what you overheard. Describe how you can voice your concern to this person about what he or she said and how you'll react if that person responds negatively.

It's two hours before tonight's end-of-the-season dinner banquet with players and parents. The team captain just told you that as high scorer for your team, you are expected to make a speech recognizing how well your team worked together. You've never spoken in front of such a big group before, and your team leader has asked you to be witty and entertaining. Since this isn't really your style, you'll have to plan quickly and creatively. Explain how you'll put together a meaningful speech to celebrate your team's success.

For future reference, you may want to put a check next to the questions you are assigning.

Public speaking isn't necessarily something some teens go looking to do, but as leaders, it helps to be prepared to stand up and express themselves effectively in different situations. In "Do Something About It" (pages 120–122 in *Everyday Leadership*), the actions offer ways teens can practice and improve their presentation and speaking skills while communicating with friends and family or in other small groups.

Do Something About It

Whether you're speaking to a small group of friends or a larger audience of strangers, first impressions make a big difference in capturing people's attention and getting your message heard. Make a point to practice public speaking skills when talking with family or other small groups.

---

122   Everyday Leadership

What I Did to Achieve My Goal(s)

Session 19: Having My Voice Heard   121

Check the goal(s) you will set to demonstrate your leadership abilities. If you have ideas you prefer, add them on the lines provided. Then write a date by which you plan to put your goal(s) into action on the "To Do By" lines and the date you completed them on the "Did By" lines. Be sure to fill in "What I Did to Achieve My Goal(s)."

	To Do By	Did By
○ I will learn 10 new words to use when speaking with others.		
○ I will volunteer as spokesperson the next time my group needs someone to talk publicly or to another organization about a particular project, event, or goal.		
○ I will practice giving a speech in front of a mirror to improve my nonverbal communication. Then I'll practice in front of a friend or trusted adult for feedback.		
○ I will publicly recognize the successes of my team by acknowledging them at our next organization-wide event.		

Other "Do Something About It" Ideas

○

○

FIND OUT MORE ABOUT IT

Getting the Point Across

Most people don't look forward to public speaking. How scary and nerve-wracking to have everyone looking at you! But speaking well can set you apart as a leader. Effective speakers get their messages heard and also build others' confidence in them.

With practice and experience, you can build confidence when trying to have your voice heard. Seize every opportunity you can—whether you're talking to the parents of kids you baby-sit, mentoring a younger student, volunteering as your youth group's spokesperson, or representing teen voices at a city council or school board meeting. Keep the following tips and techniques in mind as you practice.

Getting Ready to Speak

* If you have time to prepare, then prepare! Research your topic and your audience. Learn their interests and the issues that are important to them. Capture their attention and emotions.

* Capitalize on your strengths. If you're good at quickly putting together ideas on the spot, then only loosely organize what you want to say and let your comments flow. If your mind goes blank in front of a crowd, then write down some more detailed notes. Presenting in a way that is natural for you will be more comfortable.

* Identify what makes you feel more at ease speaking in front of a group. Most people are more confident when speaking on topics they know well.

* Organize your speech the same way you do a written paper. Include an introduction, a body, and a conclusion. Be sure also to allow time for answering any questions from the audience.

* Write notes to organize your thoughts. But use the notes for reference only and avoid reading them as if you were reading a story. Prepare the outline in a way that you won't be tempted to read it from start to finish without looking up.

* Use humor if it makes sense to include it in the presentation. Keep in mind who your audience is and avoid potentially offensive jokes or comments. Jokes can often fall flat and create an uncomfortable atmosphere, so plan what you may say afterward if the audience doesn't laugh.

Speaking to an Audience

* If you don't have time to prepare, get tense, or are unable to answer a question, first take a deep breath to calm yourself. Depending on the situation, slow down the pace of what you're saying or recheck your notes. Ask for a minute or two to put your thoughts together. Jot some notes to organize your ideas before giving your response. Or, say that you would like some time to give it more thought and will follow up later. Make sure you do. If others are presenting with you, ask someone to take over where you left off.

Getting the Point Across (continued)

* Work on your weaknesses. If you're nervous talking in front of others, avoid saying, "I'm nervous." People may not even notice you're nervous. If they do, then it's already obvious and there's no need to draw attention to it.

* If you easily connect with others individually, extend this ability in public speaking. Think of public speaking as simply having a conversation with many people instead of just one!

* Remember you're talking to real people. Maintain eye contact for a second or two with as many in the audience as possible. Notice people who are nodding in agreement or frowning in disagreement. Instead of just talking at the audience, ask people questions to grab their interest.

* Show the audience respect. You may be the expert on a topic, but avoid implying that you are more knowledgeable than the audience. They'll be more likely to remember and value what you said.

* Be passionate about your topic. Even if it's an everyday subject, connect your audience with how you feel about what you're saying.

* Allow silence. Don't feel that you have to fill every second with your voice. Audiences need time to process what they've heard. Using silence also shows that you're comfortable speaking in front of others and don't have to fill the air with noise to cover your nervousness.

* Practice good grammar. Avoid mumbling and using slang or words you really don't know. If someone asks you a question using unfamiliar words, say, "I'm not sure what you're asking. Would you please rephrase your question?" If you pretend to understand, you could potentially give a response that isn't even close!

For more about communication skills, see "What You *Don't* Say Can Say It All" on page 38 in session 7 and "Listening Blocks" on pages 44–45 in session 8.

20

MOTIVATING THE TEAM

(PAGES 123–130 IN *EVERYDAY LEADERSHIP*)

GOALS

Participants will:

- explore personal motivators
- examine motivational techniques and skills
- learn tips to help identify what motivates others
- learn tips to motivate others

MATERIALS NEEDED

- Empty shoe box
- 5 pieces of note paper
- Masking tape
- Empty 5-gallon plastic tub
- Small pad of paper and pencil
- Chart paper
- Markers

GETTING READY

You may want to make enough copies of the "Find Out More About It: Motivation: What It Takes" handout for everyone in the group.

Crumple the 5 pieces of note paper into balls and put them into the empty shoe box. Place the 5-gallon tub at the front of the room. Place three lines of masking tape on the floor, one each at 4, 6, and 8 feet from the tub.

Getting Started

Motivation is vital to encourage team members to meet goals. This session, teens gain an appreciation for how leaders need to balance what motivates individuals and what motivates the team. They also gain awareness of what motivates them personally and how that can influence their team.

To introduce motivation, begin with the activity "Take Your Best Shot." This is a fun, nonscientific way to introduce the ideas behind behavioral motivation patterns. At the start of the session, meet participants outside the room and say:

Today, each of you will participate in an experiment, one at a time. Please wait outside the room

quietly until someone calls you in—and don't peek. I'll call in the first person. After you've taken your turn, please ask another person waiting outside to come in. Don't say anything. Just wave the person in. While you're back in the room after your turn and watching everyone else take their turns, don't say anything either. When everyone's done, you'll find out more!

TEACH THIS

Take Your Best Shot

Although you tell participants you're keeping track of how many paper balls they toss into a tub, you're actually recording which line they stand on to do the throwing, the real purpose of the activity. You may want to keep track of the number of balls each person gets into the tub anyway, because they'll ask if they didn't keep track themselves. While participants don't realize it, this quick activity allows them to experience some internal and external factors that motivate them.

As each person enters the room, give the same instructions:

> Here's a box with 5 paper balls. On the floor, notice three lines various distances from the tub. Stand at one of those lines and try to throw as many balls as possible into the tub. Once you start tossing, you can't change which line you stand at. I'll keep track of how many paper balls make it into the tub.

After each person takes a turn throwing the paper balls, have that individual call in the next person waiting outside the room. Once everyone's had a turn, sit in a circle to talk. Allow 15 to 20 minutes for the activity and discussion.

Talk About It

First summarize the experiment by asking:

- **Why did you pick the line you did?**
- **Were you more concerned with trying to get the paper balls into the tub or about succeeding when tossing them from the line that posed the greatest challenge?**
- **What do you think this experiment is supposed to show?**

- **Other than the first person to go, were you influenced to choose the line you did because others were watching? Why or why not? Can you think of an everyday situation where your motivation was similarly influenced?**

Explain to teens the real point of the activity:

The goal of this experiment was not about how many paper balls you could get into the tub. For some of you, though, this was what motivated you. The real purpose of the activity was to see how far you were willing to stand from the tub to get the balls in. When keeping track of the balls, I was actually more interested in which line you threw the balls from, not how many made it into the tub. This activity is a fun, nonscientific way to explore generally what motivates a person. But don't assume that whichever line you chose today represents what motivates you. This was just an entertaining way to introduce the topic of motivation.

Next, ask the following questions:

- **Which of you stood at the farthest line? At the middle line? At the closest line? Why did you choose the line you did and what do you think your choice says about what motivates you?**
- **As a leader, how important is it for you to know what motivates you *personally* before you can motivate others? Explain.**

TEACH THIS

What Motivates Me

In this activity, teens further discuss similarities and differences in what motivates individuals. Since the activity often stimulates discussion about values, it's good to emphasize how being aware of personal motivators can help leaders motivate others. When leaders understand their personal motivators and realize everyone isn't driven by the same thing, they are able to use motivational approaches that are less "me" and more "we." This is particularly eye-opening for teens who've been uninspired to act or members of an unmotivated group.

Ask teens to turn to "What Motivates You?" on pages 124–125 in their books, read the instructions, and individually complete the ranking. After 5 minutes, invite participants to share their 5 top and bottom rankings. Encourage teens to take notes, so they know what motivates each person in future sessions and activites.

124   Everyday Leadership

TRY THIS

What Motivates You?

How often do you think about what motivates you? When you start a new project or set a personal goal? Knowing how and why you get motivated can help you understand and become more in tune with what motivates those in the group. As a leader, it's important to keep everyone wanting to work and wanting to work together until the job or task is complete.

Read the following 23 specific sources of motivation, or motivators. Next rank the items from most to least important (start with 1 being the most important). Circle your five strongest motivators and put two circles around your weakest.

- Getting good grades
- Repecting and valuing the culture and background of others
- Having a job that pays well
- Being selected for a position, such as student government, student advisory board, captain of an athletic team, camp counselor, etc.
- Having family approval
- Having friends' approval
- Being seen as a good person
- Having food
- Being able to do things my way
- Owning stuff, such as brand-name clothes and shoes, CDs, a computer, a personal music player, books, a car, etc.
- Achieving a goal I set for myself
- Partying or being social
- Being respected or having others look up to me or ask for my advice
- Being noticed or having girls or guys like me
- Doing the right thing

Session 20: Motivating the Team   125

- Following through on responsibilities and commitments
- Learning new things
- Getting a compliment
- Participating in school or community activities to help others
- Getting the part-time job I want
- Having someone to look up to
- Believing in a cause and standing up for what I believe in
- Enjoying what I am doing

Talk About It

To help connect both activities this session, ask:

- If your top 5 motivators were taken away, what would you do to motivate yourself?

- In everyday situations, do you think about what motivates you? Why or why not?

- Do you know what motivates your friends? Explain.

- Do you know what motivates those who follow your lead? Explain.

- How can you learn about what motivates others in your group?

- If team members hit a wall (can't make any more progress) while trying to accomplish something, what can you do as their leader to keep them motivated? How can you decide what is the best way to motivate them?

- Now that you have greater awareness of what motivates you personally, what will you do if what motivates you is very different than what's motivational to the rest of the group?

Ask teens to read "Motivation: What It Takes" on pages 125–128 in their books (pages 149–151 in this book). You may also want to pass out the "Find Out More About It: Motivation: What It Takes" handout. Check in to see if teens have any questions about what they've read. Briefly discuss other sources of internal or external motivation they may think of.

Wrapping Up

In "Think and Write About It" (pages 128–129 in *Everyday Leadership*), teens are asked to reflect on balancing their own motivational needs with the needs of people in their group.

Think and Write About It

Whether you aim to achieve or just not fail, think about what drives you internally and externally to do things. Think also about your experiences with others and what you've noticed helps them stay motivated. Keep all these motivations in mind as you answer the following questions. Use the lines provided to write your responses. Reread "Motivation: What It Takes" on pages 125–128, if necessary.

Describe a time when you struggled to stay motivated. What got in the way? Were you eventually able to get motivated? Why or why not? What would have helped you stay motivated?

Describe a time when it was very easy to stay motivated. What helped keep you motivated?

The actions in "Do Something About It" (pages 129–130 in *Everyday Leadership*) reinforce ways teens can explore what helps motivate them and others.

Do Something About It

The more in tune you are with what motivates you and other people you lead, the easier it is to inspire a group to get or stay motivated.

Check the goal(s) you will set to demonstrate your leadership abilities. If you have ideas you prefer, add them on the lines provided. Then write a date by which you plan to put your goal(s) into action on the "To Do By" lines and the date you completed them on the "Did By" lines. Be sure to fill in "What I Did to Achieve My Goal(s)."

	To Do By	Did By
○ I will ask an adult I trust to connect me with a younger student or neighborhood teen who needs support to stay committed to his or her homework or other goals.		

Do you tend to be a success achiever or a failure avoider, or does it depend on the situation? In what circumstances do you tend to be one or the other? Explain.

As a leader, you might face a group that is ready to give up. A motivational speech is the last thing they want to hear; they're tired of your enthusiasm and go-get-em attitude. What could you try to get the group newly inspired?

For future reference, you may want to put a check next to the questions you are assigning.

	To Do By	Did By
○ I will write a note to someone who keeps me motivated and let him or her know what this means to me.		
○ I will stay focused on a challenging group goal or project when others give up and suggest alternative ideas to get everyone thinking positively.		
○ I will talk with my friends about how I can help them stay motivated for personal goals they've set.		

Other "Do Something About It" Ideas

○ _____

○ _____

What I Did to Achieve My Goal(s)

FIND OUT MORE ABOUT IT

Motivation: What It Takes

Luck is nice to come by, but you can't always count on it. Being motivated and working hard to succeed is something you *can* count on.

Hard work and motivation often go hand in hand. Sometimes people don't know what motivates them, but a leader needs to figure out what works best for each person and for everyone as a group to accomplish both ordinary and extraordinary goals.

Some people may be very self-driven and others may need a high level of motivation to finish a task. Because people can be so different, it's important for leaders to understand various approaches to motivation.

Success Achievers and Failure Avoiders

People who tend to focus on succeeding are *success achievers*. The more success they have, the more motivated they become. For example, for an annual community holiday event, a success-achieving leader considers the occasion a success if as many people, or more, attend as the previous year. On a personal level, if you're a success achiever, getting all A's in school may be very important, because you think "nothing else is enough."

Some success achievers view *any* accomplishment beneath the highest level a failure. For example, having more people attend than the previous year is the only way the leader will measure success for the holiday event. This is unrealistic and stressful. No matter what drives you or others around you, set realistic and practical expectations.

On the other hand, people who are *failure avoiders* care more about not failing than they do about succeeding. For example, on a service project, a leader who's a failure avoider is satisfied when his or her team just finishes by the deadline. Similarly, on a personal level, if you're a failure avoider, getting a low grade in a class is fine, because you may think "at least I didn't fail."

Avoiding failure can keep people stuck at being adequate but not great. If this is the case, set standards higher to achieve more, and encourage others to do so, too.

When trying to motivate people, it's human nature to assume that what motivates you to achieve is the same for them. But to effectively inspire others, whether a team or a group of friends or family, balance what motivates you with what's meaningful and motivating to those around you.

Sources of Motivation

Researchers have studied what motivates people and have identified two types of motivators: *internal* (inside a person) or *external* (outside a person). Most people aren't motivated by only one or the other, but some combination of the two. As you learn what motivates others to act, keep in mind the following internal and external motivators.

Internal Motivations

When people are internally motivated, no amount of money, recognition, or other external item you offer, will be motivating. Internally motivated people are driven by how they feel about their own actions. Here are a few internal motivations and examples:

Achievement

The desire to achieve something, to work for the challenge rather than the reward, is the motivation.

Example: To participate in a 30-mile walk-a-thon.

Competence

The desire to master a job or do your best is the motivation.

Example: To learn how to use a power saw.

Belief in Something

The desire to uphold personal values or morals or fight for an individual belief is the motivation.

Example: To support animal rights.

External Motivations

When people are externally motivated, it's what they can get that motivates them to do or continue doing something. Externally motivated people are driven to act by money, material goods, being promoted, or receiving recognition. Here are a few external motivations and examples:

Power

The desire to seek control or have your opinions drive what others do is the motivation.

Example: To be the one who chooses which design to use for invitations to an annual event.

Affiliation

The desire to be with other people while accomplishing certain goals is the motivation.

Example: To work with the kids in the class who like science the most on a group project.

Position

The desire to "move up the ladder" in a group to the top position is the motivation.

Example: To be shift manager at a part-time job.

Hero

The desire to do well in the eyes of someone you admire or respect, or to be like that person, is the motivation.

Example: To show your coach you can do your best time ever at the final season competition.

Motivating Others: What's a Leader to Do?

To motivate people on your team or those you interact with regularly, it helps to recognize what really matters to them. Start by showing your own enthusiasm, and providing many opportunities for everyone to be involved. The more everyone participates, the easier it is to uncover what gets each person excited. And the more excited people are, the more likely they'll stay committed and energized about the project or goals. As a result, everyone wants to see *their* team succeed. Keep these additional strategies in mind to help you motivate others:

* Help people find things that match their interests.

* Make it easy for others, especially those new to a group or situation, to speak up. Allow all perspectives and listen carefully to every idea.

* Pay attention to nonverbal communication, such as facial expressions, eye contact, and posture, as well as tone of voice. If people verbally say things that seem to differ from what they're nonverbally communicating, clarify what they mean.

* Include the individual or members of the team in setting clear goals.

* Check in to see how things have been going and what may be done differently, if necessary.

* Survey everyone privately to find out how they feel about certain situations.

Once you know what motivates a person or the team, create an atmosphere that helps them maintain excitement. People are more productive and motivated when they know:

* what they're supposed to do.

* what they can do without having to ask permission.

* how what they're doing relates to what others are doing.

* what they're doing is important and not just a token job.

* what represents a "job well done."

* what they do well.

* what they can do to improve.

* you value their efforts and membership on the team.

* you'll reward them.

* you want them to succeed in a way that *they* find meaningful.

To *keep* a positive, motivating atmosphere, remember to:

* show your own enthusiasm and excitement.

* admit when you've made a mistake.

* demonstrate that you genuinely trust others by letting them make decisions without running everything by you.

* praise people publicly, and offer any constructive criticism privately.

* show and tell others you genuinely appreciate them.

21

SHOWING APPRECIATION, CELEBRATING SUCCESS

(PAGES 131–135 IN *EVERYDAY LEADERSHIP*)

GOALS

Participants will:

- learn the importance of leaders acknowledging team members' contributions and successes
- show their appreciation of other participants
- discuss ways to show their appreciation and celebrate successes

MATERIALS NEEDED

- Card stock paper to be folded in half or blank thank-you cards, one for each teen (use bigger paper or cards for larger groups)
- Chart paper or whiteboard
- Markers or dry erase markers
- Masking tape
- Party food (optional)
- Handout: "Find Out More About It: Recognition and Rewards"

GETTING READY

Make enough copies of the "Find Out More About It: Recognition and Rewards" handout for everyone in the group.

Write the following three statements on the board or a large piece of paper taped to the wall:

- One thing I appreciated about you during this leadership development experience is . . .
- One thing I learned from you during this leadership development experience is . . .
- One thing I think you deserve recognition for during this leadership development experience is . . .

If you choose to distribute certificates, make as many copies of the "Everyday Leadership Certificate" on page 158 as necessary for your group. Write each person's name, sign your name, and date the certificate on the lines provided.

If you choose to do a post-assessment, have a copy of the Everyday Leadership Skills & Attitude (ELSA) Inventory for each participant.

Getting Started

If you are choosing to conduct the ELSA again as your post-assessment tool, you will want to build in extra time or an additional session prior to this closing session. You will conduct the post-assessment using the same process as you did for the pre-assessment. Students will compare their first ELSA results to their results after completing the *Building Everyday Leadership* sessions (and any other leadership development efforts utilized in your program).

Helping teens understand the importance of showing appreciation to others and celebrating team success isn't difficult. For the most part, this is a significant part of their daily behavior with friends. Increasing awareness of doing this for their team when they're leaders is a little more difficult, only because many teen leaders get so caught up in trying to be a strong leader that they forget to mark the fun, successful, and celebratory aspects. Earning respect and achieving success as a leader rarely occurs without acknowledging and celebrating the efforts and achievements of everyone in the group.

Although this is the last session, it's useful to point out to participants that appreciating others, celebrating accomplishments, and recognizing people's contributions can (and should) take place regularly, not just at the end of a project. Incorporating recognition, appreciation, and celebration into a leader's overall role with her or his team can help maintain motivation and positive attitudes, even when a group encounters a difficult challenge.

If you haven't already done so, you may want to conduct session 20 on motivation to teens to promote a sustainable, positive attitude in their group.

Introduce the topic of honoring contributions and celebrating successes by sincerely expressing to teens what you appreciate about them as a group. Also share in what ways you've seen them develop as effective leaders. It's easy to have fun as you guide the group to recognize everyone's hard work and accomplishments throughout the sessions. Your goal is to create a fun atmosphere while encouraging teens to share what they truly appreciate about the other participants and their overall contributions to the leadership experience and the group.

TEACH THIS

Thank You Very Much

In this activity, participants write acknowledgments about their peers based on one of the three statements on the wall or board. The activity helps teens reflect on how everyone relates to one another and works together as a team and to develop their ability to recognize others they lead in the future.

Ask teens to bring a pen and sit in a circle on the floor. As you distribute the blank thank-you cards, explain:

Here's a blank thank-you card for each of you. Write your name on the front, and then pass it to the person on your right. Next, choose one of the three statements on the board (or paper) and write your thoughts about the person whose card you now have. Even though you may be tempted to write about an inside joke or make a funny comment, strive to write sincerely, commenting on how others in the group positively affected you overall in this leadership-learning experience. Write neatly so each person can read your note and make sure to sign your name. When you finish a card, pass it to the person on your right. Continue until your card returns to you with everyone's notes.

Depending on the size of your group, allow at least 15 to 20 minutes for teens to write and then silently read their thank-you cards. While teens are writing, set out any food to enjoy toward the end of the session.

Talk About It

After everyone has read their cards, ask:

- **What is the most important thing you have learned or appreciate about this leadership-learning experience? Explain.**

- **As a leader, how do you view your success? Is it reflected by what the team accomplished, how you are viewed as a leader, or something else? Explain.**

- **How do you think people you've led would describe your ability to acknowledge accomplishments and show appreciation? If you don't recognize others' accomplishments, why not?**

- If a leader never acknowledges your or other group members' efforts, how is your attitude affected? What can you do as a leader to make sure you acknowledge members' efforts?

- How can you recognize the hard work of some team members while possibly dealing with little contribution from other members?

- What are some ways you show individuals your appreciation or acknowledge their contributions?

- What are some ways to celebrate as a team?

Pass out the "Find Out More About It: Recognition and Rewards" handout and give teens a few minutes to read it. Ask if they have any questions or comments.

If you've created any certificates, pass them out. Suggest teens keep them with their leadership materials or inside their books. Invite everyone to enjoy the food and celebrate their accomplishments.

Wrapping Up

"Think and Write About It" (pages 132–133 in *Everyday Leadership*), presents several situations that help teens increase self-awareness about the value of recognizing others' efforts and successes. The different scenarios challenge them to find ways to show team members their appreciation.

Think and Write About It

As you answer the following questions, think about ways people have let you know they appreciate you, and enjoyable group celebrations that stand out for you. Write your responses on the lines provided.

How do you determine how others like to be recognized or shown appreciation?

The math team you're captain of just won the league championships. What can you do to recognize key members for their efforts and celebrate the team's success?

As the team leader for a service project, you've just learned the team's been nominated for a mayor's award for the project's success. How do you celebrate the nomination, whether or not you receive the award?

A younger kid you tutor has won an art award. You want to show how proud you are of this accomplishment. What can you do that's personally meaningful to her or him?

For future reference, you may want to put a check next to the questions you are assigning.

The goals in "Do Something About It" (pages 134–135 in *Everyday Leadership*) encourage teens to seek opportunities to appreciate and celebrate others around them in small and big ways.

Do Something About It

Showing others your appreciation doesn't need to take a lot of effort, but sincerity is important. Sometimes, just saying "Way to go!" can make a world of difference. Find new ways to let people know they're important and that you couldn't succeed without them.

Check the goal(s) you will set to demonstrate your leadership abilities. If you have ideas you prefer, add them on the lines provided. Then write a date by which you plan to put your goal(s) into action on the "To Do By" lines and the date you completed them on the "Did By" lines. Be sure to fill in "What I Did to Achieve My Goal(s)."

	To Do By	Did By
○ I will invite a trusted adult who has really made a difference in my life to lunch. I will ask friends who feel the same way to join us.		
○ I will work with my coach, mentor, teacher, or program director to make it a priority to plan a celebration for a team or committee I am on.		
○ I will talk with my family about ways we celebrate and explore ideas about how we can recognize important milestones in our lives.		
○ I will find out about a local community award and nominate a friend or someone I think deserves recognition.		

	To Do By	Did By
Other "Do Something About It" Ideas		
○		
○		

What I Did to Achieve My Goal(s)

FIND OUT MORE ABOUT IT

Recognition and Rewards

When you genuinely show other people your appreciation, you let them know they matter. It can be as simple as saying "thank you," or as grand as throwing a surprise birthday party. What's important is that people are more likely to be and do their best when they know others see that they make a difference.

Strong leaders mean it when they say, "Way to go" or "We couldn't have done it without you." They pay attention to recognizing and rewarding everyone in the group. But this doesn't mean you have to acknowledge each person exactly the same way. Instead, learn what is most meaningful to each one. Then everyone can feel you sincerely value her or his contribution to the team.

Leaders who positively acknowledge and celebrate their group members' efforts create an atmosphere where people feel important. And they also are excited to keep doing more. Effective leaders realize when and how to celebrate as a team. They recognize both the small and large efforts and successes. They don't necessarily wait until the end of a project to recognize contributions or celebrate. Instead, they regularly schedule ways to honor people without overshadowing hard work still to be done.

Find personal ways to express your gratitude to others around you for their contributions. In addition, here are more ideas for showing your appreciation and celebrating success:

* Present certificates for different accomplishments throughout the year.

* Create a special thank-you or other type of note that a person may keep.

* Ask an adult advisor for a letter of recommendation (for you or someone else) to reinforce accomplishments and promote future leadership opportunities.

* Give an award at regular meetings to recognize contributions.

* Hang a banner outside a person's house, room, or highly visible area, which recognizes what the person, or a group of people, has done.

* Give stickers or stars to put on team helmets or lockers for goals well done.

* Take your entire team to lunch.

* Create an "Everyday Leadership Oscar" event and award small trophies, such as "Best Supporting Leader," "Best Creative Thinker," or "Best Motivator."

* Hang a poster in a public place that charts your team's progress.

* Ask movie theaters for ticket discounts and take your group to see a movie.

* Ask a bookstore to donate a leadership book to your school or local library with a bookplate honoring an individual person or a group.

* Ask local teen-related businesses to donate coupons or offer discounts to team members for a job well done.

Recognition and Rewards (continued)

* Take your entire team bowling or miniature golfing to hang out and have fun.

* Design posters to hang in the windows of teen-friendly businesses that support teens.

* Collect money and make a donation in honor of a person (or your team) to an organization that the person or team values.

* Offer to have your team help an organization that supports teen issues.

* Reward a person recognized as "Volunteer of the Month" by coordinating a day for everyone on the team to help a cause that's important to that volunteer.

* Hold a potluck or have cake before a regular meeting or even in place of the meeting to celebrate your team's hard work.

* Write an article for your school or program newsletter that talks about everyone who worked hard or contributed to a project or cause.

* Honor individuals by taking them to lunch, sending flowers, or creating a bulletin board in their honor.

* Find people or businesses to sponsor someone to attend a leadership conference or workshop and support ongoing success.

* Establish and regularly update a "Leadership Hall of Fame" that includes pictures, mementos, and articles about notable leaders.

* Introduce and talk about the people who help you or your group as much as possible.

Try not to get too caught up in the challenges of being a strong, respected leader that you forget to mark your and others' achievements. Think creatively and get your own ideas going to make celebrating success fun.

Everyday Leadership

Certificate of Achievement

_____
(Name)

has completed _____ sessions of the guidebook for teens, _Everyday Leadership:
Attitudes and Actions for Respect and Success,_ and is now recognized as an Everyday Leader.

Congratulations on your success!

and

Celebrate your leadership attitude!

_____
(Adult Leader)

_____
(Date)

Everyday LEADERSHIP

Skills & Attitude (ELSA) Inventory

INCLUDES IDEAS FOR REFLECTION, EXTENSIONS, AND CURRICULAR CONNECTIONS

Instructions for Administering the ELSA Inventory

Regardless of setting, consider conducting the inventory in the following manner:

You will need one copy of the Everyday Leadership Skills & Attitude Inventory and a pencil for each participant. Establish when and where you will have your group complete the inventory. Although participants can complete the inventory on their own at home or another setting, it's preferable to have them complete it individually in your setting, where opportunities for group discussion and individual reflection exist.

Read aloud the first page of the inventory and answer any questions participants have. Reiterate that there are no right or wrong answers. Remind participants that when answering the questions, they should use the same interpretations of leadership and being a leader throughout the inventory. Encourage them to avoid overthinking the statements and to answer each statement with the first response that comes to mind.

Invite teens to find a comfortable location, independent of their peers. While you may intend to discuss the inventories as a group, completing them is an individual endeavor.

Allow participants approximately 15 to 20 minutes to read through and respond to the statements. The time necessary will depend on your audience. Even if some finish earlier than others, ask that they not turn to the last page ("What This Inventory Means to Me") until everyone is done.

When everyone has completed the statements, ask them to turn to the "What This Inventory Means to Me" page and follow the instructions. You may want to read the introductory paragraph of this page with the group. Invite participants to read and complete the page at their own pace. When everyone has completed this process, bring the group together to discuss the inventory.

You may want to consider the following questions to guide your discussion about the teens' results, whether or not you plan to engage in additional organized leadership activities.

- How did you feel as you were completing the ELSA Inventory?
- What's something new you discovered about yourself after completing the inventory?
- What do you think of the results? Were you aware of the areas you're strong in? Were you aware of the areas where you can strengthen your abilities?
- What can you do now to tap into your strengths and build up the areas where you're not as strong?
- In what ways does the ELSA Inventory help you identify ways you are a leader?
- In what ways does the ELSA Inventory help you look at ways others lead?
- What is one leadership goal you can set based on completing the ELSA Inventory?
- What steps can you take to reach your leadership goals?
- How can this group help you achieve this leadership goal?

If you have already identified extensions, connections, or enrichments (see page 169) you want to use with your group, incorporate these as appropriate in your timeframe.

Remind teens that they may practice leadership regularly even if they don't consider what they're doing to be "leadership" actions. Provide examples such as babysitting; tutoring; participating in sports, clubs, or music; working; helping in their household; volunteering; and so on. The inventory is designed to bring awareness to these skills and attitudes. It's designed to identify ways teens practice leadership every day and ways they can strengthen those actions—for themselves and others in their lives.

The Everyday Leadership Skills & Attitude (ELSA) Inventory

Being a leader and learning to lead depends as much on your leadership attitude as it does on your leadership skills. *Leadership skills* are your abilities to act as a leader—how well you communicate, work with others, or make decisions, for example. *Leadership attitude* is the outlook you have as a leader—both about yourself and about others on your team—and your ability to look at situations with leadership in mind.

For some, leadership attitude and skills come naturally. But for most people, they gain leadership skills and attitude by setting goals, trying new things, and believing that when they set their mind to something, it will happen.

This inventory provides 49 statements that explore your attitude toward leading or being a leader, and the various leadership skills necessary to put your leadership attitude into action.

Respond to each statement as it relates to your outlook and who you are TODAY—not how you hope to be in the future or how you were in the past.

Respond to each statement honestly for yourself. *There is no right or wrong answer.*

When reference is made to a team, it can mean your group of friends, a sports team, your family, your youth group, a volunteer project team, student council, a class—any group where you find yourself using (or learning to use) your leadership skills the most.

Whether or not a statement refers to a team, you may choose to think of yourself in a particular setting when responding—at school, at home, with friends, etc. If you do this, then use the same setting throughout the entire inventory.

When you have completed the inventory, you will transfer your responses to the last page. Turn to that page only after you've responded to every statement.

ELSA Inventory

Circle the number that best fits how each question describes you as a leader or your view on leadership TODAY.

Scale: **1** Not Like Me *(Never)* **3** Often Like Me *(Usually)*

2 A Little Like Me *(Sometimes)* **4** This Is Me! *(Always)*

1. I ask for feedback from others on my actions and behaviors. **1 2 3 4**

2. I show appreciation toward others who help me or my team achieve goals. **1 2 3 4**

3. I am considered a leader by others in my school, community, family, or circle of friends. **1 2 3 4**

4. I stand up for others when they are being bullied or picked on. **1 2 3 4**

5. I stay on task when working on a project. **1 2 3 4**

6. I can put myself in other people's shoes. **1 2 3 4**

7. I do my best and help others in my group do the same. **1 2 3 4**

8. I balance many responsibilities *(school, family, job/chores, friends, volunteering)* and know when to step back if things become too much to handle. **1 2 3 4**

9. I minimize competition between team members that might keep us from reaching our goals. **1 2 3 4**

10. I consider myself a leader. **1 2 3 4**

11. I am comfortable speaking in front of a group. **1 2 3 4**

12. I deal with problems directly. **1 2 3 4**

13. I get involved with projects or activities that may not directly affect me *(i.e., support clubs, events, activities that are important to friends and family).* **1 2 3 4**

14. I show initiative (take on responsibilities without being asked) often. **1 2 3 4**

15. I look for ways to use my talents and skills as best I can and I work to my potential. **1 2 3 4**

16. I share credit with those who deserve it. **1 2 3 4**

17. I represent the positive characteristics of a good leader. **1 2 3 4**

18. I listen actively (not just pretend to listen) to what others are saying. **1 2 3 4**

19. I help people reach agreement when a decision appears difficult to make. **1 2 3 4**

20. I serve others through volunteering or helping on projects (without waiting to be asked). **1 2 3 4**

21. I take calculated risks so I (or my team) can achieve certain results. **1 2 3 4**

22. I ask for help when I need it. **1 2 3 4**

23. I take time to celebrate accomplishments. **1 2 3 4**

24. I have people in my life that I can look to as leaders or mentors. **1 2 3 4**

25. I know when—and when not—to share my opinions with others on my team, and I think before I talk. ① ② ③ ④

26. I can make decisions with which I'm confident, even in difficult times. ① ② ③ ④

27. I pay attention to current events and issues that may affect my friends and me. ① ② ③ ④

28. I look for new, unique, or different ways to do things. *(I'm willing to try new ways of doing things.)* ① ② ③ ④

29. I am aware of my own strengths and weaknesses. ① ② ③ ④

30. I make sure team members cooperate and work with each other on common goals. ① ② ③ ④

31. I know what leadership and being a leader means in my life. ① ② ③ ④

32. I listen to others so I can address their needs or concerns. ① ② ③ ④

33. I do the right thing even when others may pressure me to do otherwise. ① ② ③ ④

34. I value the differences each person brings to my team and I speak up when I see or hear someone excluding others. ① ② ③ ④

35. I can set realistic goals and understand what it takes to achieve them. ① ② ③ ④

36. I understand why I do the things I do. ① ② ③ ④

37. I contribute productively to group ideas and projects. ① ② ③ ④

38. I can follow others who may be a better fit as a leader in certain situations. ① ② ③ ④

39. I speak up on issues that are important to me. ① ② ③ ④

40. I keep cool under pressure and control my temper. ① ② ③ ④

41. I accept team members who come from different races, cultures, and abilities. ① ② ③ ④

42. I strive to keep others in a group involved no matter what we're doing. ① ② ③ ④

43. I can sense how others are reacting to what I say or do as part of a group and can change my behavior if necessary. ① ② ③ ④

44. I create ways for others in a group to take on or share responsibility on projects. ① ② ③ ④

45. I believe being a leader for myself and others is an important part of who I am. ① ② ③ ④

46. I communicate openly and keep others well-informed. ① ② ③ ④

47. I ask for help when problems or decisions turn out to be more than I can handle and I can't find solutions by myself. ① ② ③ ④

48. I respect differences of opinions and approaches toward issues and projects, and I listen to other people's points of view, even when the ideas are very different from my own. ① ② ③ ④

49. I look for opportunities for me or my team to try new things or new ways to do old things. ① ② ③ ④

What This Inventory Means to Me

To learn what your responses mean with regard to your leadership skills and attitude, transfer your responses to the statements as they fall into each column below. Carefully transfer each response to its corresponding line below, then add up each column.

1. _____	2. _____	3. _____	4. _____	5. _____	6. _____	7. _____
8. _____	9. _____	10. _____	11. _____	12. _____	13. _____	14. _____
15. _____	16. _____	17. _____	18. _____	19. _____	20. _____	21. _____
22. _____	23. _____	24. _____	25. _____	26. _____	27. _____	28. _____
29. _____	30. _____	31. _____	32. _____	33. _____	34. _____	35. _____
36. _____	37. _____	38. _____	39. _____	40. _____	41. _____	42. _____
43. _____	44. _____	45. _____	46. _____	47. _____	48. _____	49. _____
_____	_____	_____	_____	_____	_____	_____
Total (SA)	**Total (WWO)**	**Total (QOL)**	**Total (CLBH)**	**Total (DMPS)**	**Total (SS)**	**Total (SO)**

Now What?

Under each column total is an abbreviation that refers to one of seven different areas of leadership and the skills and attitudes associated with that area or "category." You can read about these categories on the next page.

The total identifies your strength in each area. A high score means you are strong in that area or engage these attitudes and skills the most as a leader. A lower score means this is an area on which you might focus as you embark on any leadership experience.

If you are high in all areas, good job! More common, though, is that you'll be strong in one or a few areas and need to set some goals to achieve more in the others.

After reading each of the category descriptions and using your new self-leadership knowledge, set specific leadership goals to strengthen your skills and attitudes. Use the Everyday Leadership Skills & Attitude Inventory to become the kind of leader you want to follow.

ELSA Inventory Category Descriptions

Column One: Self-Awareness (SA)

How well do you know yourself? In times of trouble and in times of security, having a keen sense of your values and beliefs guides you as an individual and as a leader. Strength in this area indicates you understand your values and beliefs, knowing to draw upon them in any situation. If this is a challenge area, seek to gain greater awareness of your values and beliefs. Explore ways to express them with others.

(Statements 1, 8, 15, 22, 29, 36, 43)

Column Two: Working with Others (WWO)

For some, being part of a team is a sweet spot. Understanding your attitude toward teamwork, contributing to a team, promoting group well-being, and championing the contributions of others to team success demonstrates strength in this area. If this is a challenge area, find ways to build productive relationships with others as both a team member and a team leader.

(Statements 2, 9, 16, 23, 30, 37, 44)

Column Three: Qualities of Leadership (QOL)

Describing the qualities of leadership is an endless list! Clearly grasping what leadership means to you, understanding how leaders represent themselves and how others look to you as a leader, and having distinct leadership role models indicate strength in this area. If this area challenges you, seek a leadership mentor, establish a personal definition of leadership, and practice leadership behaviors every chance you get.

(Statements 3, 10, 17, 24, 31, 38, 45)

Column Four: Communicating, Listening, and Being Heard (CLBH)

Do people turn to you when they want someone to listen? Do you reliably voice your opinion? Strength in this area means you're capable of getting your point across, empathizing with the views of others, and remaining calm when discussions get heated. If this doesn't describe you, work to listen to what others are saying, formulate opinions you can vocalize, and develop skills that make others want to hear what you have to say.

These statements delve into your skills as a communicator. They also explore how you feel about speaking up and speaking out.

(Statements 4, 11, 18, 25, 32, 39, 46)

Column Five: Decision Making and Problem Solving (DMPS)

Facing and solving problems can be difficult and require more than a positive attitude. Strength in this area means you understand different approaches for solving problems, possess an ethical compass, act with integrity, and capably set goals. If this area poses a challenge, use the statements to guide you to develop skills that help you make decisions and deal with problems.

(Statements 5, 12, 19, 26, 33, 40, 47)

Column Six: Social Solutions (SS)

Whether it's being a social influencer or an activist change agent, leadership skills in this area come easily to some. Strength at finding social solutions means you are comfortable with those different from yourself, have keen awareness of social issues, and are committed to serving others. If it's harder for you to take action like this, explore ways to take a stand on a personally important issue, interact with new and different people, or find a cause you can openly support.

(Statements 6, 13, 20, 27, 34, 41, 48)

Column Seven: Seeking Opportunities (SO)

If you're inspired by outside-the-box thinking, creativity, and taking risks that lead you or your team to greater heights, this is an area of strength for you. But not everyone seeks the road less traveled, and if this is you, building skills in this area means trying new things, pushing yourself out of your comfort zone, and finding mentors and peers who support you in appropriately stretching your leadership boundaries.

(Statements 7, 14, 21, 28, 35, 42, 49)

More About You

I am a (circle one):   Boy   Girl

I am (mark what applies):

_____ American Indian or Alaska Native alone

_____ Asian alone

_____ Black or African-American alone

_____ Native Hawaiian or other
Pacific Islander alone

_____ White alone

_____ Mixed race _____

_____ Some other race alone

Age: _____   **Grade in school:** _____

The place where I live is:

_____ Urban (Near or in a big city)

_____ Rural (Not near a big city—only small
towns, farms, ranches, or the country)

_____ Suburban (outside a big city but not
in the country)

Why I completed this inventory:

_____ For a class

_____ For a program or activity in which
I'm involved

_____ For myself

_____ Other

I'm involved in these leadership activities and programs (mark all that apply and provide details if relevant):

_____ I'm not involved in any leadership activities/
programs

_____ Community group (Girl Scouts/Boy Scouts;
Boys/Girls Club; 4-H; camp; fraternity/
sorority etc.):
What program? _____

_____

_____ Volunteering (what type?): _____

_____

_____ Work part time (approximately 10–20 hours
a week)

_____ Work full time

_____ Youth group at my place of worship

_____ Babysitting

_____ Music and fine arts activities: _____

_____

_____ Athletics: _____

_____

_____ I have a mentor (how'd you get your
mentor?): _____

_____

_____ I am a mentor/tutor
(ages you work with): _____

_____ Other: _____

More about a leadership program I'm involved in
that's not on this list: _____

_____

Reflecting on My ELSA Inventory Results

This sheet is for you to write thoughts that arose during and after completing your ELSA Inventory. Treat it as you would a journal—write what comes to mind without worrying what others think. Pick one question or respond to them all.

How did I feel as I was completing the ELSA Inventory?

_____

_____

_____

_____

What is something new I discovered about myself after completing the inventory?

_____

_____

_____

_____

What do I think of my results? Was I aware of the areas where I'm strong? Was I aware of the areas where I can strengthen my abilities?

_____

_____

_____

_____

What can I do now to tap into my strengths and build up the areas where I'm not as strong?

_____

_____

_____

_____

MORE ➡

Reflecting on My ELSA Inventory Results (continued)

In what ways does the inventory help me identify the ways I'm a leader?

_____

_____

_____

_____

In what ways does the ELSA Inventory help me look at the ways others lead?

_____

_____

_____

_____

What is one leadership goal I will set based on completing the ELSA Inventory?

_____

_____

_____

_____

What steps will I take to reach my leadership goals?

_____

_____

_____

_____

How can this group (or another group to which I belong) help me achieve my leadership goals?

_____

_____

_____

_____

ELSA Extensions and Enrichments

Conducting complementary activities and extensions with teens will strengthen skills and attitudes. Here are some tips for selecting activities, extensions, and enrichments that support leadership development related to the inventory:

- Identify activities from your own "bag of tricks" that you've used in the past and correlate them with any of the seven categories on the inventory.

- Have teens recall activities in which they've participated that support skills in any of the seven categories of the inventory.

- Select from teen suggestions and conduct those activities with the group.

- When reviewing new resources and activities, identify how they might support and strengthen skills in any of the seven categories of the inventory. Point this out during discussion or debriefing of the activity.

- Develop a list of reflection statements or questions to use with activities or group discussions that build on the seven categories of the inventory; general examples are in the next column.

- Make connections on a daily basis to material teens are reading, events they're planning, projects on which they're working, volunteer activities, interactions with peers, athletics, and other leadership lifestyle situations.

- Make connections to programs and events you experience (i.e., professional development, training courses, conference workshops, etc.), incorporating activities you have found worthwhile with teens.

The activities and sessions in this book and the bonus activities in the digital content can be used to build skills in more than one category of the ELSA Inventory. Observe what takes place during the activities and then choose from the following questions to help teams apply what they learned from the process. Add other questions if you see certain behaviors (positive or negative) arise as the team works through the initiative. Each activity also includes a set of activity-specific Talk About It questions.

General questions:

- **What happened in this activity?**

- **What leadership skills were needed for your team to accomplish the activity? (Examples include: communication, listening, teamwork, finding a leader, delegating [spreading out the work], setting goals, having a vision, overcoming obstacles, decision-making, creative thinking, taking risks, treating others with respect, valuing different opinions, positively dealing with conflicts, and so on.** If your group struggles with identifying skills as "leadership," give them examples or rephrase with: **What did your team need to do during this activity in order to accomplish it?)**

- **How does this activity support your personal or group ELSA Inventory goals?**

- **What happened when people on your team made mistakes?**

- **How did you treat each other as you were trying to reach your goal?**

- **Was it necessary for your team to have a leader in order to succeed? Why or why not?**

- **What did you learn from this activity that makes sense in your own life (with friends, with family, at school, in the community, at place of worship, in sports, etc.)?**

ELSA Inventory Curriculum Connections

The ELSA Inventory can be used in conjunction with the *Building Everyday Leadership* curriculum as well as many other leadership products and programs. Use these activities and sessions to help students develop specific leadership qualities.

Using the Inventory with *Building Everyday Leadership In All Teens*

Using the Inventory with *Teambuilding with Teens*

(by Mariam G. MacGregor, M.S., Free Spirit Publishing, 2008. See page 212 for more information.)

Using the Inventory with Other Resources

Here is a limited list of additional resources that contain activities and ideas to help develop leadership skills and attitudes. Include them with the great resources you already use.

The Complete Guide to Service Learning: Proven, Practical Ways to Engage Students in Civic Responsibility, Academic Curriculum, & Social Action by Cathryn Berger Kaye (Free Spirit Publishing, 2010). While not leadership-specific, this book is a collection of service activities, community service project ideas, quotes, reflections, and resources that support leadership skills and attitudes.

The Courage to Be Yourself: True Stories by Teens About Cliques, Conflicts, and Overcoming Peer Pressure edited by Al Desetta, M.A., and Educators for Social Responsibility (Free Spirit Publishing, 2005). A collection of short essays by young people who have faced the challenge of being different from the norm and finding ways to survive. These real-life stories help teens and tweens navigate life and apply personal leadership strengths especially when encountering unpopular circumstances. A *Leader's Guide* is also available.

Everyday Leadership Cards: Writing and Discussion Prompts by Mariam G. MacGregor (Free Spirit Publishing, 2009). This deck of leadership cards contains 120 prompts and a booklet with directions and suggestions for using the prompts. Topics include: Qualities of Leadership, Working with Others, Self-Awareness, Power Play, Creative Thinking & Risk Taking, Social Issues, Communication, Doing the Right Thing, and Leadership Through Time.

Girl Scout Leadership Experience (leadership journeys for various ages). The Girl Scout leadership journeys address age-appropriate, girl-specific topics of self-understanding related to peer pressure, relationships, cyberbullying, tolerance, understanding the greater world, communicating, making decisions, taking action, and making a difference. Journeys are organized by age and leadership themes. Find general information, including links to order books, at www.girlscouts .org/program/journeys.

Search Institute (various resources). Books and materials published by Search Institute support the nonprofit's mission of helping create healthy communities for every young person. Leadership education encompasses the 40 Developmental Assets identified by Search, and many of the resources published promote leadership attitudes in teens and the adults working with them. Find information and products at www.search-institute.org.

Student Leadership Planner: An Action Guide to Achieving Your Personal Best by James M. Kouzes and Barry Z. Posner (Jossey-Bass Publishing, 2005). A customizable tool for guiding teens and tweens deeper into personal leadership exploration. While aligned with the Student Leadership Practices Inventory, this tool also correlates to everyday leadership issues and challenges identified when completing the ELSA Inventory.

Talk with Teens About What Matters to Them: Ready-to-Use Discussions on Stress, Identity, Feelings, Relationships, Family, and the Future by Jean Sunde Peterson (Free Spirit Publishing, 2011). A collection of field-tested guided discussions providing ways to reach out to young people and address their social and emotional needs. Many of the topics addressed correlate directly to everyday leadership issues and dilemmas.

Making Academic Connections

Opportunities exist in every academic area to investigate, educate, and explore the topic of leadership. Some educators may be overwhelmed with the idea of incorporating leadership concepts in the classroom, however leadership development can naturally improve classroom culture and climate without detracting from academic subject matter. To succeed, any educator or youth worker responsible for leadership in their setting can strengthen success by engaging all stakeholders in the process. To build allies, remember to:

- Highlight how leadership efforts add depth to affective development and cocurricular activities.

- Promote co-teaching between leadership "expert" (coach, youth worker, counselor, social worker) and subject-area instructor to maximize educator confidence.

- Invite teachers and/or administrators to observe your students in action.

- Promote the accomplishments of student leaders.

- Rotate leadership classes or groups in the academic schedule, particularly if it requires teens to leave their classroom for leadership responsibilities or otherwise interrupts.

- Give teachers ample warning when students will be missing their classes for leadership activities or conferences.

- Invite teachers to be cosponsors and/or to accompany students attending leadership conferences and workshops.
- Relate leadership development efforts to leadership and/or academic standards. (Information and links to leadership standards are found on pages 206–214; information for academic standards by U.S. state can be found at your state's department of education website.)
- Have peer mediators or other student leaders present at faculty meetings or "school improvement" meetings.
- Encourage teachers and administrators to talk with students who have taken on leadership roles at school, especially with those students who have had a hard road getting there!

Here are brief summaries of how leadership can appropriately and profoundly be incorporated into curricula without compromising the integrity of curricular standards.

Language Arts

Have students:

- Study leaders in literature as well as conflicts between fiction and nonfiction representations of literary leaders.
- Study heroes (fiction and nonfiction).
- Interpret well-known speeches by leaders.
- Incorporate public speaking into classroom presentations.
- Prepare for and participate in oral debates.
- Create projects that depend upon autobiographical and biographical readings, research, and investigation.
- Utilize Socratic seminar approach to language arts content.
- Analyze editorials for expressions of leadership.
- Write "Letters to the Editor" as expressions of leadership.
- Demonstrate learning through participation in group projects.
- Serve as peer mentors or tutors.

Mathematics

Have students:

- Utilize and interpret statistics for national problems, solving for positions presented by global leaders.
- Research leaders in the mathematical world and their impact on modern society.
- Apply math concepts, theories, and algorithms to everyday decisions.
- Learn and practice group dynamics and teambuilding.
- Incorporate mathematical problem-solving techniques to real-life situations.
- Practice communication skills and presentation abilities by explaining problem solving.
- Interpret historical significance and societal reliance on mathematical theories.
- Make a connection between math and leadership styles and decisions.
- Investigate exponential impact of personal decisions using mathematical principles.
- Understand linear and abstract processing, and practice patience.
- Serve as peer mentors or tutors.

Physical Education/Athletics

Have students:

- Learn and practice teambuilding and manage group dynamics.
- Learn and practice standards of fairness.
- Practice good communication and listening skills.
- Participate in team activities with individuals different from themselves.
- Utilize ethical decision-making during group and individual athletic pursuits.
- Practice serving as role models to peers and younger athletes.
- Identify and demonstrate standards of sportsmanship and humility.
- Learn the long-term value for leaders to live balanced lifestyles.
- Practice appropriate confrontation and conflict resolution skills related to rules and regulations (both group- and self-monitored).
- Serve as peer mentors or tutors.

Science

Have students:

- Apply concepts of ethics and ethical decision-making.

- Learn and practice skills of investigation and interpreting abstract conclusions.

- Explore concepts of diversity, extinction, and handling change.

- Learn and practice teambuilding and collaborative skill-building (lab partners; group work).

- Debate and utilize public speaking skills (as when discussing controversies in sciences).

- Research leaders in science throughout history.

- Research contributions of scientific investigation in sociological reference (impact on greater society).

- Trace international space exploration "leadership" (or superiority) through time.

- Participate in productive discussions on controversial science-related topics.

- Research and debate the role of leaders and decision-makers on global science-related policies.

- Serve as peer mentors or tutors.

Social Studies

Have students:

- Explore and discuss concepts of diversity, tolerance, prejudice, and social norms.

- Apply concepts of ethics and ethical decision-making.

- Interpret historical significance and impact of economics for global leaders.

- Research, discuss, and debate various philosophies of leaders and leadership.

- Research leadership styles and impact of U.S. and world leaders.

- Discuss leadership decisions relative to various social policies such as education, environment, international relations, international corporate culture, etc.

- Explore leadership in context of different religions and spiritual beliefs.

- Research the role of leaders relative to social change and justice.

- Participate in service learning activities and civic action.

- Serve as peer mentors or tutors.

Visual Arts/Practical Arts/Fine Arts

Have students:

- Practice and demonstrate resourcefulness.

- Practice appropriate risk-taking and creative-thinking skills.

- Practice communication skills through nonverbal expressions.

- Learn and practice teambuilding and collaborative skill building (project partners; group work).

- Explore and discuss concepts of diversity, tolerance, prejudice, and social norms relative to artistic expression.

- Compare and contrast personal expression versus freedom of speech in art, including countries where freedom of speech is not a right.

- Research artistic expression throughout history.

- Apply concepts of ethics and ethical decision-making (for example, unding the arts, NEA controversies, selecting public art, etc.).

- Form and defend personal opinions relative to art and music.

- Research personal standards versus societal standards relative to art and music.

- Research leaders in art.

- Explore artistic expression as a means for meaningful dialogue among international leaders.

- Serve as peer mentors or tutors.

Making Social Connections

In many ways, it's easier to make leadership connections in community programs than it is in schools because these programs aren't affected by prioritizing of academic subjects. Leadership education in these settings is also less bound by instructional minutes. Great success comes when the opportunities created and encouraged in community programs are approached with similar standards and clarity as are established with school-based curricula.

In addition to the typical mission statements and desired outcomes identified by organizations to justify funding and guide program direction, describing measurable learning outcomes helps teens know what leadership skills they can expect to gain from their participation. These learning outcomes also help teens link experiences that take place outside of school with those that occur at school. For dropouts and stop-outs (kids who take time away from school yet return later, such as teen parents, teens who are ill, those who have family issues, and so on), participation in community-based programs that have clearly identified leadership outcomes may provide enough connection and motivation to reengage in school.

Leadership development connections can be made in service learning and volunteer activities, Boys and Girls clubs, probation and diversion programs, adult mentoring programs (like Big Brothers Big Sisters), teen pregnancy programs, anti-violence initiatives, community programs (like Girl Scouts, Boy Scouts, Camp Fire, 4H, and recreation center activities), and others.

The following list provides examples of leadership development outcomes one can expect teens to gain by participating in leadership experiences and training. The ELSA Inventory is particularly effective for measuring these gains when instituted as a pre-assessment and post-assessment tool.

- Learning to be sensitive to diverse populations and community needs
- Learning tolerance and communication skills
- Learning and practicing empathy
- Recognizing one's role as an active member of the community
- Understanding community priorities and needs
- Learning to put words into action
- Learning how to navigate funding programs and learn resourcefulness
- Leading others toward a common goal
- Learning how to build allies and coalitions
- Identifying strengths and developing challenge areas
- Learning skills around setting goals, maintaining motivation, and recognizing one's importance as a contributing member of the community
- Making appropriate and positive choices in their lives
- Learning how to access assistance, help, and support in their community
- Learning ethical decision-making
- Learning how to be responsible
- Resolving one's violation through reparative justice (diversion/probation programs)
- Alternatives for problem solving, communicating, and decision-making without violence
- Practicing appropriate conflict resolution skills
- Making healthy choices
- Taking responsibility for choices and the implication of consequences
- Having opportunities to develop a vision and goals for themselves
- Learning how to ask for help and learning about support systems in the community
- Identifying appropriate role models and mentors to rely upon
- Learning to balance needs and wants, and learning the skills to fulfill both
- Having opportunities to practice decision-making, problem solving, and working with others while receiving guidance from a mentor
- Understanding role as a parent for developing children as leaders (teen parent programs)
- Learning resourcefulness as a leader in one's own life and the lives of others

Everyday LEADERSHIP

SUPPLEMENTAL MATERIALS

Class Sequence

The recommended class sequence (on pages 179–180) is based on conducting the sessions in *Building Everyday Leadership* in the order presented. Additional supplemental sessions are included to accommodate related projects and exams. Suggestions also are provided for when to use optional material. For example, you can collect the pre-assessment tool during your second session, whatever session topic you choose to explore.

Since most school semesters usually run 18 weeks (36 for the entire year), you might consider conducting *Building Everyday Leadership* using one of the following options:

- Meet once a week for the entire school year. This would allow for completing the 29 recommended sessions, plus 7 weeks to also do leadership and service projects, host speakers, or view theme-related films (see "Resources and Additional Reading" on pages 206–214).

- Meet twice a week for a semester. This would allow for completing the 29 recommended sessions, plus 7 other sessions to do volunteer activities, host speakers, or view theme-related films (see "Resources and Additional Reading" on pages 206–214).

- Meet three times a week for a quarter (9 weeks). This, however, would require fitting in two additional supplemental sessions for two weeks (meeting four times in one week) or extending a meeting time to accommodate two sessions once during the week for two weeks.

- Meet every day for a semester. This would allow for using the sessions as part of your overall curriculum. Additional days could provide opportunities to talk about what was learned the previous day or to continue an engaging or unfinished discussion, as well as allow time to do volunteer activities, host speakers, or view theme-related films (see "Resources and Additional Reading" on pages 206–214).

Determining your sequence for conducting the sessions depends on several factors:

- the size and makeup of your group
- the frequency and length of meetings
- the necessity of exams and related projects
- the outcomes you expect

Copy the "*Building Everyday Leadership* Class Sequence" on pages 179–180 either to follow or to customize for your particular group. If you want to follow the recommended sequence, make copies of "*Everyday Leadership* Class Sequence" on pages 179–180 to distribute to participants at the first session. Or you may distribute copies of your own sequence. Be sure to tell teens dates for each session, including any supplemental sessions for project presentations and exams.

Building Everyday Leadership Class Sequence

Session 1: Introducing Leadership

Optional Material: Review the class sequence and any major deadlines, as well as the class syllabus and grading standards. Distribute the ELSA Inventory (see page 160) to be completed by the next session.

Session 2: What Leadership Means to Me

Optional Material: Collect the ELSA Inventory distributed in the first session. Make copies of "Guidelines for Observing an Organization" and "Notes for Observing an Organization" on pages 185–188. Decide if you will have teens do the optional letter writing or PowerPoint design in addition to the summary presentation. Hand out the guidelines and form for writing notes to review with participants. Assign the date (or refer teens to the class sequence) for giving the presentations after conducting sessions 1–16. These sessions cover many of the topics addressed in the project. For teens who want to work with another person, provide a few minutes to identify partners and exchange contact information and schedules.

Session 3: The Leaders in My Life

Session 4: What I Look for in a Leader

Session 5: Leaders and Followers

Session 6: Power Play

Session 7: Communicate with Style

Session 8: Hear, There, Everywhere: Active Listening

Session 9: My Values

Session 10: Doing the Right Thing

Session 11: He Says, She Says

Optional Material: Make copies of "Guidelines for Researching a Leader" and "Notes for Researching a Leader" on pages 191–195 to hand out and review with teens. Assign deadlines (or refer participants to the class sequence) for submitting the name of a leader and book title for completing the project. For teens who want to work in small groups (1 to 2 others), provide a few minutes to identify partners and exchange contact information and schedules.

Supplemental Session A: Add a session here for the "Midterm Exam." If you're periodically collecting teens' books, do so now and return them at the next session.

Supplemental Session B: Add a session here to return and review the "Midterm Exam."

Session 12: Choosing Tolerance

Session 13: Strength in Numbers

Session 14: Turning Conflict into Cooperation

Session 15: All in Favor, Say "Aye"

Session 16: All for One and One for All

Supplemental Session C: Add a session here to have teens give their 3- to 6-minute summary presentations for the "Observing-an-Organization Project."

Supplemental Session D: Add another session here if needed to continue "Observing-a-Leader Project" presentations (depending on your group size).

Session 17: Taking Chances

Session 18: Thinking Creatively

Session 19: Having My Voice Heard

Optional Material: Distribute the ELSA Inventory as a post-assessment (see page 160) to be completed by the next session.

Supplemental Session E: Add a session here to have teens give their 5- to 10-minute presentations for the "Researching-a-Leader Project."

Supplemental Session F: Add another session here if needed to continue "Researching-a-Leader Project" presentations.

Session 20: Motivating the Team

Optional Material: Collect the ELSA Inventory.

Supplemental Session G: Add a session here to conduct the "Final Exam."

Supplemental Session H: Add a session here to return and review the "Final Exam" and discuss differences between pre- and post-assessments.

Note: It's nice to end the leadership learning experience with session 21, which covers the topics of appreciation and celebrating success, rather than the final exam. You may prefer, though, to schedule supplemental sessions G and H after session 21, since the final exam covers session 21. Teens can answer the relevant questions on the final exam without necessarily doing session 21.

Session 21: Showing Appreciation, Celebrating Success

Everyday Leadership
Class Sequence

Welcome to "Everyday Leadership." In this class, we will be meeting on the dates indicated to learn about leadership topics and to develop effective leadership skills. Session numbers correspond to the sessions in your book *Everyday Leadership*. This schedule also includes exam dates and project deadlines.

Session Date   **Session Topic**

_____   1. Introducing Leadership

Look over this class sequence and any major deadlines, as well as the class syllabus and standards for grading, if required. Complete the pre-assessment tool by the next session, if required.

_____   2. What Leadership Means to Me

Turn in the pre-assessment tool if distributed in session 1. Read the handouts "Guidelines for Observing an Organization" and "Notes for Observing an Organization." Write the assigned deadline on "Notes for Observing an Organization." If you want to work with another person, exchange contact information and schedules.

_____   3. The Leaders in My Life

_____   4. What I Look for in a Leader

_____   5. Leaders and Followers

_____   6. Power Play

_____   7. Communicate with Style

_____   8. Hear, There, Everywhere: Active Listening

_____   9. My Values

_____   10. Doing the Right Thing

_____   11. He Says, She Says

Read handouts "Guidelines for Researching a Leader" and "Notes for Researching a Leader." Write the assigned deadlines on "Notes for Researching a Leader." If you want to work with one or two other people, exchange contact information and schedules.

MORE ➔

Session Date	**Session Topic**
_____	Supplemental Session A. Midterm Exam
_____	Supplemental Session B. Review the Midterm Exam
_____	12. Choosing Tolerance
_____	13. Strength in Numbers
_____	14. Turning Conflict into Cooperation
_____	15. All in Favor, Say "Aye"
_____	16. All for One and One for All
_____	Supplemental Session C. "Observing an Organization" presentations
_____	Supplemental Session D. "Observing an Organization" presentations
_____	17. Taking Chances
_____	18. Thinking Creatively
_____	19. Having My Voice Heard
_____	Supplemental Session E. "Researching a Leader" presentations
_____	Supplemental Session F. "Researching a Leader" presentations
_____	20. Motivating the Team

Turn in the post-assessment tool if distributed in Session 19.

_____	Supplemental Session G. Final Exam
_____	Supplemental Session H. Review the Final Exam and compare pre- and post-assessments
_____	21. Showing Appreciation, Celebrating Success

Everyday Leadership
Class Syllabus

This class is designed to help you discover and develop your talents as a leader. Everyone has the potential to lead, and every day provides you with opportunities and possibilities to lead. Instead of sitting and taking notes, you'll learn about leadership by getting involved in activities, engaging in group discussions, writing your thoughts, and setting goals to act. As you learn leadership by connecting it to everyday life, you will gain greater confidence in your potential and your abilities. Fun and interesting sessions will help you improve skills to become an effective leader and have a good time.

Goals

The overall goals of "Everyday Leadership" are to support you in:

* developing a basic understanding of leadership ideas and how to lead others.

* learning practical leadership skills through fun and challenging activities, discussion, observation, reading, writing, and goal setting.

* building a positive attitude about leadership.

* increasing awareness of your abilities, strengths, and style of leadership.

* acting in small or big ways to make a difference by inspiring and leading others.

Grading

In addition to regular attendance and participation in the sessions, your grade also will be based on the following:

* Reflective writing in "Think and Write About It" in your books

* Goal setting in "Do Something About It" in your books

* Achieving personal goals set in your books

* Completing the "Observing-an-Organization Project"

You'll pick an organization you're interested in learning more about and attend one of its meetings to observe how the group works together. You'll receive guidelines and a form to help focus your observations and prepare a summary presentation of your findings.

* Completing the "Researching-a-Leader Project"

You'll read a biography or autobiography of a leader (alive or dead) you're interested in learning more about. Then, choosing from several formats (for example, written paper, mock interview, impersonation), you'll summarize the person's style of leadership and reflect on her or his impact on society. This is *not* a book report, but an analysis of the person's leadership style and any experiences that guided him or her to become a leader. You'll receive guidelines and a form to help you evaluate the leader's life and prepare a presentation.

* Completing exams

A midterm and a final exam give you the opportunity to demonstrate your basic understanding of the leadership topics and lessons learned throughout the sessions.

Observing-an-Organization Project

Observing how an organization conducts a meeting is an excellent way to see leadership in action. Although this is an optional project for evaluation purposes, it is valuable to have teens observe an organization even if they aren't participating in the *Everyday Leadership* sessions in a class setting.

This project allows teens firsthand experience applying what they are learning about everyday leadership. They get to see how other leaders and their groups function. Meetings held by city council, workplace staff, school faculty, school-improvement teams, student clubs, athletic teams, youth groups, community organizations, or volunteer programs all offer excellent opportunities for teens to choose from.

To complete this project, teens are to:

- review the instructions "Guidelines for Observing an Organization" on pages 185–186

- choose an organization and obtain permission to attend one of its meetings

- observe the meeting, fill out the form "Notes for Observing an Organization" on pages 187–188, and turn in the form for your review

- give a 3- to 6-minute presentation to the class summarizing their observations

To extend the project further or to offer extra credit, consider inviting teens to choose from one of the following:

- Write a letter to the leader of the group, giving advice and feedback about their observations. Teens don't need to send the letter, but they can format it as a business letter.

- Create a PowerPoint presentation as if they were leadership consultants asked to provide feedback to the organization. They can highlight the group's strengths and offer tips to help the group run meetings more effectively.

Assign this project during session 2 and schedule completion of it following session 16, as recommended in the sample sequence for conducting sessions (see page 179). This way teens will have learned a wide range of leadership skills and can more fully appreciate what they see going on in the meeting they attend. Applying what they've learned from the sessions while using the "Outline for Observing an Organization" helps teens focus on what to look for during the meeting.

Before explaining the project to participants, make enough copies of both the instructions and the guidelines for each person. Consider allowing teens to partner with one other individual to complete the project. Have both teens fill in his or her own "Outline for Observing an Organization" form. They are to participate equally when presenting their observations to the class. Decide also if you want to invite teens to choose from one of the options listed previously to extend the project.

Depending on the size of your group and a preferred organization to observe, you might choose to have the entire group attend a meeting together. Then you can take time later to discuss what each person observed and wrote on his or her form.

Distribute to teens copies of the guidelines and the outline during session 2, per the recommended class sequence. Allow a few minutes for teens to read this information. Ask them to write down the project due date on the outline. Emphasize the importance of contacting an organization to make sure it's okay to attend a meeting rather than just showing up at one. Answer questions teens may have at this time. Encourage them to check in with you if they have more questions while completing the project.

When teens summarize their observations for the class, allow about 3 to 6 minutes for each presentation. This limited time encourages participants to capture the essence of what they observed and provides an opportunity to practice speaking abilities. Ask teens to hand in their completed outline following their presentations.

Guidelines for Observing an Organization

Observing how an organization conducts a meeting is a great way to see leadership in action. This project gives you firsthand experience applying what you're learning about everyday leadership.

To complete this project, you are to:

* choose an organization and obtain permission to attend one of its meetings

* observe the meeting and fill in the form "Outline for Observing an Organization" to turn in

* give a 3- to 6-minute presentation to the class summarizing your observations

You can choose to work with one other person on this project. If you work with a partner, you are each to fill in your own "Outline for Observing an Organization" form as well as participate equally during your class presentation.

When you observe the group you select, keep in mind the wide range of leadership skills you've already learned. Apply what you've learned from the sessions while filling in the "Outline for Observing an Organization." This will help you focus on what to look for and appreciate what you see going on in the meeting.

Follow these steps to help you prepare for and complete this project:

1. Identify an organization that interests you. Meetings held by city council, workplace staff, school faculty, school-improvement teams, student clubs, athletic teams, youth groups, community organizations, or volunteer programs are all good options.

2. Plan ahead. Some groups meet only once a month. If you wait too long to inquire about attending, you may miss attending the meeting before the project deadline. Contact a few organizations to explain your project, why you'd like to attend a meeting, and if that would be possible. Since some groups hold closed meetings (nonorganization members may not attend), your first choice may not work.

3. Get the information you need. You'll also want to find out when the organizations' upcoming meetings are scheduled and the number of people expected to attend. Ideally, visit a group meeting that includes at least 7 to 10 people. More participants will make the meeting more interesting and allow you to get a better sense of how the leader and group work together.

4. Make an appointment. To attend the meeting you prefer, call back the organization to confirm you can and will be there. Write down the date, time, and location. Get directions if necessary. Inform any other organizations that said it'd be okay to attend one of their meetings of your plans so they aren't left wondering if you're coming or annoyed if you don't show up. You might say:

> **Thank you so much for agreeing to let me attend your meeting, but I will be attending a different organization's meeting that fits better with my schedule. I appreciate your help.**

5. Take notes. When you attend the meeting, use the "Outline for Observing an Organization" to write down your observations. Pay attention to how group members work together, the leader's style, and the goal and outcome of the meeting. Be sure to note the group's strengths and challenges, and suggestions for how you think members may work together more effectively.

6. Report back to the group. Prepare a 3- to 6-minute summary of your observations to present to your class. Avoid reading through the entire form. Instead, organize your thoughts to provide some general overview of your experience. Begin with the name of the organization and the specific meeting you observed.

7. Turn in your notes. After giving your presentation, be sure to turn in your completed outline.

Notes for
Observing an Organization

This project is due on _____.

Use this form to guide your observations of the meeting you attend. It includes some general statements to respond to, with additional questions to the side. You don't need to answer each one of the side questions. Use them to help you focus on various interactions that may take place during the meeting. If you're working with a partner, each of you should write notes on your own forms.

1. The name of the group I'm observing: _____

2. Why I chose this group: _____

3. A brief description of the group, its purpose, and who the members are:

_____

_____

_____

_____

4. This is how I understand the group is organized:

_____

_____

_____

_____

> Who leads, controls, or influences the group? Does the leader use formal or informal power?

5. This is what I saw about how the group operates:

_____

_____

_____

_____

> How are decisions made or tasks and responsibilities assigned? Are all members involved or only a few? Who makes things move forward or keeps the group at a standstill?

Notes for Observing an Organization (continued)

6. This is what I observed about how the group communicates:

_____

_____

_____

_____

> Do people understand what's going on? Do they ask questions? Do they seem comfortable speaking up? Who talks? How often and for how long? Do speakers project their voices or mumble?

7. This is what I noticed about how the group communicates nonverbally:

_____

_____

_____

_____

> What obvious nonverbal communication do people use? Do speakers seek approval from others or dismiss others' ideas through gestures or body language?

8. This is my view of how members of the group work together:

_____

_____

_____

_____

> How well do members work together? How does the leader keep people interested? Does the group use consensus rule, majority rule, a combination, or something else, to make decisions? How do people react when they encounter conflict?

9. This is how the atmosphere of the meeting felt:

_____

_____

_____

_____

> Was the atmosphere warm, friendly, cool, hostile? Did it change when certain people spoke? If people expressed opposing views?

10. This is a summary of my general observations about this group:

_____

_____

_____

_____

> In what ways did the group successfully work together? In what ways could the group be more productive and effective? What advice would you give to the leader? If you were leading this group, what would you do similarly or differently?

Researching-a-Leader Project

Researching the life and experiences of a well-known leader is an excellent way to gain greater understanding of leadership in action and how leadership can be an everyday part of who a person is. Although this is an optional project for evaluation purposes, it is valuable to have teens explore leaders that interest them even if they aren't participating in the *Everyday Leadership* sessions in a class setting.

This project allows teens to recognize how diverse leaders are, but also how similar leadership behaviors and expectations can be. It also helps them distinguish between a leader's likeability and skill; everyone may not like a particular leader, but they can still identify how that person demonstrates skillful leadership. Researching leaders also brings to light differences in style, character, behavior, and judgment among successful leaders.

To complete this project, teens are to:

- review the "Guidelines for Researching a Leader" on pages 191–192

- select a leader (dead or alive) to research who interests them

- select an autobiography or one or more biographies about the leader to read and submit the title(s) for your approval; they may also look at additional resources

- read the selected primary book(s) and fill in "Notes for Researching a Leader" on pages 193–195 to turn in

- choose a format to give a 5- to 10-minute presentation to the class about the person's leadership style and reflect on the leader's impact on society and on teens' outlook as everyday leaders

Rather than write a book report or summarize information they read, teens are to evaluate the leader's life based on the book(s). Teens also may view a documentary, as well as use encyclopedias (bound or online) or other references or resources to supplement the autobiography or biography, but they're not to use them as their primary source. In a less formal setting, you may want to offer viewing a documentary as an alternative to reading a book. Generally, however, reading a biography or autobiography supports building stronger literacy skills and may be more accurate or complete.

Instruct teens to use the "Notes for Researching a Leader" to highlight the following details and to prepare for their presentations to the class:

- why they selected the leader they did

- what her or his leadership means to them

- what the leader's life was or is like, including facts as well as teens' opinion of the person as a leader

- what occurred in the person's life that influenced who he or she was or is; for example, whether a significant incident inspired her or him to be a leader or if becoming a leader happened by default

- the person's leadership style

- why people consider this individual a leader

- what impact this person has had on society

To give their 5- to 10-minute presentation to the class, consider allowing teens to choose from various formats. You might suggest the following general ideas and parameters:

- present a 5- to 7-page research paper, typed, double-spaced

- perform a short synopsis about a particular time in the leader's life

- give a speech impersonating (pretending you're) the leader

- conduct a mock interview of the person, discussing important influences or a pivotal event in the individual's life as a leader

- act out a TV or movie scene starring the leader and demonstrating her or his leadership in action

Assign deadlines for teens to turn in the name of their selected leader, book title, and project format during session 11 and schedule completion of the project following session 19, as recommended in the sample class sequence (see pages 179–180). This allows teens to have learned a wide range of leadership skills and more fully appreciate the impact a leader has had on society and on themselves. Applying their learning from the sessions while using the "Notes for Researching a Leader" helps teens assess the leader they've chosen.

Before explaining the project to teens, make enough copies both of the guidelines and the outline form for each person. You may choose to let participants work in teams of 2 to 3 people. Have small groups choose at least one book that each member will read. If you prefer, assign groups as necessary to support their productivity or to represent diverse perspectives in each group. Tell small groups each member is to complete her or his own outline. They also are to participate equally when giving their presentation to the class.

Distribute copies of the guidelines and notes handouts during session 11, as noted in the recommended class sequence. Ask teens to write the project due date on the outline form. Read through the guidelines together and answer any questions. Encourage teens to check in with you if they have more questions while completing the project. Stress that they are to document all online sources with the website URL, date accessed, and original author if available. Emphasize they are to think analytically and creatively as they explore who their selected leader is and what he or she achieved.

When teens present projects to the class, allow about 5 to 10 minutes for each person or small group. Ask teens to turn in their completed outlines following their presentations.

Guidelines for Researching a Leader

Researching the life and experiences of a well-known leader is an excellent way to gain greater understanding of leadership in action and how leadership can be an everyday part of who a person is.

This project helps you recognize how diverse leaders are, as well as how similar leaders' behaviors and people's expectations of them can be. Learning about a particular leader also can bring to light the distinction between how well a leader is liked and how skilled a leader is. Everyone may not like a particular leader, but they can still identify how that person effectively leads others. Leaders can be successful yet differ greatly in style, character, behavior, and judgment.

To complete this project, you are to:

* select and get approved a leader (dead or alive) to research who interests you

* select and get approved an autobiography or one or more biographies about the leader to read; you may also look at additional resources

* select and get approved a format to give a 5- to 10-minute presentation to the class about the person's leadership style and your reflections on the leader's impact on society and on your outlook as an everyday leader

* read the selected primary book(s), fill in the "Notes for Researching a Leader," and prepare your presentation

* give your presentation and turn in the "Notes for Researching a Leader"

To choose a leader to research, you may want to consider the following ideas:

* topics that interest you and leaders who are experts on that topic

* social issues that interest you and leaders who have made a difference on that issue

* cultural, gender, or religious issues in your own life and leaders who have focused on those issues

* leaders who have created strong disagreement in society

* up-and-coming leaders who others may not know a lot about

* important leaders where you live or have lived

* leaders from different time periods

* leaders from professional fields or involved in hobbies you enjoy

Rather than write a book report or summarize information, evaluate the leader's life based on the book(s) you read. Use the "Notes for Researching a Leader" to highlight the following details and to prepare your presentation:

* why you selected the leader you did

* what her or his leadership means to you

* what the leader's life was or is like, including facts as well as your opinion of the person as a leader

* what occurred in the person's life that influenced who he or she was or is; for example, whether a significant event inspired her or him to be a leader or if becoming a leader happened by chance

* the person's leadership style

✻ why people consider this individual a leader

✻ what impact this person has had on society

You may choose to work with one or two other people on this project. If you work in a small group, you are each to fill out your own "Outline for Researching a Leader" as well as participate equally during your class presentation. You may also use encyclopedias (bound or online) or other references or resources to supplement an autobiography or biography but don't use them as your primary source. Document all online sources with the website URL, date accessed, and original author if available.

To give your 5- to 10-minute presentation to the class, here are some ideas about what format you may choose to complete your project:

✻ present a 5- to 7-page research paper, typed, double-spaced

✻ perform a short synopsis about a particular time in the leader's life

✻ give a speech impersonating (pretending you're) the leader

✻ conduct a mock interview of the person, discussing important influences or a pivotal event in the individual's life as a leader

✻ act out a TV or movie scene starring the leader and demonstrating her or his leadership in action

After you have finished your presentation, turn in your "Notes for Researching a Leader."

Be creative. Think critically. Have fun. See what interesting and unusual things you can discover about important leaders in our world.

Notes for Researching a Leader

This project is due on _____.

Use this form to write notes as you research the leader you've chosen. It includes some general statements to respond to and space for factual information, descriptions, and opinions. Be sure to list all your sources with complete references.

1. The leader I chose is: _____

2. I selected this person because: _____

3. This is what his or her leadership means to me:

_____
_____
_____
_____

4. This is what this person's life was/is like:

_____
_____
_____
_____

5. This is what I think of this person as a leader:

_____
_____
_____
_____
_____

MORE →

Notes for Researching a Leader (continued)

6. This is what influenced this person to be a leader (for example, happened unexpectedly, was inspired by a significant event or major life situation):

_____

_____

_____

_____

_____

7. I would describe this person's leadership style as:

_____

_____

_____

_____

_____

8. People who influenced this leader and the ways in which they did so include:

_____

_____

_____

_____

_____

9. People consider this person a leader because:

_____

_____

_____

_____

Notes for Researching a Leader (continued)

10. This leader has had (or will have) an overall impact on society because:

_____

_____

_____

_____

_____

The books and resources I used to complete this project:

_____

_____

_____

_____

_____

_____

_____

_____

_____

_____

Midterm and Final Exams

If you're using *Building Everyday Leadership* in a class setting, the midterm and final exams on pages 197–199 and 201–204 can assist you with academic evaluation. Both exams broadly cover the information in all 21 sessions. The midterm exam assesses what teens have learned from sessions 1–11, and the final exam assesses what teens have learned from sessions 12–21.

The exam questions are framed in different formats to encourage teens to think about and clearly explain what they have learned. Most of the questions are geared toward addressing major points in the sessions rather than all specifics. Consider that the number of sessions you conduct may influence which questions will be most appropriate. If you cover only some of the topics or conduct the sessions in a different order than presented, you might use the exams for guidance in creating your own assessment.

Some of the questions also explore participants' personal experience in the sessions. It's important to get feedback from teens to help you modify sessions if necessary in the future. Personal reflection in an assessment format can help you determine what works and resonates best with teens, so you can teach leadership most effectively.

Everyday Leadership
Midterm Exam

What have you learned about yourself while learning to lead? Answer the following questions to show your knowledge of what it means to take the lead and to be an effective leader. Write clearly and use complete sentences.

1. Write three sentences to define leadership.

_____

_____

_____

2. From the following list, circle a quality you look for in a leader, and one quality you think isn't necessarily important in a leader. Then write two to three sentences for each word explaining why you chose it.

Ambitious	Experienced	Confident	Trustworthy	Popular
Outspoken	Inspirational	Dependable	Ethical	Loyal

_____

_____

_____

_____

3. People in a group can be seen as "Y" people or "X" people. Each type is more likely to work best under a certain style of leadership. Write "Y" or "X" next to the style of leadership that fits best. Briefly explain why each style best fits each type of person.

_____ Leader-Centered Leader

_____

_____

_____ Group-Centered Leader

_____

_____

MORE ➡

Everyday Leadership Midterm Exam (continued)

4. In the following sentences, circle *influence* or *authority* to indicate which style of power is being used:

a. While working on a project with a tight deadline, the leader of your group uses her **influence/authority** to force everyone to stay late to finish up.

b. Except for a handful of people, everyone in your group is working hard to prepare a float for the parade. Your leader asks you to use your **influence/authority** to motivate the others to contribute.

c. To get your candidate elected, you use your **influence/authority** to encourage your friends and family to get out and vote.

d. When a child you're babysitting won't listen to you, you use your **influence/authority** to get him to follow the rules.

e. You explain to some new camp counselors you're training that if safety is an issue, it's important for counselors to use their **influence/authority** to get campers to do certain things. In other situations, it's helpful to use their **influence/authority** to inspire shy campers to participate in activities.

5. Give examples for one of the following:

• What are three things you can do to show you're actively listening in a conversation?

• What are three things that show someone is not actively listening in a conversation?

_____

_____

_____

_____

_____

_____

6. How does knowing your values and being aware of others' values help you make effective leadership decisions?

_____

_____

_____

_____

_____

_____

7. Texas Congresswoman Barbara Jordan said, "All my growth and development led me to believe that if you really do the right thing . . . you're going to be able to do whatever you want to do with your life." Do you agree or disagree? Explain.

_____

_____

_____

_____

8. Read the phrases below and write "T" or "M" to indicate whether they describe a traditional or modern style of leading, communicating, and working with a team.

_____ a. Emphasizes competitiveness and individual responsibility

_____ b. Views relationships as important in and of themselves

_____ c. Is enthusiastic, energetic, and willing to express emotion

_____ d. Objectively directs members to do their jobs and isn't influenced by emotions

_____ e. Is willing to take risks

_____ f. Is usually willing to help out the team in any situation

_____ g. Trusts a feeling

_____ h. In times of conflict, favors avoiding it or trying to control the outcome

9. Compare how you saw yourself as a leader when you started this class to how you see yourself now.

_____

_____

_____

_____

10. What is the most meaningful thing you have learned about leadership in this class so far?

_____

_____

_____

_____

Answer Key to Everyday Leadership Midterm Exam

The following key will assist you in assessing participants' completed exams. Specific answers are provided where applicable. For some questions, a range of specific or general answers is possible. For guidance in evaluating teens' responses, relevant session(s) are noted, except for a few questions that explore teens' personal connection to leadership.

1. See sessions 1 and 2

2. See sessions 3 and 4

3. See session 5
    "X" for Leader-Centered Leader
    "Y" for Group-Centered Leader

4. See session 6
    a. authority
    b. influence
    c. influence
    d. authority
    e. authority, influence

5. See sessions 7 and 8

6. See session 9

7. See session 10

8. See session 11
    a. T
    b. M
    c. M
    d. T
    e. T
    f. M
    g. M
    h. T

9. Variable depending on teen's experiences and participation.

10. Variable depending on teen's experiences and participation.

Everyday Leadership
Final Exam

What have you learned about yourself while learning to lead? Answer the following questions to show your knowledge of what it means to take the lead and to be an effective leader. Write clearly and use complete sentences.

1. "Diversity may be the hardest thing for a society to live with, and perhaps the most dangerous thing for a society to be without," said American activist and clergyman William Sloane Coffin Jr. Write a brief paragraph explaining how you feel about this quote, the issue of tolerance, and ways to address conflicts between diverse groups.

_____

_____

_____

_____

2. Read the following sentences and write "G" or "T" to indicate whether they describe a group or a team.

_____ a. Members want or choose to join others and are proud of their membership.

_____ b. Members may share responsibilities but also do things themselves because they aren't sure they can count on others.

_____ c. Members see conflict and mistakes as opportunities to complain about others.

_____ d. Members share duties because they know they can count on others.

_____ e. Members aren't always aware of what the goals are.

_____ f. Members want to see how decisions are made and put into action.

_____ g. Members prefer not to take on leadership roles.

_____ h. Members are interested in how they can interact with one another.

3. In the following sentences, circle *majority rule* or *consensus rule* to indicate which would be the most effective decision-making approach.

a. To make a quick decision regarding this year's homecoming theme, your group uses **majority rule/ consensus rule**.

b. After collecting surveys and hosting many discussions, your group uses **majority rule/consensus rule** to finally make a decision about vending machines offering soda.

c. The rec center is considering expanding the youth soccer program but wants as many people committed to a decision as possible. The director hosts a community meeting to help make the decision using **majority rule/consensus rule**.

d. As teen representative to the school board, you express that students won't support a uniform change if they don't get to be part of the discussion. You inspire the superintendent to listen to students' opinions and use **majority rule/consensus rule** to make a widely supported decision.

e. One of your friends tends to make all the decisions for your group. With spring break coming up, you get your friends to meet and talk about new things to do during the time off and use **majority rule/consensus rule** to consider everyone's ideas. With so many ideas suggested, you use **majority rule/consensus rule** to pick the top two choices.

4. What would you say to a group of younger kids about how you decide whether a risk is appropriate to take?

_____

_____

_____

_____

5. From the following list, circle two "locks" or attitudes that keep people stuck or unable to think creatively. Then describe a way you can inspire creative thinking in yourself and others to get past each "lock" you circled.

Looking for the Right Answer   Thinking Something Isn't Logical

Following the Rules   Being Practical

Avoiding Uncertainty   Believing There's No Place for Mistakes

Thinking Playing Around Isn't Important   Doing the Bare Minimum

Avoiding Foolishness   Thinking "I'm Not Creative"

_____

_____

_____

_____

_____

_____

6. List three specific steps you can take to prepare yourself so that when you speak as a leader, people pay attention to what you say.

_____

_____

_____

_____

7. Select one *internal motivator* (for example, achievement, competence, belief in something) and one *external motivator* (for example, power, affiliation, position, hero) and explain the personal importance of these in keeping you motivated.

_____

_____

_____

_____

_____

_____

_____

_____

_____

8. What is the strongest leadership skill you've discovered about yourself from this leadership experience?

_____

_____

_____

_____

_____

_____

_____

9. Based on your leadership experience in this class, what advice would you give other teens who don't think they have what it takes to be a leader?

_____

_____

_____

_____

_____

_____

_____

10. Write a response to one of the following:

• Describe a time when you showed someone your appreciation and how the person responded.

• Describe a time when someone showed you his or her appreciation and how you responded.

_____

_____

_____

_____

_____

_____

_____

_____

Answer Key to Everyday Leadership Final Exam

The following key will assist you in assessing participants' completed exams. Specific answers are provided where applicable. For some questions, a range of specific or general answers is possible. For guidance in evaluating teens' responses, relevant session(s) are noted, except for a few questions that explore teens' personal connection to leadership.

1. See sessions 12 and 14
2. See session 13
   a. T
   b. G
   c. G
   d. T
   e. G
   f. T
   g. G
   h. T

3. See sessions 15 and 16
   a. majority rule
   b. majority rule
   c. consensus rule
   d. consensus rule
   e. consensus rule, majority rule

4. See session 17

5. See session 18

6. See session 19

7. See session 20

8. Variable depending on teen's experiences and participation.

9. Variable depending on teen's experiences and participation.

10. See session 21

Resources and Additional Reading

Preface: Inspiring Teens to Take the Lead

Council for the Advancement of Standards in Higher Education

www.cas.edu

The Student Leadership Programs Standards and Guidelines: Self-Assessment Guide aids educators developing college leadership programs with guidelines that translate well into teen leadership programs. The standards assist educators with determining strengths and weaknesses of current leadership programs and provide a frame of reference for improvement. (See NASET on this page and NYLC on page 217 for leadership and service learning standards for K–12 education.)

Gardner Carney Leadership Institute (gcLi)

6155 Fountain Valley School Road

Colorado Springs, CO 80911

719.391.5349 • gclileadership.org

The Institute conducts a summer training retreat focused on training teachers at all levels to teach leadership to children and young adults. Although the Institute primarily serves educators in private and independent schools, the experience can be valuable for public educators as well. At their website, click on "Origins," then "gcLi Founding White Paper" for an informative research article, "Creating a Context for Leadership: The Teacher's Forum," written by Todd M. Warner and Catherine O'Neill Grace in 2003 to support the creation of the institute.

Journal of Extension (JOE)

www.joe.org

An online journal of the U.S. Cooperative Extension System, *JOE* seeks to expand and update research and knowledge for extension professionals and other adult educators to improve their effectiveness. Particularly relevant is the article "Leadership Skill Development of Teen Leaders" written by Scott Kleon and Susan Rinehart (June 1998, vol. 36, no. 3), which summarizes a study about teens' perceived leadership development after participating in Ohio's 4-H Teen Community Leadership College. Click on "Journal," then "Back Issues," then "1998, Volume 36—June."

Journal of Leadership Education (JOLE)

www.leadershipeducators.org/page-1014283

Published by the Association of Leadership Educators online, *JOLE* provides a forum for scholars and professional practitioners engaged in leadership education to share information about leadership education theory and practice worldwide.

National Alliance for Secondary Education and Transition (NASET)

c/o National Center on Secondary Education and Transition

Institute on Community Integration, University of Minnesota

6 Pattee Hall

150 Pillsbury Drive SE

Minneapolis, MN 55455

612-624-5659 • www.nasetalliance.org

NASET is a national voluntary coalition of more than 40 organizations and advocacy groups representing special education, general education, career and technical education, youth development, multicultural perspectives, and parents.

National Collaborative on Workforce and Disability (NCWD/Youth)

c/o Institute for Educational Leadership

4301 Connecticut Avenue NW, Suite 100

Washington, DC 20008

877-871-0744 • www.ncwd-youth.info

Composed of partners with expertise in disability, education, employment, and workforce development issues, NCWD/Youth provides numerous resources and publications, including a "Background Paper" on youth development and youth leadership. From their homepage, look under "Publications," then "White Papers," and then "Youth Development & Leadership White Paper."

SOAR: Multicultural Youth Leadership

www.childrenandyouth.org

SOAR builds and strengthens effective partnerships to support children and youth. Their Multicultural Youth Leadership curriculum is for youth professionals to address culture, leadership, identity, and empowerment with diverse teens ages 14 to 18.

Introduction: Leading the Way

Leaders: Strategies for Taking Charge by Warren G. Bennis and Burt Nanus (New York: Harper Business, 2007). Discusses four key strategies for effectively managing others: attention through vision, meaning through communication, trust through positioning, and the deployment of self.

The Leadership Challenge: How to Make Extraordinary Things Happen in Organizations by James Kouzes and Barry Posner (San Francisco: Jossey-Bass, 2012). Although originally geared toward business settings, *The Leadership Challenge* provides information relevant for young people as emerging leaders. Based on the authors' extensive research, this book features numerous case studies and examples, which show the Five Practices of Exemplary Leadership in action around the world.

Leadership for Student Activities
www.nassp.org
A magazine for middle and high school student leaders and their advisors working with student councils and Honor Society chapters. Issued monthly during the academic year, it covers leadership activities and topics such as diversity awareness, bullying, community service, and school decision making. *Leadership for Student Activities,* published by National Association of Secondary School Principals (NASSP), is a benefit of membership in the National Association of Student Councils, the National Honor Society, and the National Junior Honor Society. Check with your school student council or honor society, teacher advisor, or principal to join one of the groups and receive the magazine.

On Becoming a Leader: The Leadership Classic—Updated and Expanded by Warren Bennis (New York: Basic Books, 2009). Examines the qualities inherent in strong leaders and offers practical strategies for improving leadership skills with updated references and real-world examples.

The Student Leadership Challenge: Five Practices for Becoming an Exemplary Leader by James Kouzes and Barry Posner (San Francisco: Jossey-Bass, 2014). The Five Practices of Exemplary Leadership principles written in a specific context for youth leaders (high school and college), guiding students through concrete actions they can take to become exemplary leaders.

Core Leadership Competencies

Teens participating in all 21 sessions in *Building Everyday Leadership* can expect to acquire and enhance 12 core leadership competencies that align closely with developing or established content standards for leadership, service learning, or workplace preparation in various locations. The following sources provide information on specific content standards as well as websites for further information.

Sample Leadership Content Standards
mariammacgregor.com/wp-content/uploads/2014/02/Sample-Leadership-Content-Standards.pdf

Arizona's College and Career Ready Standards
www.azed.gov/azccrs

Content Knowledge: A Compendium of Standards and Benchmarks for K–12 Education (online edition)
www2.mcrel.org/compendium
A searchable compilation of content standards for K–12 curriculums. Draws upon the best of education research to create practical, user-friendly products for educators to create classrooms that provide all students with opportunities for success. Provides guidance for aligning leadership efforts within other academic areas without specifically addressing leadership education.

Hawaii Content & Performance Standards III (HCPS III) Database (Honolulu, HI: Hawaii Department of Education, 2007)
standardstoolkit.k12.hi.us

Linking Leadership to Instruction: A Leadership Development Curriculum for Virginia Public Schools
www.doe.virginia.gov/instruction/leadership/leadership_curriculum.pdf
Provides a well-rounded rubric of curriculum-based standards related to helping teens define leadership (specific to schools in the State of Virginia and easily transferable to other states/settings).

Maine Career and Education Development (Augusta, ME: Maine Department of Education, 2007)
www.maine.gov/doe/careerandeducation

Michigan Career and Employability Skills Standards (Ann Arbor, MI: Michigan Teacher Network, 2004)
www.michigan.gov

Montana Standards for Career and Vocational Technical Education (Helena, MT: Montana Office of Public Instruction, 2000)
opi.mt.gov/pdf/Standards/ContStds-CareerTech.pdf

New Jersey Cross-Content Workplace Readiness Curriculum Framework (Trenton, NJ: New Jersey Department of Education, 2001)
www.state.nj.us/education/archive/frameworks/ccwr

Pennsylvania Career Education and Work Academic Standards (Harrisburg, PA: Pennsylvania State Board of Education, 2006)
www.education.pa.gov/K-12/PACareerStandards/Pages/default.aspx#tab-1

Other Assessments

In conjunction with using the ELSA Inventory (page 159), the following leadership development tool can provide an added dimension to understanding personal leadership strengths, particularly in older students:

Student Leadership Practices Inventory by James M. Kouzes, Ph.D., and Barry Z. Posner, Ph.D. (San Francisco, CA: Jossey-Bass, 2005).
www.studentleadershipchallenge.com/Assessments.aspx

Session 1: Introducing Leadership

National Resource Center for Youth Services (NRCYS)
Schusterman Center
4502 E. 41st Street, Bldg. 4W
Tulsa, OK 74135
918- 660-3700 • nrcys.ou.edu
Offers current news and research in the field of youth development and ways to engage youth.

Wisconsin's Youth Leadership Certificate Program
Department of Public Instruction
125 S. Webster Street, PO Box 7841
Madison, WI 53707
800-441-4563 • dpi.wi.gov/cte/skills-standards/youth-leadership
Includes a leadership portfolio transcript to use to keep track of leadership building activities in six areas: personal management; communication and critical creative-thinking skills; media and technology; interpersonal, conflict management, and democratic organizational and small group skills; practicing ethical standards and behaviors; and democratic discussion and problem solving, and reasoned action skills.

Session 2: What Leadership Means to Me

Guidelines to Understand Literature About Leadership by Carter McNamara, M.B.A, Ph.D. (Minneapolis: Authenticity Consulting, 1999)
managementhelp.org/leadership/development/literature.htm
This online article examines various points of view and definitions of leadership, provides suggestions from authors of leadership literature, and includes links to other leadership articles.

SOAR: Multicultural Youth Leadership
(See the listing under "Preface" on page 206.)

"Youth Development & Youth Leadership: A Background Paper" by Andrea Edelman, Patricia Gill, Katey Comerford, Mindy Larson, and Rebecca Hare (2004)
www.nj.gov/dcf/documents/behavioral/providers/YouthDevelopment.pdf
A paper created by the National Collaborative on Workforce and Disability for Youth (NCWD/Youth) to assist youth service practitioners, administrators, and policy makers in defining, differentiating, and providing youth development and youth leadership programs and activities.

Session 3: The Leaders in My Life

Big Brothers Big Sisters of America
2202 North Westshore Boulevard, Suite 455
Tampa, FL 33607
813-720-8778 • www.bbbs.org
Dedicated to helping kids and teens, ages 6 through 18, develop positive and lasting relationships.

MENTOR/National Mentoring Partnership
201 South Street, Suite 615
Boston, MA 02111
617-303-4600 • www.mentoring.org
A premier advocate for expanding mentoring initiatives. Works with a strong network of state and local partnerships to ensure that mentoring organizations receive support and tools to effectively serve young people.

Who Mentored You?
Harvard Mentoring Project
Center for Health Communication
Harvard School of Public Health

677 Huntington Avenue
Boston, MA 02115
617-432-1038
sites.sph.harvard.edu/wmy
Celebrities and prominent figures reflect on the importance of their mentors.

Session 4: What I Look for in a Leader

Giraffe Heroes Project
PO Box 759
Langley, WA 98260
360-221-7989 • www.giraffe.org
A national nonprofit organization that honors people who stick out their necks for the common good, inspires others to do the same, and gives them the tools to succeed.

My Hero Project
1278 Glenneyre Street, Suite 286
Laguna Beach, CA 92651
949-376-5964 • www.myhero.com
A not-for-profit educational Web project to inspire people of all ages with an ever-growing archive of hero stories from around the world. Editor of *My Hero: Extraordinary People on the Heroes Who Inspire Them* (New York: Simon & Schuster, 2005).

Session 5: Leaders and Followers

ChangingMinds.org
www.changingminds.org
Devoted to the art of persuasion, this site provides substantive information on theories, techniques, and styles of leadership and followership. Click "Disciplines," then "Leadership."

Kid President
www.kidpresident.com
A collection of inspirational videos expressing life lessons, many of which highlight attitudes and behaviors kids (and adults) who strive to be positive leaders and followers can demonstrate.

Session 6: Power Play

"The Role of Power in Effective Leadership" by Vidula Bal, Michael Campbell, Judith Steed, and Kyle Meddings (The Center for Creative Leadership, 2008) www.ccl.org/leadership/pdf/research/roleOfPower.pdf
A research white paper evaluating the role of power,

and although data was collected from a predominantly male, adult control group, some of the research findings are surprisingly applicable to youth leadership settings.

Simulation Training Systems
PO Box 910
Del Mar, CA 92014
800-942-2900 • www.simulationtrainingsystems.com
Provides experiential training programs (simulations) for schools, charities, and businesses. One called "StarPower" is a real-time, face-to-face, non-computer-based activity in which students experience the problems, challenges, and decisions individuals face in an organization of differentiated power. Often available to borrow from a local college or university by contacting the Student Affairs, Leadership, or Residential Life departments.

Session 7: Communicate with Style

Communication Skills Profile by Elena Tosca (San Francisco: Jossey-Bass, 1997). A 48-item, self-assessment tool to help individuals measure and improve communication skills. Takes about 10 to 20 minutes to complete, and 10 to 15 minutes to score. Includes a comprehensive profile analysis and action planning guide.

4-H Youth Development Building Bridges: Reaching People Through Communication by Trisha Day and Greg Lampe, edited by Wayne Brabender
4h.uwex.edu/pubs/showdoc.cfm?documentid=11399
A collection of curriculum materials and instructional resources for teaching communication skills (and conflict resolution) to teens, parents, and adults who work with kids.

Toastmasters International
PO Box 9052
Mission Viejo, CA 92690
949-858-8255 • www.toastmasters.org
A nonprofit organization devoted to helping individuals improve communication and presentation skills in supportive group environments. Provides members resources on public speaking and advice on how to use its communication methods with teen groups.

Session 8: Hear, There, Everywhere: Active Listening

Are You Really Listening? Keys to Successful Communication by Paul J. Donoghue, Ph.D., and Mary E. Siegel, Ph.D. (Notre Dame, IN: Sorin Books, 2005). Addresses the importance of listening and provides practical steps to improve specific communication skills: paying attention, listening, and being heard.

How to Talk So Kids Will Listen & Listen So Kids Will Talk (New York: Scribner, 2012) and *How to Talk So Teens Will Listen & Listen So Teens Will Talk* (New York: HarperCollins, 2005) both by Adele Faber and Elaine Mazlish. Each book contains practical listening and communication strategies for adults to improve relationships with kids and teens. Includes tips, examples, and practice exercises.

Mastering Soft Skills for Workplace Success: Soft Skill #1 Communication (U.S. Department of Labor Office of Disability Employment Policy) www.dol.gov/odep/topics/youth/softskills /Communication.pdf A collection of activities designed for teens to learn appropriate communication skills in various settings.

Session 9: My Values

Character Counts! Coalition National Office
9841 Airport Boulevard, #300
Los Angeles, CA 90045
310-846-4800 • www.charactercounts.org
A national, diverse partnership of schools, communities, and organizations committed to using the Six Pillars of Character—trustworthiness, respect, responsibility, fairness, caring, citizenship—in individual and joint programs.

Character.org
1634 I Street NW
Washington, DC 20006
202-296-7743 • character.org
An umbrella organization that facilitates incorporating character education into schools and communities. Provides a wide range of links through its website and resources, research, and recommendations to foster developing ethical, responsible young people.

just keep livin Foundation
1107 Glendon Avenue
Los Angeles, CA 90024
310-857-1555 • www.jklivinfoundation.org
This nonprofit started by Matthew and Camila McConaughey is dedicated to empowering high school students nationwide by providing them with the tools to make healthy choices for a better future.

Session 10: Doing the Right Thing

Center for Spiritual and Ethical Education (CSEE)
910 M Street NW, Suite 722
Washington, DC 20001
800-298-4599 • www.csee.org
Although primarily partnering with independent schools, CSEE provides resources connected to the latest evidence-based research on developing resilient, compassionate, intrinsically motivated young people. The information translates to public schools and community-based settings.

The Good, the Bad & the Difference: How to Tell Right from Wrong in Everyday Situations by Randy Cohen (New York: Broadway Books, 2003). A collection of ethical case studies written in "Q & A" format from the author's popular *New York Times* column.

Institute for Global Ethics
10 East Doty Street, Suite 825
Madison, WI 53703
888-607-0883 • www.globalethics.org
An independent, nonsectarian, nonpartisan, nonprofit organization that promotes ethical action and provides numerous case studies to use with young people and adults.

Junior Achievement Student Center
One Education Way
Colorado Springs, CO 80906
719-540-8000 • www.jamyway.org
An online tool to help students prepare for the workforce. Includes multi-age curriculum and classroom activities related to ethics in business. See "Learn About Ethics" at their website.

Markkula Center for Applied Ethics
Santa Clara University
500 El Camino Real
Santa Clara, CA 95053
408-554-5319 • www.scu.edu/ethics
Provides a forum for students and educators to explore ethics through case studies, articles, research, ethics camps, and other programming.

Session 11: He Says, She Says

"The Gender Revolution" in *The Washington Post*, March 22–26, 1998
www.washingtonpost.com/wp-srv/national/longterm/gender/gender22a.htm (accessed February 16, 2015)
In this five-part series, various reporters investigate the changing roles men and women have experienced at home, with family, and in the workplace since the 1950s.

Girls Leadership Institute
111 Myrtle Street, Suite 101
Oakland, CA 94607
866-744-9102 • www.girlsleadership.org
Girls Leadership offers programs, workshops, camps, and resources to teach girls the skills they need to know who they are, what they believe, and how to express it, empowering them to create change in their world.

IGNITE National
www.ignitenational.org
A nonprofit, nonpartisan organization dedicated to inspiring and preparing young women to become civic and political leaders by connecting them to opportunities where they can exercise these skills. IGNITE's work is informed by national research on gender differences in political ambition.

Phillips Academy—Brace Center for Gender Studies
180 Main Street
Andover, MA 01810
978-749-4000 • andover.edu/academics/programinfo/bracecenterforgenderstudies/pages/default.aspx
The Brace Center strives to advance an understanding of gender and its influence on individual achievement of boys and girls. Their website includes a collection of gender papers and an additional list of gender resources.

Resources for Gender Issues in Education, Ohio Literacy Resource Center
literacy.kent.edu/Oasis/Resc/Educ/gender.html
A collection of online links related to research, resources, and organizations focused on gender equity in the lives of young people.

Why Gender Matters: What Parents and Teachers Need to Know About the Emerging Science of Sex Differences by Leonard Sax, M.D., Ph.D. (New York: Doubleday, 2005). Challenges gender theories by examining the biological differences between the sexes and analyzing the ways these differences affect kids' and teens' behavior.

Session 12: Choosing Tolerance

America's Civil Rights Movement: A Time for Justice directed by Charles Guggenheim
(Montgomery, AL: Teaching Tolerance, 1995)
www.tolerance.org/kit/america-s-civil-rights-movement-time-justice
Using documentary footage and eyewitness reports, this film examines the history of inequality and intolerance in the United States. The film kit is free to educators and includes a discussion guide and lesson plans.

A Class Divided (Frontline) directed by William Peters
(Boston, MA: WGBH Educational Foundation, 1985)
www.pbs.org/wgbh/film/class-divided
A provocative documentary on Jane Elliott's famous "Blue-Eyed/Brown-Eyed" exercise first tried in 1970, in which white college students were required to accept treatment given to minorities.

Mighty Times: The Children's March (Montgomery, AL: Teaching Tolerance in association with HBO)
www.tolerance.org/kit/mighty-times-childrens-march
Mighty Times tells the story of how the young people of Birmingham, Alabama, braved fire hoses and police dogs in 1963 and brought segregation to its knees. Their heroism complements discussions about the ability of today's young people to be catalysts for positive social change. The film kit is free to educators and includes a discussion guide and lesson plans that align with standards in language arts, music, and social studies.

Teaching Tolerance
A Project of the Southern Poverty Law Center
400 Washington Avenue
Montgomery, AL 36104
334-956-8200 • www.tolerance.org
Dedicated to promoting tolerant, inclusive, hate-free environments at home and in schools and communities. Provides resources for kids, teens, teachers, and other adults. Publishes classroom materials and discussion guides, as well as the *Teaching Tolerance Magazine,* which showcases innovative tolerance initiatives in schools.

Session 13: Strength in Numbers

Association for Experiential Education (AEE)
PO Box 13246
Denver, CO 80301
866-522-8337 • www.aee.org
Governs accreditation for experiential education programs such as outdoor adventure team building programs and camps. Links provide research, resources, and activities, including best-used practices of hands-on immersion learning.

Project Adventure, Inc.
Corporate Office
719 Cabot Street
Beverly, MA 01915
800-468-8898 • www.pa.org
An innovative teaching organization that provides leadership in adventure-based experiential programming. Research supporting adventure-based, outdoor education, and experiential training as well as publications and other resources are available.

Teambuilding with Teens: Activities for Leadership, Decision Making, and Group Success by Mariam G. MacGregor (Minneapolis: Free Spirit Publishing, 2007). This collection of 36 hands-on activities supplement the lessons taught in the *Building Everyday Leadership* curriculum.

Session 14: Turning Conflict into Cooperation

The Conflict Resolution Information Source
c/o Conflict Information Consortium
University of Colorado
580 UCB
Boulder, CO 80309
303-492-1635 • www.beyondintractability.org
Offers a broad collection of research, articles, educational methods, and links about productive conflict resolution.

Engaging Schools
23 Garden Street
Cambridge, MA 02138
800-370-2515 • www.engagingschools.org
A national, nonprofit organization devoted to making teaching social responsibility a core education practice. Offers conflict resolution programs for middle school students, peer mediation and social skills lessons for secondary education, and conflict resolution training for educators.

4-H Youth Development Building Bridges: Reaching People Through Communication
(See the listing under "Session 7" on page 209.)

Style Matters: The Kraybill Conflict Style Inventory by Ron Kraybill (Harrisonburg, VA: Riverhouse ePress, 2005). Gives a simple five-styles framework to assess styles of dealing with differences. Includes "Hot Tips" for working with each style; also available in Spanish.

Thomas-Kilmann Conflict Mode Instrument (TKI) by Kenneth W. Thomas, Ph.D., and Ralph H. Kilmann, Ph.D. (Mountain View, CA: CPP, Inc., 2002)
www.kilmanndiagnostics.com/catalog/thomas-kilmann-conflict-mode-instrument
A handy tool for identifying and understanding different conflict-handling styles. Provides strategies for peaceful, pragmatic conflict resolution.

Session 15: All in Favor, Say "Aye"

Learning to Give
www.learningtogive.org
An online educational effort to introduce children and teens to the world of philanthropy and civic involvement. Offers lesson plans on majority rule, consensus, and other topics. Also provides content standards,

research, and relevant links for parents as well as teachers and youth workers and students.

"Making Civics Real Workshop #7: Controversial Public Policy Issues"
www.learner.org/workshops/civics/workshop7/teacherperspec/consensus.html
This high school social studies lesson available through Annenberg Learner explores a complex civic issue and achieves consensus on social policies related to it.

Robert's Rules of Order by Henry M. Robert III, Daniel H. Honemann, and Thomas J. Balch, with the assistance of Daniel E. Seabold and Shmuel Gerber (Boston, MA: Da Capo Press, 2011). An introduction to the intricacies of voting systems and processes.

Session 16: All for One and One for All

Learning to Give
(See the listing under "Session 15" on page 212.)

Tools to Build Consensus: Facilitate Agreement in Your Group by Ron Kraybill (Harrisonburg, VA: Riverhouse ePress, 2005). A booklet that provides clearly written, practical steps for guiding a group to consensus. Includes specific ways to deal with difficult moments and how to test for consensus.

Session 17: Taking Chances

The Endurance: Shackleton's Legendary Antarctic Expedition directed by George Butler (Sony Pictures, 2001). This G-rated documentary, based on Caroline Alexander's book of the same title (New York: Knopf, 1998), presents Ernest Shackleton and his amazing story of survival in icy Antarctica.

Leadership on the Line: Staying Alive Through the Dangers of Leading by Ronald A. Heifetz and Marty Linsky (Cambridge, MA: Harvard Business School Press, 2002). Advice on how to manage the risks and hazards of leadership.

Shackleton's Way: Leadership Lessons from the Great Antarctic Explorer by Margo Morrell and Stephanie Capparell (New York: Penguin Books, 2002). Examines the leadership techniques of Ernest Shackleton during the two years he was stranded with his crew in Antarctica.

Session 18: Thinking Creatively

Creative Think
creativethink.com
Links to books and other resources from Roger von Oech, a well-known expert on creative thinking.

Creative Whack Pack App by Creative Think (available through iTunes store)
itunes.apple.com/us/app/creative-whack-pack/id307306326?mt=8
Interactive activities to promote and engage creativity for brainstorming and problem solving.

The Pursuit of Wow! Every Person's Guide to Topsy-Turvy Times by Tom Peters (New York: Vintage/Knopf Publishing Group, 1994). The more than 200 tips for thinking creatively are timeless.

Six Thinking Hats by Edward de Bono (New York: Back Bay Books, 1999). Practical strategies to stimulate creative brainstorming and decision making.

Session 19: Having My Voice Heard

The History Channel Archives of Great Speeches
www.history.com
Offers video and audio clips of some of the most inspirational and influential speeches of the 20th and 21st centuries.

The History Place
www.historyplace.com
An independent website unaffiliated with any political organization that provides a fact-based approach to the history of humanity. To access the collection of famous historical speeches, click "Speech of the Week," then "Great Speeches Collection."

"Lessons in Leadership: How Young People Change their Communities and Themselves"
www.theinnovationcenter.org/files/Lessons_in_Leadership_exec.pdf
An executive summary of the evaluation of the Youth Leadership for Development Initiative by the Innovation Center for Community and Youth Development (funded by the Ford Foundation, December 2003).

National Youth Rights Association
www.youthrights.org
A national, nonprofit corporation that seeks to engage young people and adults in creating social justice in the lives of young people every day through school and community programs, resources, and leadership training, workshops, and presentations. Two relevant programs include: the Freechild Project (www.freechild.org), whose activities include training, networking, research, and project development around social change, and SoundOut (www.soundout.org), which promotes student voice in schools.

Teen Ink
www.teenink.com
An online and print magazine designed specifically as a way for teens to have their voices heard through creative arts. All *Teen Ink* publications are supported by the nonprofit organization the Young Authors Foundation, Inc., which is devoted to helping teens share their own voices, while developing reading, writing, creative, and critical-thinking skills. All proceeds from the print magazine, website, and *Teen Ink* books are used exclusively for charitable and educational purposes to further the goals of *Teen Ink*.

Session 20: Motivating the Team

Managing with Carrots: Using Recognition to Attract and Retain the Best People by Adrian Gostick and Chester Elton (Salt Lake City: Gibbs-Smith, 2001).
Advice on how to motivate new generations of leaders.

Psychology Today—Motivation
www.psychologytoday.com/basics/motivation
Updated on ongoing basis with articles, tips, studies, and other resources related to motivation, goal-setting, and achievement.

Various films including:
Dreamer (PG, Dreamworks, 2005)
Loosely inspired by the true story of a promising racehorse injured during a race, this film follows the relationship between a daughter and her father, who has nearly given up on the things that mean the most to their family.

Hoosiers (PG, MGM, 1986)
Based on the true story of a small-town Indiana basketball team that made the state finals in 1954, this film chronicles the attempts of a volatile, former star-player-turned-alcoholic coach leading a small-town basketball team on an improbable run to the Indiana high school championship game.

October Sky (PG, Universal Pictures, 1999)
The true story of Homer Hickam, a coal miner's son, who, against his father's wishes, was inspired by the first *Sputnik* launch to take up rocketry.

Rudy (PG, TriStar Pictures, 1993)
This classic film is about the real-life story of underdog Rudy Ruettiger, who inspired many people with his tireless determination to play college football.

Soul Surfer (PG, Sony Pictures, 2011)
A film about Bethany Hamilton, a teenage surfer who overcomes the odds and her own fears of returning to the water after losing her left arm in a shark attack.

Session 21: Showing Appreciation, Celebrating Success

Building Your Team's Morale, Pride, and Spirit by Gene Klann (Greensboro, NC: Center for Creative Leadership Press, 2004). Ideas for how to create a positive group dynamic and improve team morale.

Encouraging the Heart: A Leader's Guide to Rewarding and Recognizing Others by James M. Kouzes and Barry Z. Posner (San Francisco: Jossey-Bass, 2003). Emphasizes using encouragement and appreciating excellent performance.

101 Ways to Reward Team Members for $20 (or Less!) by Kevin Aguanno (Ontario, Canada: Multi-Media Publications, 2004). Inexpensive ways to recognize and motivate team members.

Additional Resources

Books, Magazines, and Movies

Are You Really Listening? Keys to Successful Communication by Paul J. Donoghue, Ph.D., and Mary E. Siegel, Ph.D. (Notre Dame, IN: Sorin Books, 2005). Teaches you how to improve listening and other communication skills including paying attention and being heard.

Climb On! Dynamic Strategies for Teen Success by John R. Beede (Henderson, NV: Sierra Nevada Publishing House, 2005). A fictional story about a teen who learns how to set goals, deal with situations, and gain insight into life by learning how to rock climb.

Developing Ethical Student Leaders edited by Mike Pardee and David Streight (CSEE Publications, 2011). Collection of program highlights of successful student leadership programs (primarily private schools, but concepts translate to public settings) across the United States.

The Good, the Bad & the Difference: How to Tell Right from Wrong in Everyday Situations by Randy Cohen (New York: Broadway Books, 2003). A collection of ethical case studies written in "Q & A" format from the author's popular *New York Times* column.

Leadership for Student Activities
(See the listings under "Introduction" on page 207.)

The Leadership Workbook: A Practical Guide to Self-Development for Emerging Young Leaders by New Leadership Learning Center (Baltimore, MD: New Leadership Learning Center, Inc., 2012). A holistic, step-by-step guide to leadership development, this book provides a tangible, clear path for young people to become catalysts in their communities, schools, and in the lives of their peers.

My Hero: Extraordinary People on the Heroes Who Inspire Them by the My Hero Project (New York: Simon & Schuster, 2007). A collection of essays by well-known public figures about the people who influenced their lives. A few examples include Muhammad Ali on Nelson Mandela, Dana Reeve on Christopher Reeve, Paul Newman on his father Arthur Newman, and Wynton Marsalis on Duke Ellington.

New Directions for Youth Development: Youth Leadership edited by Max Klau, Steve Boyd, and Lynn Luckow (Issue 109, Spring 2006) onlinelibrary.wiley.com/doi/10.1002/yd.v2006:109/issuetoc Collection of essays and research exploring issues and ideas related to youth leadership.

101 Ways to Reward Team Members for $20 (or Less!) by Kevin Aguanno (Ontario, Canada: Multi-Media Publications, 2004). Inexpensive ways to recognize and motivate team members.

Rudy directed by David Anspaugh (TriStar Pictures, 1993).
(See the listing under "Session 20" on page 214.)

The 7 Habits of Highly Effective Teens by Sean Covey (New York: Touchstone Books, 2014). Provides a step-by-step guide to help you improve self-image, build friendships, resist peer pressure, achieve goals, and much more.

The Student Leadership Challenge: Five Practices for Becoming an Exemplary Leader by James M. Kouzes and Barry Z. Posner (San Francisco: Jossey-Bass, 2014). The book guides students through concrete actions they can take to become exemplary leaders. Includes code for online access to *The Student Leadership Practices Inventory*, a tool that evaluates how individuals engage in five practices of leadership behaviors identified and researched by Kouzes and Posner.

Take Action! A Guide to Active Citizenship by Marc Kielburger and Craig Kielburger (Hoboken, NJ: John Wiley & Sons, 2002). Covers all the basics for how you can participate in social action issues and have fun at the same time. Provides easy-to-follow guidelines for making a difference in people's lives worldwide.

Teen Leadership Revolution: How Ordinary Teens Become Extraordinary Leaders by Tom Thelen (Lowell, MI: Character Programs, 2012). Provides teens with the reasons and methods for developing rock solid character, building authentic relationships, and growing leadership qualities for the long haul.

Teens Can Make It Happen: Nine Steps for Success by Stedman Graham (New York: Touchstone, 2000). Bridges the gap between education and the real world to help you make plans for your goals and dreams.

Tools to Build Consensus: Facilitate Agreement in Your Group by Ron Kraybill (Harrisonburg, VA: Riverhouse ePress, 2005). A booklet that provides clearly written, practical steps for guiding a group to consensus. Includes specific ways to deal with difficult moments and how to test for consensus.

A Whack on the Side of the Head: How You Can Be More Creative by Roger von Oech (New York: Grand Central Publishing, 2008). Describes how to give your creative thinking a jumpstart and look at things from alternative viewpoints.

What Do You Really Want? How to Set a Goal and Go for It! A Guide for Teens by Beverly Bachel (Minneapolis: Free Spirit Publishing, 2016). A step-by-step guide to goal setting to help you identify goals and put them in writing, set priorities and deadlines, overcome roadblocks, build a support system, use positive self-talk, celebrate successes, and more.

What Do You Stand For? For Teens: A Guide to Building Character by Barbara A. Lewis (Minneapolis: Free Spirit Publishing, 2005). Ideas, activities, and resources to help you explore who you are and develop positive traits such as caring, good citizenship, empathy, respect, peacefulness, and responsibility.

"Youth Development and Leadership in Programs (Info Brief Issue 11)" www.ncwd-youth.info/information-brief-11 This brief describes how administrators and policymakers can use the concepts of youth development and youth leadership in developing and administering programs that serve all teens and activities specifically geared toward students with disabilities. The brief is based on a longer paper, "Youth Development and Youth Leadership, A Background Paper," published by the National Collaborative on Workforce and Disability for Youth (January 2005)

Organizations and Websites

Annenberg Learner
www.learner.org/resources/lessonplanbrowse.html
This website provides teacher resources and professional development across the curriculum; it includes a wide range of content-related lessons that inspire leadership discussions and development.

Big Brothers Big Sisters
2202 North Westshore Boulevard, Suite 455
Tampa, FL 33607
813-720-8778 • www.bbbs.org
Dedicated to helping kids and teens, ages 6 through 18, develop positive and lasting relationships with a mentor (a caring adult or an older teen) who can spend one-on-one time together and provide helpful, positive guidance. Some local Big Brothers Big Sisters agencies have a program called "High School Bigs," which trains and matches up high school students with younger students. Contact your local Big Brothers Big Sisters agency to see if this program is available.

DoSomething.org
19 West 21st Street, 8th Floor
New York, NY 10010
212-254-2390 • www.dosomething.org
Strives to make community service something fun and interesting for young people to do through various programs. Middle and high school students in the United States and Canada can apply to serve for a year as representatives of a 30-member Youth Advisory Council, which influences DoSomething.org programs.

Giraffe Heroes Project
PO Box 759
Langley, WA 98260
360-221-7989 • www.giraffe.org
A national nonprofit organization that honors people who stick out their necks for the common good, inspires others to do the same, and gives them the tools to succeed.

High Mountain Institute
531 County Road 5A
Leadville, CO 80461
719-486-8200 • www.hminet.org
Offers several outdoor adventure and leadership learning experiences for high school students including

academic and wilderness programs and summer programs. Teens from diverse backgrounds have the opportunity to learn lifelong leadership skills and put them into action.

The History Channel Archives of Great Speeches
www.history.com
Offers video and audio clips of some of the most inspirational and influential speeches of the 20th and 21st centuries.

Hugh O'Brian Youth Leadership (HOBY)
31255 Cedar Valley Drive, Suite 327
Westlake Village, CA 91362
818-851-3980 • www.hoby.org
Offers leadership seminars for high schoolers to be effective, ethical leaders at home, school, work, or in the community. Teens are selected annually from the United States and around the world.

Mariam G. MacGregor
mariammacgregor.com
mariam@youthleadership.com
Author Mariam G. MacGregor's online resource for youth leadership education and program development

MENTOR/National Mentoring Partnership
201 South Street, Suite 615
Boston, MA 02111
617-303-4600 • www.mentoring.org
Works with a strong network of state and local partnerships to provide mentors. To find a local mentor at their website, enter your zip code in the "Connect to Mentoring Opportunities" box at their home page.

My Hero Project
www.myhero.com
Offers an ever-growing Internet archive of hero stories from around the world to inspire people of all ages.

National 4-H Council
7100 Connecticut Avenue
Chevy Chase, MD 20815
301-961-2800 • 4-h.org
Serves millions of young people around the United States learning leadership, citizenship, and life skills. "4-H" stands for "Head, Heart, Hands, and Health," representing the four values members work to develop through participation in 4-H programs.

National Teen Leadership Program (NTLP)
101 Parkshore Drive
Folsom, CA 95630
800-550-1950 • ntlp.org
This nonprofit organization offers three-day intensive leadership camps and one-day workshops to instill important leadership concepts in young people.

National Youth Leadership Council (NYLC)
1667 Snelling Ave N., Suite D300
St. Paul, MN 55108
651.631.3672 • nylc.org
An organization dedicated to developing young leaders by providing leadership opportunities, training, and resources to address issues that matter to them.

PeaceJam Foundation
11200 Ralston Road
Arvada, CO 80004
303-455-2099 • www.peacejam.org
An international education program built around Nobel Peace Laureates who work personally with teens to share their leadership spirit, skills, and wisdom. Aims to inspire a new generation of peacemakers to change local communities and the world.

Tolerance.org
www.tolerance.org
Dedicated to promoting tolerant, inclusive, hate-free environments at home and in schools and communities. Provides ideas, activities, and daily news about groups and individuals working for tolerance and fighting hate. Encourages teens to "Mix It Up" by venturing outside of usual social groups and boundaries in school and the community.

Youthbuild USA
www.youthbuild.org
An expanding network of more than 250 local programs serving rural and poor communities in 46 states. Provides leadership growth opportunities for young people through academic and career programs and civic engagement to build affordable housing locally and nationally.

Youth Leadership Institute (YLI)
940 Howard Street
San Francisco, CA 94103
415-836-9160 • yli.org
YLI provides training and technical assistance services
to support and build the capacity of organizations
to engage teens in several key areas of community
change, including food access, youth philanthropy,
educational equity, civic engagement, and prevention
of alcohol, tobacco, and other drug use.

Youth Service America (YSA)
1620 I Street NW, Suite 501
Washington, DC 20006
202-296-2992 • ysa.org
A resource center that coordinates Global Youth
Service Day and partners with thousands of organizations to engage young people, ages 5 to 25, in community service and leadership activities locally, nationally,
and globally.

INDEX

Page references in **bold** refer to reproducible forms and handouts.

Mariam G. MacGregor, M.S., worked with college student leaders at Syracuse University, Santa Clara University, and Metropolitan State College of Denver before serving as the school counselor and coordinator of leadership programs at an alternative high school in Colorado. While there, she received honorable mention for Counselor of the Year. Now, she's a nationally recognized leadership consultant who works with schools (K–12 and higher education), nonprofit agencies, faith groups, and communities interested in developing meaningful, sustainable leadership efforts for kids, teens, and young adults.

Mariam is the former youth volunteer trainer for Night Lights (a respite care program that serves families with kids with special needs) and EPIC Mentors (a program started by one of her sons at his elementary school that pairs peer mentors with kids with learning challenges). She consults with organizations and presents workshops on designing meaningful and sustainable youth leadership experiences in both school- and community-based settings. Contact Mariam at **mariammacgregor.com**. She lives in Texas with her husband and three kind kids.

Other Titles by Mariam G. MacGregor

Everyday Leadership
Attitudes and Actions for Respect and Success (A Guidebook for Teens)
by Mariam G. MacGregor, M.S.,
foreword by Barry Z. Posner, Ph.D.
For ages 11 & up.
144 pp.; paperback; 7" x 9"

Everyday Leadership Cards
Writing and Discussion Prompts
by Mariam G. MacGregor, M.S.
Grades 6–12.
60 cards; 2-color; 3" x 4½"

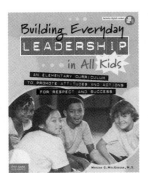

Building Everyday Leadership in All Kids
An Elementary Curriculum to Promote Attitudes and Actions for Respect and Success
by Mariam G. MacGregor, M.S.
For teachers, grades K–6.
208 pp.; paperback; 8½" x 11";
includes digital content

Teambuilding with Teens
Activities for Leadership, Decision Making, and Group Success
by Mariam G. MacGregor, M.S.
Grades 6–12.
192 pp.; paperback; 8½" x 11";
includes digital content

Other Great Resources from Free Spirit

The Complete Guide to Service Learning
Proven, Practical Ways to Engage Students in Civic Responsibility, Academic Curriculum, & Social Action
by Cathryn Berger Kaye, M.A.
For teachers, grades K–12.
288 pp.; paperback; 8½" x 11"; includes digital content

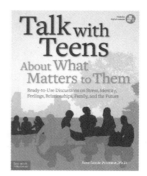

Talk with Teens About What Matters to Them
Ready-to-Use Discussions on Stress, Identity, Feelings, Relationships, Family, and the Future.
by Jean Sunde Peterson, Ph.D.
Grades K–8. 288 pp.; paperback; 8½" x 11"; includes digital content

What Do You Really Want?
How to Set a Goal and Go for It!
A Guide for Teens
(Revised & Updated Edition)
by Beverly K. Bachel
For ages 11 & up. 160 pp.; paperback; 2-color; 6" x 9"

What Do You Stand For? For Teens
A Guide to Building Character
by Barbara A. Lewis
For ages 11 & up.
288 pp.; paperback; B&W photos and illust.; 8½" x 11"

Building Character with True Stories from Nature
by Barbara A. Lewis
Grades 2–5.
176 pp.; paperback; illust.; 8½" x 11"; includes digital content

The Kids' Guide to Working Out Conflicts
How to Keep Cool, Stay Safe, and Get Along
by Naomi Drew, M.A.
For ages 10–15. 160 pp.; paperback; 2-color; illust.; 7" x 9"

Leader's Guide
Includes 36 reproducible handout masters. For teachers, grades 5–9.
128 pp.; paperback; 8½" x 11"

The Kid's Guide to Service Projects
Over 500 Service Ideas for Young People Who Want to Make a Difference
(Updated 2nd Edition)
by Barbara A. Lewis
For ages 10 & up. 160 pp.; paperback; 2-color; 6" x 9"

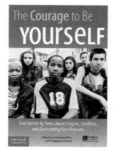

The Courage to Be Yourself
True Stories by Teens About Cliques, Conflicts, and Overcoming Peer Pressure
Edited by Al Desetta, M.A., with Engaging Schools
For ages 13 & up. 160 pp.; paperback; 6" x 9"

Leader's Guide
For teachers, social workers, and other adults who work with youth in grades 7–12.
168 pp.; paperback; 8½" x 11"

Interested in purchasing multiple quantities and receiving volume discounts?
Contact edsales@freespirit.com or call 1.800.735.7323 and ask for Education Sales.

Many Free Spirit authors are available for speaking engagements, workshops, and keynotes.
Contact speakers@freespirit.com or call 1.800.735.7323.

For pricing information, to place an order, or to request a free catalog, contact:

Free Spirit Publishing Inc. • 6325 Sandburg Road • Suite 100 • Minneapolis, MN 55427-3674
toll-free 800.735.7323 • local 612.338.2068 • fax 612.337.5050
help4kids@freespirit.com • www.freespirit.com